THE ROOTS OF POPE FRANCIS'S SOCIAL AND POLITICAL THOUGHT

From Argentina to the Vatican

Thomas R. Rourke

ROWMAN & LITTLEFIELD
Lanham • Boulder • New York • London

Published by Rowman & Littlefield
A wholly owned subsidiary of
The Rowman & Littlefield Publishing Group, Inc.
4501 Forbes Boulevard, Suite 200, Lanham, Maryland 20706
https://rowman.com

Unit A, Whitacre Mews, 26-34 Stannary Street, London SE11 4AB, United Kingdom

Copyright © 2016 by Rowman & Littlefield
First paperback edition 2018

All rights reserved. No part of this book may be reproduced in any form or by any electronic or mechanical means, including information storage and retrieval systems, without written permission from the publisher, except by a reviewer who may quote passages in a review.

British Library Cataloguing in Publication Information Available

The hardback edition of this book was previously cataloged by the Library of Congress as follows:
Names: Rourke, Thomas R., author.
Title: The roots of Pope Francis's social and political thought : from Argentina to the Vatican / Thomas R. Rourke.
Description: Lanham : Rowman & Littlefield, 2016. | Includes bibliographical references and index.
Subjects: LCSH: Francis, Pope, 1936-
Classification: LCC BX1378.7 .R6275 2016 (print) | LCC BX1378.7 (ebook) | DDC 261.8092—dc23
LC record available at https://lccn.loc.gov/2016023172

ISBN 978-1-4422-7271-2 (cloth : alk. paper)
ISBN 978-1-5381-1555-8 (pbk. : alk. paper)
ISBN 978-1-4422-7272-9 (electronic)

∞ ™ The paper used in this publication meets the minimum requirements of American National Standard for Information Sciences Permanence of Paper for Printed Library Materials, ANSI/NISO Z39.48-1992.

Printed in the United States of America

Praise for
The Roots of Pope Francis's Social and Political Thought

"Everybody views Pope Francis through a particular lens, acknowledged or not. The reader in search of a much wider lens for viewing the first Jesuit pope will naturally be drawn to this rich and perceptive volume, which probes the myriad historical, religious, and social factors that made Francis who he is today. Thomas R. Rourke draws from extensive knowledge of the culture, politics, and even the literary heritage of Argentina that shaped Jorge Mario Bergoglio at pivotal junctures in his eventful life. The complex picture that emerges is fascinating in every way."
—**Thomas Massaro, SJ,** Jesuit School of Theology of Santa Clara University; author of *Living Justice: Catholic Social Teaching in Action*

"Among the more creative, provocative, and controversial social critics and commentators of the day, Pope Francis occupies a place in the first ranks. In *The Roots of Pope Francis's Social and Political Thought*, Thomas R. Rourke provides an illuminating analysis that utilizes many sources unavailable in English while bringing to his project extensive personal experience of Francis's native Argentina and a comprehensive familiarity with the social doctrine of the Catholic Church. This is a useful and important piece of work."
—**Russell Shaw,** author of *Catholics in America*

"This book meets a real need: it takes Pope Francis seriously as a thinker, and it shows that his pastoral practice is guided by a profound and coherent—if not systematic—social and political vision. Rourke digs deep into Bergoglio's writings and speeches and sheds fascinating new light on some of the lesser-known influences on his thought, such as the Jesuit reductions and Suárez. What emerges is a Pope who—immersed in the Incarnation—always favors the concrete over the abstract, and common people over the domineering, homogenizing, and destructive forces of our time. This is an important book. It points the way ahead to Catholic social thought and action in the Francis era."
—**William T. Cavanaugh,** DePaul University

CONTENTS

Acknowledgments		vii
1	The Pope from the South	1
2	Historical-Theological Roots I: The Development and Destruction of the Jesuit Missions	15
3	Historical-Theological Roots II: From Vatican II to the Theology of Liberation and the Vatican Response	47
4	Historical-Theological Roots III: From the Theology of the People to Pope Francis's Vision for the Church Today	71
5	Culture and Its Religious Roots	101
6	Bergoglio and the Political Order	133
7	Economics: Globalization, Poverty, and Work	167
Epilogue: Perennial Challenges to Inculturation and *Laudato si'*		195
Bibliography		209
Index		215
About the Author		221

ACKNOWLEDGMENTS

This book required the translation into English from the original Spanish of approximately two thousand pages of materials from Father Jorge Bergoglio's published works. For this work of translation I owe a great debt to my Argentine wife, Dr. Rosita Amelia del V. Chazarreta Rourke, who helped me with many difficulties in translating terms specific to Argentina's history, culture, literature, and idioms. She was also my indispensable aide in editing and revising. And yet my debt goes much deeper than this. I owe to her the experiential knowledge I have of Argentina, as well as love of things Argentine, including Cardinal Bergoglio, now Pope Francis. I discovered long ago that no amount of study can replace real experience of a people and their culture. My interpretation of Argentina is mediated through Rosita. This book would have been unthinkable without her.

I would also like to thank my in-laws, the Chazarreta Goitea family, the late Arturo B. and Zulema, Dr. Ana María, and Arturo C., for all the years of hospitality, during which I was able to follow the trajectory of the inspirational Bishop, then Archbishop and Cardinal of Buenos Aires, Father Jorge Bergoglio.

I would like to thank the *Journal of Catholic Social Thought* for permission to publish portions of my previously published article, "Pope Francis: The Historical-Theological Roots and Development of His Social Thought" 13, no. 2 (Summer 2016): 285–309. In addition, I would like to thank Dr. Barbara Wall, editor in chief at the journal, for her timeliness and collegiality in the permissions process.

I would like to thank Ginger M. McGiffin, of the Carlson Library's interlibrary-loan desk at Clarion University, who was always extremely helpful to me in accessing any materials I needed in the process of researching this book.

I would like to thank Sarah Stanton, Carli Hansen, Alden Perkins, and all the helpful staff at Rowman & Littlefield for helping me through the processes of acquisition, copyediting, and production. Rowman & Littlefield remains a highly professional and, at the same time, user-friendly publisher of scholarly books.

Finally I thank my home institution, Clarion University of Pennsylvania, for granting me a full-year sabbatical to pursue the research and writing of this work. Without this time I could not have completed the book.

I

THE POPE FROM THE SOUTH

Pope Francis's long-time friend, Alberto Methol Ferré, a brilliant autodidact who had long participated in the Conference of Latin American Bishops, held the view that in the history of the Church one could distinguish regional churches as either "source churches" or "reflection churches."[1] The former reflect the signs of the times in the best sense, implementing the Gospel in the manner best suited to the circumstances of the age. They have a depth of evangelical renovation that makes them more self-sufficient, and they play a leadership role in the Church universal. The latter, reflection churches, on the other hand, rely on the source churches. Clearly Latin America was historically mostly a reflection church, befitting its status as newly evangelized and an image of Spain and Portugal on many levels. In Methol Ferré's view—last expressed just prior to the Fifth General Conference of the Bishops of Latin America and the Caribbean, held in Aparecida, Brazil (2007)—Latin America was on the verge of becoming a source church.

Methol Ferré had come to that conclusion because he had been able to discern a line of thinking that had emerged in Latin America beginning at the time of Pope Paul VI's papacy (1963–1978)—particularly in light of Vatican II's 1965 document *Gaudium et spes* (GS).[2] It was at this time that the themes of freedom and liberation were developing very strongly in Latin America, in ways deeper than the topic of freedom had been treated at the Second Vatican Council (1962–1968), which had more narrowly focused on liberty of conscience in religious matters in the context of Church-state relations. The new Latin

American development was a more ample treatment of the theme of liberation, as it came to be called, and included the conviction that world poverty and underdevelopment had to be addressed. Paul VI's *Populorum progressio* (*PP*), published in 1967, was a great encouragement to this development, but the influence was not one-way.[3] It is often forgotten that Paul VI himself went to the Second General Conference of Latin American Bishops in Medellín, Colombia, in 1968. In his opening discourse, he made very specific references to a number of contributions from the Latin American Church, giving them in a sense equal weight to his own encyclical. These documents were, specifically, the written conclusions of bishops' conferences in Bolivia, Brazil, and Mexico, a seminar for priests in Chile, and, furthermore, extensive statements produced by Jesuit and Salesian provincials who had met that same year. All of these spoke of poverty and liberation. Paul VI affirmed these lines of thinking while underlining the importance of development, particularly for those living in inferior and inhuman conditions.[4] The strong call for social change that emerged in Latin America from the now-legendary conference was in continuity with Paul VI's opening allocution.

The subsequent history of the development of Latin American thinking has been inadequately appropriated here in the United States, especially, where the elements of Marxist revolution in the popular movements and the theme of the Cold War were given almost unique emphasis. Although these elements were real, there was a lot more going on in Latin America that was missed in the North. A deeper look reveals that the Marxist bent in theory and practice was an option many tragically took in Latin America. Although not a move in the right direction, which both Paul VI and the Latin American bishops generally realized, it was a response to genuine evils that had not been adequately addressed or for that matter recognized. Even today many believe that there is really nothing to do but buy into the dominant model of globalized capitalism and accept whatever the results might be as the best possible. Whatever one's point of view, such a conclusion was not the line suggested by either *Populorum progressio* or the Latin American bishops. Moreover, neither the Pope nor the bishops were advocating the "warmed-over Marxism" derided by critics.[5]

Two important developments occurred in Latin America that were largely missed in the North. First, Latin America had and has its own wells to drink from, religiously, culturally, and in terms of political thinking. One notable development was a line of thinking in Argentina called *la teología del pueblo*—or "the theology of the people," which overlapped with the better-known theology of liberation yet departed from it in significant ways. This theology of the people saw a kind of liberation that emphasized Latin America's historical uniqueness, particularly with respect to religion and culture. An authentic liberation could only come about if the people were in touch with their own historically constituted identity. This line of thought and practice particularly found merit and depth in the traditions of popular regional religiosities. The problem with the most politically radical strand of the theology of liberation was that it carried the discourse of external oppression so far that it came to see in Latin American culture nothing but the fruits of the oppressor. This was not a view that could withstand sustained historical scrutiny. The uniformly negative reading of Latin America's own history and culture was often grounded in European modes of thinking that had come down from the Enlightenment. As a young, promising Jesuit Provincial, Father Jorge Mario Bergoglio, S.J., with reference to his native Argentina, could see abundant examples and models of progress within the Christian civilization that had emerged in Latin America. In his Argentine history, he could think of the perennially valid moral vision from the great epic poem *Martín Fierro* or the heroic and visionary life of Manuel Belgrano, and, perhaps above all, the great work of evangelization and civilization that was the Jesuit missions, begun in the 1500s, in the region of contemporary Argentina, Paraguay, and Brazil. Whatever the sins of the Spaniards, whatever their excesses, in many cases an authentic inculturation of the Gospel had indeed emerged in Latin America. Moreover, it is still there, embodied in what Bergoglio would come to call *el santo pueblo fiel de Dios*—or the holy, faithful people of God. For the future Pope, liberation had to come from them and through them. It could not come from a self-appointed vanguard group embodying schools of thought in many ways alien to the people's traditions.

A second development the North failed to notice in Latin America is related to the first. Although the theology of the people was in a sense distinctly Argentine, it reflected a developing, broader consensus among the bishops of Latin America, a way of thinking that was to find expression in 1979 in the Third General Conference of Latin American

Bishops. The interpretation of that conference was often dominated by the discussion of the degree to which it did or did not support the theology of liberation. The radical elements in the liberation school were generally not pleased with Puebla but found enough support in its final document to keep moving forward with their agenda.[6] However, the most important feature of the Puebla conference was its shift to an emphasis on culture. Naturally, the need for political and economic changes were reiterated, but the conference produced clear language echoing the line of thinking in the theology of the people, affirming the value of the people's historic Christian identity as the source for needed change. This realization would culminate in the Fifth General Conference of Latin American Bishops, held in Aparecida, Brazil, in 2007. Then-Cardinal Bergoglio, a longstanding sympathizer with the theology of the people, put his imprint on that conference and became the redactor of the final document. Although Alberto Methol Ferré died in 2007 and did not live to see the election of Jorge Mario Cardinal Bergoglio to the Chair of Saint Peter on March 13, 2013, one could say it represented the ascendance of the Church in Latin America to source church.

As Methol Ferré also suggests, frequently parallels between the developments in the Latin American Church and the universal Church go unseen. A dialogue between Rome and the currents of Latin American thinking, in the final analysis, affirmed the developments of thinking that had developed in the region, helping to purify them of false utopianism and revolutionary, political messianism. Vatican documents *Libertatis nuntius* (1984) and *Libertatis conscientia* (1986) were often narrowly interpreted as criticizing the theology of liberation.[7] Methol Ferré, on the other hand, sees in these directives an affirmation of other trends in the region concerning theological reflection on liberation. Methol Ferré sees in the first lines of *Libertatis nuntius*, not a European quashing of a Latin American development, but, rather, nothing less than a development of and continuity with properly Latin American thinking: "Redemption is liberation in its most profound sense, because it frees us from the most radical evil: sin and the power of death."[8] Those who had followed Latin American developments, as Methol Ferré had, could see the validity of the claim. Concerning liberation, Latin America had its own wells of theological reflection, moral insight, and culture from which it could draw. The region did not have to follow the path determined for it by European rationalism generally or Marxism in particular. Moreover, as the theology of liberation had said, poverty in the region was indeed the result of sin and was closeness to death.

For his part, Father Jorge Bergoglio—when Provincial and during his trajectory from auxiliary bishop in Buenos Aires to Archbishop and then Cardinal—developed his own social thought along these lines. As is generally recognized, his life has been that of a pastor. He exercised this role in a set of circumstances as trying as any. He became Jesuit Provincial in 1973 at age thirty-six in the midst of severe social and political conflict that was reflected in the Church, his Province, and his city, Buenos Aires. Circumstances dictated that he take a stand. In truth, he already had one, rooted in the original vision of inculturating the Gospel as exemplified in the work of the Jesuit missionaries in his region. As we shall see, the activity of the old Jesuit missionaries was to remain paradigmatic for Bergoglio, impacting his entire view of the Church and the world, up to and including today. Moreover, the currents of thought that surrounded him clearly impacted his development. He had to consider the theology of liberation line, the restorationists, and the theology of the people. He always remained independent of the first two, but not in the sense of being closed off and unwilling to dialogue. As Provincial, Bergoglio helped people who had taken the more politically radical line, even though his thinking differed.[9]

To understand Bergoglio one must understand Argentina religiously, culturally, and politically, a knowledge not common in the United States. One must particularly appreciate the different ways religion and politics intersect there, which relates to unique features of Argentine history in particular and Latin America generally. For example, it is common for the Primate of Argentina, the Cardinal, to speak to civil officials and to the broader society, particularly on the patriotic celebrations on May 25 and July 9. The first commemorates the beginning of the independence movement, while the latter is the actual Independence Day, recalling the signing of the act that declared the independence of the "United Provinces of the South."[10] As the Catholic Church played such an important role in the history of the nation, from the time of the independence movement, it is simply part of the national life. Today there is still a Te Deum ceremony in the Metropolitan Cathedral on both days. Particularly in difficult times, which have been the norm for a long time, people listen to and take note of what the Cardinal has to say about the state of the nation. Over and above these two important civic holidays, the Cardinal has a national audience on many occasions when addressing matters of pertinence. August 7, for example, the Feast of San Cayetano (Saint Cajetan), "Father of Providence," has traditionally been a day of prayers for work and bread. With the nation's explosion of poverty in the 1980s, Cardinal Bergoglio expanded the feast-day homily's themes to include reflection on social justice far more broadly considered. Moreover, even aside from special days, if the Cardinal makes comments on social, political, or economic developments, he may receive national press coverage.

Bergoglio, during his time as Cardinal, came to be seen in many ways as the conscience of the nation. This led him into conflict with the Kirchner regime, which first came to power in the midst of the political and economic disarray in 2003. Though the Kirchners—Néstor and Cristina—had become millionaires specializing in mortgage-foreclosure cases, they took the political line of the seventies left. Their interpretation of the nation's problems was textbook ideology: the bad guys were uniquely the old oligarchy, the military, big industries, foreign interests, and much of the Catholic Church's hierarchy. Surely there was much valid criticism to be made of those quarters. However, to listen to the Kirchners, the left never kidnapped anyone, killed anyone, or initiated any acts of violence worth recalling. The nation's Catholic culture, as its past, mattered for nothing, except insofar as they could selectively mine its history to their own advantage. They stirred up old hatreds, recalling the violence of the seventies in a one-sided way, prompting political divisions from which they believed they could profit. They were destined to clash with Bergoglio, who always pleaded for national unity and integration and wished to discuss the problems of poverty, exclusion, and even corruption in public addresses. Although Bergoglio was always willing to admit the Church's historical errors, particularly in the seventies, President Néstor Kirchner and his wife, subsequent president Cristina Fernández de Kirchner, saw Bergoglio as an enemy—perhaps *the* enemy, given his popularity. One of the more amusing anecdotes since the Pope's election is how then-president Cristina Fernández de Kirchner made a dramatic about-face after an initially cool response to his election as Pope. In Argentina, Bergoglio is a national hero, very widely respected, and she could see it was not in her political interest to exhibit any further hostilities.

Bergoglio's preaching and teaching have never centered on the Kirchners or any other political leader or movement. Rather the themes of his preaching have been consistent for decades, flowing from the same sources. These will be the focus of this book. First and foremost is the theme of inculturation, deeply embedded in him by his Jesuit roots generally and the history of the Jesuit missions in his region particularly. Moreover, although Pope Francis thoroughly rejects any project of mere restorationism in nostalgia for days gone by, Catholic roots drive his social thinking. For him inculturation of the Gospel leads to a better civilization. Although willing to respect modern arrangements of Church and state, and clearly eschewing any notions of a Catholic Church with political power, Bergoglio's sense of the ideal is that the Gospel should be free to penetrate every dimension of life. The roots of his thinking are incompatible with secularist assumptions about the social and political order. Inculturation of the Gospel also informs his thought as to what the permanent enemies are—that is, "imperial projects." The paradigm for this category is the European centralization of power that spelled doom for the Jesuit missions in the 1700s. Imperial projects always target the people in their historically constituted identity to prepare the way to dominate them. The Pope today sees "ideological colonization" in the uniform and liberalizing tendencies of globalization, which are both cultural and economic. Inspired by the writings of Romano Guardini, Pope Francis sees a disturbing tendency toward centralizing power unaccompanied by a corresponding ethics to limit it. Indeed, power today hides behind the impersonal facade of a kind of technocratic–financial–market power juggernaut that speaks in a language of universality, progress, utility, welfare, and inevitability. Moreover, the Pope has always thought that the key to resistance is to be found in the history of the people; liberation is inseparable from recouping one's identity, particularly culturally and religiously. One of the unique features of his thought is that, although he may be willing to discuss the topic of the day, his discourse is always rooted in the difficult and long-term dimensions of contemporary problems. Hence, in the midst of crisis he does not predominantly make policy proposals but speaks to the need to develop a civic culture based on the people's history.

In chapters 2 through 4 of this book we explore in depth the historical and theological roots of Pope Francis's social thought. These are the keys to his thinking, and they overlap the subsequent, more specific discussions of culture, politics, and economics. In chapter 2 we consider first and foremost Jorge Mario Bergoglio's Jesuit history, which roots his thinking and pastoral action. We will quickly see that to be in his presence is to be in the presence of a man who has for many years been contemplating Christ in the Gospels according to the Ignatian method. Years of prayer inform his discussions of the social implications of the Gospel. In the spirit of Saint Ignatius, the Pope is always a man both radically contemporary and thoroughly traditional. He counsels the Catholic Church to march to the peripheries and engage the world in all its change and newness—but to do so immersed in the Gospels and the tradition of the Church. In the spirit of the original Jesuit missions, inculturation emerges as the central theme of his social thought. Rooted in a deeply historical sense of the way the Gospel has been inculturated in Latin America, Bergoglio has always seen through the false and ultimately self-centered paths of vanguard progressivism and a restorationism that seek to enshrine the past. Wisdom means understanding the necessary connection between past, present, and future. Those with sapience informed by faith see the totalitarian nature of projects that purport to build a future without the past, which always means stripping the people of their identity so as to mold them into whatever one desires. Wisdom also sees that one cannot take refuge in the past and that attempts to build such a world can never bring it back but merely a caricature of it as an expression of the will of those now in power. This, too, is an authoritarian project. Of importance here will be the treatment of the great Jesuit thinker Francisco Suárez, whose reflections on popular sovereignty shed much political light on the past as well as the present.

In chapter 3 we explore Bergoglio's more contemporary influences, with a focus on changes in the Catholic Church writ large and the Latin American Church in particular—from the Second Vatican Council, closing in 1965, through the Vatican responses to liberation theology in the 1980s. Everyone in a leadership position in the Catholic Church since Vatican II has been informed by that great ecumenical council, where on social matters the last conciliar document, *Gaudium et spes*, is paramount. Pope Paul VI's *Populorum progressio* (1967) and *Evangelii nuntiandi* (1975) help configure and confirm Francis's thinking on the themes of development, evangelization, inculturation, the dangers of ideology, and the importance of popular religion. These developments in the universal Church melded with those in the Latin American and specifically the Argentine Church. The Second General Conference of Latin American Bishops, held in Medellín, Colombia, in 1968, marked a decisive turn in focus in the direction of social justice in the region. This turn dovetailed with the development of the theology of liberation, which was to become the most decisive influence in Latin America from the sixties through the eighties. Concerned over politicized readings of the Gospel emanating from the latter theology, the Vatican issued two documents in 1984 (*Libertatis nuntius*) and 1986 (*Libertatis conscientia*) to clarify the Church's stance with respect to liberation theology.

In chapter 4 we focus on Bergoglio's own development in Argentina more specifically. Steering a path between radical expressions of theology of liberation and restorationists sympathetic to the barbaric project of the national security state, Bergoglio, we will see, found in the *teología del pueblo* a way of thinking consistent with his Jesuit roots concerning inculturation and respect for the presence of Christ already in His faithful people. This school of thought, embodied in the works of Lucio Gera, Rafael Tello, and Juan Carlos Scannone, among others, was an Argentine alternative to liberation theology. Sympathetic to the latter's aims to create a just society, these Argentine theologians nonetheless distanced themselves from what they saw as liberation theology's Enlightenment, European, and rationalist roots. Additionally this chapter recognizes that no treatment of Bergoglio's roots could fail to mention Alberto Methol Ferré, who supported Bergoglio's thinking on the faithful people and the shift to an emphasis on Latin America's historical culture at the Puebla conference. In this gathering, the Latin American bishops underlined that change had to be rooted in the history and culture of the region more so than by foreign ideological influences. Moreover, Methol Ferré's insights would help Bergoglio see the implicit atheism at work in the world of contemporary relativism and consumerism. Chapter 4 concludes with an examination of the Pope's vision for the Catholic Church at large, an ecclesial vision that strongly shapes his social thought.

Chapter 5 treats culture. Bergoglio believes that the recognition of transcendence is absolutely necessary for the health of culture; human centeredness without reference to God always tends in the authoritarian direction. Culture must be seen in its reality, which is a present with both a past and future. The failure to appropriate past and future with the present accounts for why both the young and the old tend to be discarded. In an increasingly utilitarian culture, the people, understood in their historical fullness, are in a sense *the* cultural resource. Popular religion in particular is an ever-present source of cultural wisdom and depth. Globalization has distinctively uniform tendencies in the cultural area, and these are to be seen as part of an imperial project to be resisted. Two very characteristic cultural trends in Pope Francis's papacy are in his calls for a "culture of encounter" and various forms of "dialogue." These are no vacuous liberalizing trends but calls to bring Christ into the culture, into every encounter with a cultural world wherein the faith is no longer the driving force. The ahistorical, uniformizing, materialistic, and utilitarian tendencies in contemporary culture cause a great deal of uprootedness and fragmentation as people lose their historical-cultural roots. The Catholic Church must respond to all these forms of brokenness.

In chapter 6 we explore Bergoglio's political thinking. Surely his greatest contribution here has been his personal witness of social and civic engagement, an attitude he fosters in others, particularly the young. Although his thought is rich, it is not systematic; it must be understood in reference to some of the broader themes in Catholic social teaching, which he references: the common good, the role of the state, the principles of solidarity and subsidiarity, and freedom. The more original dimensions of his thinking are in the areas of political anthropology and political culture, where he examines the ways the broader cultural problems discussed in the previous chapter have particularly deleterious effects on the political world. At times echoing his predecessor, the present Pope laments how contemporary politics descends into nominalism, secularism, and relativism. Worst of all, politics gives way to the imperatives of the technocratic paradigm, surrendering the substance of the common good to powerful global interests. In the process, politics becomes more authoritarian under the guise of democracy but ironically loses credibility as well. The people can see, protestations to the contrary, that the political system is not solving the problem of exclusion but often accentuating it. Admiring the nobility of politics in its classical meaning, in the manner the Catholic Church has always understood it—as the pursuit of the common good—Bergoglio sees in these developments a great loss. There are no easy fixes here. He speaks at length to the people of Argentina how they can find models of a successful political culture, appealing to the great epic poem *Martín Fierro*, the great Argentine founder Manuel Belgrano, the civic-minded "Cura Brochero," and the Gospel narrative of the Good Samaritan.

In chapter 7 we explore Bergoglio's thinking on economics, which has actually received the most notoriety, although a good deal of the discussion is simply uninformed. As with the discussion of politics, the Pope's treatment is to be understood in light of the Church's received teaching, a debt he readily acknowledges. The understanding of property as private but with social obligations is the moral root of his teaching. From this he proceeds to the characteristic commitment to the universal destination of goods in the context of a regulating state that recognizes the principle of subsidiarity. Although recognizing the possibilities of globalization, Bergoglio's analysis tends to echo his treatment of globalization on culture; it is a uniform tendency that tends to be hegemonic, domineering particularly with respect to the developing world. He reaffirms the doctrine of the preferential option for the poor, insisting on its theological roots. Influenced by John Paul II's *Laborem exercens*, Pope Francis sees work as the key to the social question.[11] He affirms the priority of labor over capital. However, he doubts this well describes what economic globalization generally does. He particularly emphasizes the "new idolatry of money" and the dominance of the financial sector, clearly echoing Pope Pius XI's denunciations in *Quadragesimo anno*.[12] Finally, he discusses the "social debt" as a way to offset the more typical discussion of Third World debt, which focuses on how to make sure financial institutions in the global North get their money back from developing nations. Pope Francis's emphasis is on how these projects of debt repayment have unjustly squeezed the poor for decades and that the true debt, the "social debt," is owed first to the excluded—the poor and those who have lost their jobs. It is in the forcefulness of his language—"This economy kills," he declares—that we find what is characteristic of Pope Francis's economics teaching; he echoes traditional teaching with the language of the prophets.

In chapter 8, the epilogue, we recapitulate the major themes of the book along with a brief treatment of the contribution of *Laudato si'*.[13] Thought of as primarily a document on the environment, Francis's second encyclical also echoes the larger framework of the social question framed in this book.

NOTES

1. Alberto Methol Ferré and Alver Metalli, *El papa y el filósofo* (Buenos Aires: Editorial Biblos, 2013), 79–80.

2. Paul VI, *Gaudium et spes*, The Holy See (Vatican website), December 7, 1965, http://www.vatican.va/archive/hist_councils/ii_vatican_council/documents/vat-ii_const_19651207_gaudium-et-spes_en.html. (Hereafter cited in text as *GS*.)

Throughout the book, when ecclesiastical documents are referenced, I shorten the titles to a two-letter abbreviation—as in *GS* here. When the reference is to a specific passage or section of the document, the abbreviation will be followed by a comma, then the numbered paragraph of the document—for example, "*GS*, 65". Readers should note that ecclesiastical documents generally have numbered paragraphs and that the number written is *not* a page number. The only exception will be in chapter 3, in the discussion of the documents from the 1968 Second General Conference of Latin American Bishops at Medellín. As that conference produced a series of named documents—not just one—the name of the individual document will be cited in the text, followed by the paragraph number. All ecclesiastical documents pertaining to the universal Church can be found on the Vatican's website, The Holy See, http://w2.vatican.va/content/vatican/en.html.

3. Paul VI, *Populorum progressio*, The Holy See (Vatican website), March 26, 1967, http://w2.vatican.va/content/paul-vi/en/encyclicals/documents/hf_p-vi_enc_26031967_populorum.html.

4. Methol Ferré and Metalli, *El papa y el filósofo*, 181.

5. See Peter Steinfels, "An Unsparing View of Economic Ills," *New York Times*, February 20, 1988, http://www.nytimes.com/1988/02/20/world/an-unsparing-view-of-economic-ills.html.

6. See, for example, John Eagleson and Philip Scharper, eds., *Puebla and Beyond: Documentation and Commentary*, trans. John Drury (Maryknoll, NY: Orbis Books, 1979).

7. Congregation for the Doctrine of the Faith, *Libertatis nuntius*, The Holy See (Vatican website), August 6, 1984, http://www.vatican.va/roman_

curia/congregations/cfaith/documents/rc_con_cfaith_doc_19840806_theology-liberation_en.html; and Congregation for the Doctrine of the Faith, *Libertatis conscientia*, The Holy See (Vatican website), March 22, 1986, http://www.vatican.va/roman_curia/congregations/cfaith/documents/rc_con_cfaith_doc_19860322_freedom-liberation_en.html.

8. Methol Ferré and Metalli, *El Papa y el filósofo*, 183.

9. See Nello Scavo, *Bergoglio's List: How a Young Francis Defied a Dictatorship and Saved Dozens of Lives*, trans. Bret Thoman (Charlotte, NC: Saint Benedict's Press, 2014).

10. At this time, 1816, these United Provinces went beyond contemporary Argentina, including all or parts of Paraguay, Uruguay, and Bolivia.

11. John Paul II, *Laborem exercens*, The Holy See (Vatican website), September 14, 1981, http://w2.vatican.va/content/john-paul-ii/en/encyclicals/documents/hf_jp-ii_enc_14091981_laborem-exercens.html.

12. Pius XI, *Quadragesimo anno*, The Holy See (Vatican website), May 15, 1931, http://w2.vatican.va/content/pius-xi/en/encyclicals/documents/hf_p-xi_enc_19310515_quadragesimo-anno.html.

13. Francis, *Laudato si'*, The Holy See (Vatican website), May 24, 2015, http://w2.vatican.va/content/francesco/en/encyclicals/documents/papa-francesco_20150524_enciclica-laudato-si.html.

2

HISTORICAL-THEOLOGICAL ROOTS I

The Development and Destruction
of the Jesuit Missions

Pope Francis is already identified by some characteristic turns of phrase that define the pastoral direction of his pontificate. He wants to avoid the temptation for the Catholic Church to be a "self-enclosed Church," symbolized by closed doors, but instead to be "an outreach Church," which goes "to the streets," to the "existential peripheries," and in the process incarnates the Gospel in all dimensions of life and the social order.[1] Less known is how his pastoral direction was most deeply formed within him during his decades of reflection on the original Jesuit missions in his native Argentina. This is where we begin. In this chapter, we explore the Argentine roots of Pope Francis's thought, with a special focus on his understanding of the theology and practice of the original Jesuit missions in his native country. The theology and missionary direction of the latter centered on an evangelization that would lead to a full flowering of the Incarnate Word in every dimension of the life of the people, an inculturation that would encompass the social, political, and economic orders. As Bergoglio himself refers to the missions as the time of Jesuit thinker Francisco Suárez, we will examine Suárez's theory of popular sovereignty, itself closely related to the incarnational theology informing the missions. Although this theory would be significant to the development of republican and democratic thinking in the West, in the 1700s it threatened the sovereignty of European monarchs intent on centralizing power in the state. Therefore, the Spanish and Portuguese Crowns destroyed these increasingly independent missions. Bergoglio's reflections on this tragedy establish a kind of paradigm for his social thought—that is, a conflict between Gospel inculturation, on the one hand, and ideological absolutism, on the other. Moreover, he eventually came to view forms of rationalism inspired by the Enlightenment as serving to justify the related political and economic imperialism.

One of the most significant theological elements in the thought of Jorge Mario Bergoglio is his ongoing reflection on and pastoral implementation of the theology of the Incarnation. Furthermore, the greatest influence on his thinking with respect to this theme is the theory and practice of the early Jesuits, particularly in their missionary activity in the southern part of the American continent (from 1565 in what is today northeast Argentina, southeast Paraguay, and southern Brazil). The Jesuits collaborated in the Council of Trent (1545–1563), the catechesis of which inspired their missionary activity. Key to their Tridentine theology and pastoral practice was the conviction that, in light of the Incarnate Word, human beings were wounded by sin but not totally corrupted. This conclusion was central to the Jesuit spirituality of contemplating and attempting to imitate Christ. If human nature were thoroughly and hopelessly corrupted, then the sinless Christ could not realistically be any kind of exemplar for fallen humans; salvation might mean forgiveness and redemption for the next life, but a thoroughly corrupt human nature cannot transform the world as an extension of the activity of the Incarnate Word. Grounded in Trent's understanding of human nature in relation to the Incarnation, the Jesuits had a hopeful, even optimistic, view of the capacity of the native peoples to be transformed by the Gospel in all dimensions of their lives. As Bergoglio himself said more than thirty-five years before assuming the Chair of Saint Peter, the grace of salvation "would not be a mere juridical title, external to man, but a transforming force, and because man did not lose completely the radical goodness that God the Creator placed in his heart, it did not seem utopian to them to launch themselves into the enterprise to catholicize a continent."[2] In order to accomplish this, the interior dimension was central, an interiority similarly rooted in the Incarnation. Saint Ignatius emphasized that the only valid spirituality was through the sacred humanity of Christ. The Jesuit had to contemplate this humanity in the Gospels and enter into it in practice. As Bergoglio put it, "We will contemplate the Passion in the flesh of Christ, in our flesh."[3] Because of human sinfulness, this path necessitates sacrifice and often suffering, but it is the only true path.

Following the mandate of Saint Ignatius, going to the peripheries of their time in the New World, and rooted in the incarnationalist theology of Trent, the Society of Jesus came to Argentina in 1565.[4] Following Saint Ignatius, they believed that God delivered His Reign "in earthly garments," offering the native Guaraní salvation understood as assuming their true identity as a people both within their historical sojourn and before the transcendent God. In order to do so, the members of the Company had to divest themselves of all that was theirs, following the Master's path of kenosis—total renunciation. Self-renunciation opened them to take on the characteristics of the people, to adapt to their history, their culture, even their geography. Concerning the self-abnegation and incorporation of the Jesuits into the lives of the people, Bergoglio cites a letter in reference to Padre Alonso de Bárzana, the first Jesuit who arrived in Argentina's oldest city, Santiago del Estero, in 1585. Describing the Jesuit priest in old age, the letter states that he "was already very old and without teeth and with no desire to preach to the Spaniards. . . . [He lived] in extreme poverty, with a most profound humility . . . becoming old together with the old Indian man and woman, with them now part of this land, seated in these lands to win them for Christ, and with the chiefs and other members, boys and children, with so much desire to take them to the Lord that it seems to burst his heart."[5]

The self-renunciation was always with the view to bringing the Gospel to penetrate every dimension of the personal and social lives of the people. Their problems—hunger, drought, and illness—became the Jesuits' problems. They understood that the behavior of many of their countrymen, the encomenderos,[6] in the latter's attempts to exploit and enslave the people, were an obstacle to the penetration of the Gospel. Therefore, the Jesuits changed the sinful structure of economic relations through their own work embodying justice. To form better a conscience respecting justice and freedom, they not only taught the Guaraní to abandon practices such as raiding and concubinage, they also undertook many works of human promotion. They brought to the people the tools and economic possibilities of the Iron Age, involving them in great works of construction, agriculture, and culture. The Incarnation of the Word was present in their work—getting dirty, building, preparing meals, teaching trades, taking care of the sick, and catechizing. In all of this, the Jesuits understood the Incarnation to imply the use of material and cultural elements present in the life of the people. They translated the catechism into Guaraní and Quechua. When they saw how external instruments (musical instruments, local art forms) were effective in attracting the native people to the faith, they did not hesitate to employ them. The Jesuits established schools and chapels for singing and made musical instruments for liturgical use. Moreover, indigenous artisans captured the mysteries of the faith in painting, sculpture, and architecture, presenting them with distinctively American "sense and color. . . . The baroque altarpieces assumed in their ornamentation praise to the One Lord of all, of our particular flora and fauna."[7] Many marvel even today not only at the economic achievements of the reductions,[8] which brought about the jealousy of the European elites, but also at the great works of art and music, which have been partially preserved.[9] In addition to being a great work of evangelization, the missions were, in Bergoglio's view, also a great work of civilization. Naturally the narratives flowing from the European centers, dominated in the 1700s by the Enlightenment and Protestantism, saw the missions differently.[10]

Lest it be thought that the Pope's thoughts on the subject of the missions is somehow distant from his thinking today, he referenced the missions very specifically during a pastoral trip to Latin America in 2015, during which he visited Ecuador, Bolivia, and Paraguay. In Paraguay on Saturday, July 11, he spoke at the Sanctuary of the Virgin of Caacupé. What made this particular discourse fascinating was his reiteration of an old theme in his thought—that is, the old Jesuit reductions as a model for inculturated evangelization today.

> Paraguay is known in the world for having been the land where the reductions started, one of the experiences of evangelization and social organization most interesting in history. . . . In them, the Gospel was soul and life of communities where there was no hunger, nor unemployment, nor illiteracy, nor oppression. *This experience teaches us that a more human society today is possible. When there is love for man, and the will to serve, it is possible to create conditions so all have access to necessary goods, with no one discarded. . . .* [You

Paraguayans] have the living memory of a people that has made flesh the word of the Gospel.[11]

In this passage we see the Pope's concern for the poverty that engulfs the people, coupled with the conviction that the existing economic system and the powers that be are largely responsible for it. Characteristically, his focus remains on the real people as historically constituted. The people have, within their own history and experience, valuable lessons that can serve to respond to today's challenges. The answers do not originate from modern ideologies, born of the Enlightenment; the latter, elitist in nature, never bend down to learn from the poor in history.

In 1988, when Jesuit Provincial, Bergoglio addressed a critique from the left-leaning, progressive wing in the Catholic Church, which referred disparagingly to pastoral activity focusing on corporal works of mercy as mere "assistancism" (in Spanish, *asistencialismo*), which is to say that merely assisting people in their daily problems is a kind of secondary issue pastorally speaking; the critique went further to claim that the more important focus should be a "reform of the structures" that perpetuate injustice. Resistance to this kind of thinking would become a hallmark of Bergoglio's thought and pastoral practice. A related criticism set up a distinction between mere "sacramentalism," which allegedly focused on mere church-related matters, and "evangelization," which implied the breadth of social, cultural, and political perspectives. In the 1970s and 1980s, this criticism often led the left to a kind of disparaging attitude toward Bergoglio's pastoral activity in Buenos Aires, which focused on helping people with the specific details of their problems. For example, he showed up to a twenty-five-acre area near his pastoral base in San Miguel one day "with four cows, four pigs, and six sheep." At the time, food prices were high. Before long, barns, sheds, fences, and vegetable farming had sprung up in the area.[12] To progressives focused on changing political and economic systems, this kind of activity was often seen as missing the boat, getting bogged down in programs of short-term assistance. Bergoglio never negated the need for political and economic changes, but he forcefully took issue that this could ever be a pretext for failing to serve the actual needs of people in the present moment. Nor did he ever see in this a mere difference in theological preference or tactics. For Bergoglio, the issue went to the core of the Gospel and the Jesuit charism itself as received from Saint Ignatius. The pursuit of justice in love, as part of evangelization, does not admit of dichotomies of the kinds progressives were promoting. Referring back to the original missions as the point of reference, during a conference given on the occasion of the canonization of the Martyrs of the Río de la Plata,[13] Bergoglio underlined that in accord with the integral life and message of Christ the Jesuits did not emphasize any supposed conflict either between reforming structures and manual labor or between work and preaching. More importantly the Jesuits understood that in doing works such as trying to cure a small pox lesion they were far from getting bogged down in unimportant details but were, rather, witnessing to the action and reality of the transcendent God made present in Christ. Bergoglio writes, "In the same wound they cured they found the one victimized on the road from Jerusalem to Jericho . . . and this same wound, and the work dedicated to it—for the Catholic conception that inspired them—pointed out to them the way of transcendence: in the first place from the action itself toward the dignity of the person, in second place toward God."[14]

Another example of Bergoglio's appropriation of the Jesuit sense of transcendence is found in his discussion of the role of baptism in the reductions. Baptism was central to the community life, given that conversion played such a fundamental role. Baptism and the sacramental life generally were integrated into a unified community life, in a way that included both the sense of integration and the transcendent importance of the sacrament. This was grounded in the Jesuit understanding that in the life of the mission the Word was continually being incarnated. The Word was made flesh most explicitly in the sacramental life but also in the other activities of the day, all of which were oriented to promoting the dignity of the natives under God. However, baptism was always an especially singular event. Bergoglio describes such a day, quoting from a Padre Del Valle:

> The catechumens entered the Church with palms in their hands and signs of great joy. . . . Our poor church was profusely adorned with arranged flowers, especially in the baptistery. . . . The solemnity lasted all afternoon until sunset. The catechumens were placed in two lines, and I with the sacred ornaments in the middle. As soon as I started I was overcome by emotion, to the point that only with great efforts amidst tears could I continue the ceremonies. Finishing the

baptisms I arranged the order of the procession: in front were the children, followed by the men, the women and at the end the recently baptized. The procession left the church, went through the town and returned to the church, where the solemnity concluded with the Te Deum.[15]

In a meditative reflection on the spiritual exercises of Saint Ignatius given to fellow religious, Bergoglio emphasized that any kind of "progressivism" deemphasizing the concrete needs of the people in favor of an alleged higher justice of structural reform was an abandonment of the Gospel itself. His approach to justice begins with a commitment to being poor himself, as did the early Jesuits. Moreover, the poor work, and to be poor is to be like them, to see justice from their perspective. Jesuits, like everyone else, are tempted to avoid the struggles of the world of those who toil daily. As religious intellectuals their temptation is to get caught up in justice in the abstract, but theories of justice, even when grounded in theology, do not give life to the people; to get caught up in this kind of theological vanguardism is a form of vainglory. In acceding to this temptation one avoids the daily labor of Jesus in his Father's workshop, dreaming of something more spectacular and more quickly realized. However, for Bergoglio this is empty egoism, not true love for God's people. Some pastors seek refuge in justice as a fantasy because the actual work of the Kingdom does not appeal to their egos and is demanding. The people demand many things. Bergoglio gives many concrete examples from his own experience of actions that pastors must take but that probably weary them on a daily basis: someone comes to ask if they can change "una promesa,"[16] another wants a certificate so they can be baptized in the great shrine in Luján, yet another wants to have a Mass said for a deceased relative, but on a very specific day. For Bergoglio, a pastor cannot neglect these in the name of God, because to refuse to serve these concrete daily needs is no transcendence but a descent, an act of self-enclosure. One can temporarily take refuge in other tasks, but these collide with the woman who requests that you walk some blocks or travel some kilometers to go bless her home.[17]

In today's theological vocabulary, all of what has been related here is called *inculturation*, and it would be difficult to overestimate the centrality of this theme in Bergoglio's thought. He has long emphasized that inculturation has been a feature of the entire Latin American world for over five hundred years. Latin America became thereby an original culture, the fruit of the planting of the seed of the Gospel in America, which generated a cultural and ethnic mix, a veritable new creation.[18] He understands Latin America to be the ongoing history of a people who have and continue to respond to the Incarnation of the Word and have become thereby an extension of it. "The Gospel," Bergoglio writes, "does not only refer to examples of the life of God but also to our own history; it is something immanent, inherent in our Christian being."[19] In the attempt to bring the Gospel to any particular community, time, and place, one very simple and useful approach is to attempt to be a good citizen, which Paul recommends in his letter to the Romans.[20] Bergoglio writes, "This is the instinct for the value of inculturation: fully living the human experience in any culture and in any city makes for a better Christian and bears fruit for the city [by winning hearts]."[21] Today, in a time when the culture is in many ways less infiltrated by faith perspectives, there is a strong temptation to "fail to look" or "fail to see" certain dimensions of what is going on. These failures are often rooted in fear of the discomfort that often results when faith demands that we challenge or confront elements that are in contradiction with the Gospel. However, inculturation cannot occur if disparate elements are not challenged. One must always return to one's roots, to who we are as a subject, which is the people of God, the one Church, a subject with two thousand years of history and with whom we are called to unite ourselves, so that we as subject can continue our sojourn through time. This subject is not an abstraction divined from sociological, political, or economic theories but is a true, real, historically constituted community in which we must choose to remain members by our choices. Failures to inculturate the Gospel occur whenever we lose the sense of our concrete identity or begin to lose the sense of the real subjectivity of those around us, something the Gospel forbids us to do. One of the most frequent manifestations of this failure today is when we allow abstract ideological perspectives to replace the Gospel-based view of people as created in the image and likeness of God.[22] We see it in discussions of the economy that tell us all is well because certain abstract indicators register positively, such as the stock market or gross national product or a trade surplus, while failing to consider that thousands or millions might be suffering regardless; others praise the development of "women's rights" even when the concept includes putting thousands or millions of unborn children to death.

Crucial to the development of Bergoglio's thought related to inculturation is the Ignatian understanding and appropriation of the universal and the particular. As Bergoglio sees it, the ideal, rooted in the Incarnation, is that the universal is made concrete in the particular. This was the principle that the Jesuits applied to the Incarnation of the Gospel in different cultures, which underlies their entire missionary thrust. He writes, "The Society [of Jesus] initiates an evangelization of real inculturation in Asia and America, which, facing the political absolutist particularism [of the European monarchs] or the Protestant abstractionism, places in opposition the real sense of universality; this *versus in unum* born from the reality of the concrete universal of the people. In other words, the response of the Church and the Society facing the project of the evil spirit, in its very roots is competitive. Our faith is combat."[23] More broadly, the universal in the particular applies to the variety of ways individual persons unite to form cohesive groups. For example, the principle extends to the Society itself: "The unity of the Society," he writes, "is a unity in diversity."[24] This is possible because the eternal Word made flesh, Jesus Christ, is the concrete universal; and hence the authentic spread of the Gospel will always manifest the universal truth, goodness, and beauty in the particular. By implication, universality is present in diversity, in as many ways as there are people and cultures. It is the work of the Holy Spirit to bring about unity in diversity in concrete ways in all dimensions of life: "The Church," Bergoglio writes, "incites us to place in common that which diversifies us—which is to say, the personal charism of each one, the personal belonging of each one to groups, to political parties, to nongovernment organizations, to parishes, to diverse sectors. This particularity that diversifies us, the Church asks us to place in common so that from this diversity the same Holy Spirit that gifts us with diversity gives us a multifaceted unity."[25]

To achieve unity in diversity is difficult and on the natural plane well near impossible at times. The difficulties are observable in almost any community. One person or group underlines the importance of unity in a way that compromises another person or group's conception of their proper autonomy. Or, on the other hand, a person or group insists on autonomy in a way that to others seems to compromise the group's unity. Saint Ignatius was fully aware that religious communities were in no way immune from such struggles. Following Saint Ignatius, Bergoglio emphasized that the only solution to such problems in a Christian community is via the spiritual life. The Jesuit who prays first of all experiences unity in diversity interiorly. Saint Ignatius is perhaps most known in the annals of spirituality for his treatment of the discernment of spirits. An important component of that is the discernment among licit decisions, wherein the Jesuit must discern among what Ignatius terms *counterpositions*. The Jesuit in prayer must deal with a variety of ideas, emotions, interior images, and movements. The Jesuit method of discernment assists him to conduct an interior dialogue through which he resolves various conflicts. The emerging solution, Bergoglio teaches, is neither in a synthesis that annuls conflicting elements in the original polarities nor in the affirmation of one polarity to the exclusion of others nor even in a subordination of one to another. Rather, "the tensions are resolved on a higher plane, maintaining—in the harmony newly achieved—the virtuality of the diverse particularities."[26] This is not for Saint Ignatius some specialized method of resolving conflicts that may emerge from time to time but the way of life of a disciple whose end is the eternal Word while living in the world of diversity and conflict. Saint Ignatius, the young Provincial Bergoglio reminds his fellow Jesuits, in no way feared conflict among legitimate counterpositions, whether they were interior, in community life, in the apostolic life, or even in the Church itself. In fact, Ignatius was suspicious when a Jesuit doing the spiritual exercises does not manifest such tensions.[27]

Bergoglio underlined a paragraph in the Jesuit Constitutions that cast light on a significant implication of this Ignatian concept of unity in diversity. It states that in the Society there must be no partiality in favor of one or another sector of the social and political hierarchy. On the contrary, what must prevail is a universal love toward all, even if the sectors are at odds with one another. Of equal importance is that this same disposition must prevail within the Society in opposition to any tendency that would interfere with unity of wills. Ignatius returns to the original idea—that universality in the real and concrete must be initially discovered interiorly—through ongoing resolution of counterpositions. Bergoglio reminds his listeners that this remains the Jesuit way, referring to a passage from the General Congregation that even conflicts that appear to threaten unity can truly be moments of grace for the community. However, this is only the case when conflicts are seen in conjunction with the interior, spiritual approach that Saint Ignatius indicated.[28]

Bergoglio referred to Saint Ignatius's treatment of this at length in his opening address to the provincial congregation in 1978.[29] Ignatius explained with his characteristic perspicacity four categories of counter-positions, or *antinomies*—four areas where tensions along legitimate and good ends regularly occur. First, there is the tension between availability and apostolic commitment. The Jesuit, he remarks humorously, is "neither a groundhog nor a butterfly."[30] Inculturation for the Jesuit demands flexibility to and availability within changing circumstances and new ministries—yet always in the context of disciplined commitment. Second, there is the tension between maintaining union of wills and dispersion, a tension both apostolic and geographic. Under circumstances where members of the community live in different places and have different apostolates, temptations to disunity whereby each emphasizes the value of his own location and work are real. Nevertheless, if the Jesuits keep the apostolic mission that flows from Christ first, they can harmonize whatever differences may arise. Third is the tension between faithfulness to and appreciation of what has been built up from the past and courage to face the new. This is the root of the age-old tension between valuing what has been accomplished and is embodied in tradition with the need to face what is new with new practices and approaches. Characteristically, neither Ignatius nor Bergoglio seek refuge in the escapes of either traditionalism or vanguard progressivism. The true path will be faithful to both sets of demands, willing to let go of methods that perhaps no longer serve the apostolate but without ever abandoning what was of permanent value. This cannot be done through purely rational calculation but must be rooted in prayerful commitment to the One who is at the same time ever the same and ever new. Finally, there is the unending tension between maintaining personal piety and zeal for the apostolate. A religious may think he or she needs to spend more time praying or undertake more apostolic work. The tension to balance those conflicting demands is real. Yet, in the Jesuit's true offering of himself to the Eucharistic Lord, and keeping his mission always first and foremost, the Jesuit knows that piety and apostolic zeal are mutually necessary and mutually supportive.

I. FRANCISCO SUÁREZ, POPULAR SOVEREIGNTY, AND THE IMPERIAL INVASION

Concerning the inculturation of the faith in Latin America, there is an important link to political theory central to Bergoglio's thought, and that is the developing theory and practice of democracy, particularly with respect to the core concepts of natural rights and popular sovereignty. A full exposition of the Jesuit contribution would take us too far afield here, but some understanding of Francisco Suárez (1548–1617) is necessary for the comprehension of the directions Bergoglio will go with his own thinking. The background to Suárez's theory was the ongoing development of what it meant to say that human beings are created in the image and likeness of God. The increasing sense of dignity imparted to the human person would have substantial repercussions on the consideration of the origins of political authority in a community of God's people. The more immediate factor that led Suárez to formulate his theory was the tendency to political centralism and absolutism in the early modern period, most prominently in the theory of the divine right of kings. European monarchs wanted to incorporate the Catholic Church, creating "national churches." The Jesuits were the principal intellectual opponents of such developments, defending the integrity and freedom of the universal Church and the people against political encroachments. In the process Suárez developed a fully articulated theory of popular sovereignty, rooted in Saint Thomas Aquinas, against aberrant theories of political absolutism.[31]

Echoing his Thomistic roots, Suárez begins by affirming the primacy and naturality of human community. "Human society," he writes, "is twofold: imperfect, or domestic; and perfect, or political." Elaborating, Suárez explains that, although the union between man and wife is "in the highest degree natural," it lacks perfection in the sense that it is not self-sufficient. For this reason the family requires the existence of a larger community, the political. Being self-sufficient, this community is more fully natural.[32] Because it is in the strictest sense a product of human nature, it precedes the existence of any political institution, including the state itself.

The natural need for a more self-sufficient community entails the creation of "a power to which the government of that community pertains." As "nature is never wanting in essentials," and "as a perfect community is agreeable to reason and natural law, so also is the power to govern such a community, without which there would be the greatest confusion therein."³³ There is, moreover, an a priori reason that supports this conclusion. Drawing on Saint Thomas, Suárez contends that "no body can be preserved unless there exists some principle whose function it is to provide for and seek the common good." He writes further that "each individual member has a care for his individual advantages, and these are often opposed to the common good, while furthermore, it occasionally happens that many things are needful to the common good, which are not . . . provided for . . . as common . . . needs; and therefore, in a perfect community, there necessarily exists some public power whose official duty it is to seek after and provide for the common good."³⁴ To assert the necessity of political authority in this way is to assert the necessity of human law, which is also necessary for the common good. The necessity of human law, he says:

> is founded on the fact that man is a social animal, requiring by his very nature a civil life and intercourse with other men; therefore, it is necessary that he should live rightly, not only as a private person, but also as part of a community; and this is a matter which depends to a large extent upon the laws of the individual community. It is furthermore necessary that each person should take counsel not only for himself, but also for others. . . . Those points which relate to the common good of men, or of the state, should be accorded particular care and observance; yet, men as individuals have difficulty in ascertaining what is expedient for the common good . . . ; so that, in consequence, there was a necessity for human laws that would have regard for the common good by pointing out what should be done for its sake and by compelling performance of such acts.³⁵

Following Saint Thomas, the principle of the common good serves as a limitation on the power of lawmakers. "It is inherent," Suárez writes, that law "should be enacted for the sake of the common good; that is to say, it should be formulated with reference to that good."³⁶ A law contrary to the common good would be unjust and hence contrary to the very nature of law itself. Such a law "is not a law, nor does it possess any binding force; indeed, on the contrary, it cannot be obeyed."³⁷

Suárez defended the proposition that political authority is instituted by God—but not in the way the divine-right theorists did. God does not institute political authority via a special or particular act of creation, Suárez concluded. Hence, God in no way ordains monarchy as the regime to govern human communities; even less does God appoint particular monarchs and ordain them with absolute power. For Suárez and the Jesuits generally, such modern readings of an expansive state had no grounding in either Scripture or Church tradition. Rather, God ordained political authority not via any special act of creation but as a power inherent in the nature of a political community, which itself was an expression of human nature as social. In Suárez's own words, the grant of political authority is given as a "characteristic property resulting from nature" and not "by a special act or grant distinct from creation."[38] In other words, God grants civil authority but not through any particular grant distinct from the generation of human nature itself; civil authority takes place as a consequence of the creation of human nature.[39]

Where, then, does this power reside by nature? In one of the most important points ever made in the development of democratic thinking, Suárez answers decisively that this power "resides not in any individual man but rather in the whole body of mankind."[40] This is because of "the fact that in the nature of things all men are born free; so that, consequently, no person has political jurisdiction over another person . . . nor is there any reason why such power should, in the nature of things, be attributed to certain persons over certain other persons."[41] Therefore, civil authority resides by nature in the community itself.[42] In this regard, "By the nature of things," Suárez writes:

> this power resides only in the community, inasmuch as it is necessary to the preservation of the latter and inasmuch as it can be manifested by the judgment of the natural reason. But all that the natural reason shows is that this power is necessary in the community as a whole; it does not show that this is necessary in one person or a senate; therefore, insofar as it is from God immediately, it is merely understood to be in the community as a whole. . . . The natural reason cannot conceive of any cause by which political power would be determinately placed in one person, or in a definite group of persons within the community. . . . Therefore, insofar as it is procured by nature, political power does not reside immediately in any subject except the community itself.[43]

Suárez clarifies that in saying political power resides in the "whole body of mankind" he does not mean mankind as a simple aggregate without order but with respect to the common act of will by which humans agree to constitute themselves as a political community for the purpose of pursuing their common good.[44]

The community may legitimately transmit its authority to a particular regime—such as a monarchy, aristocracy, or democracy—but Suárez's theory of popular sovereignty underlines that political regimes absolutely must be chosen by the people and must act for their common good, as mandated by the natural law. This raises an important question: If political authority resides in the people as a whole and is brought into existence by their common consent, then does it follow that God institutes democracy? Some subtlety is necessary here—and clarification of what exactly is meant by *democracy*. If we mean a type of regime that we can place in contrast with other forms of political regime, then the answer is no, and for the same reason it is necessary to reject the divine-right theory. God does not ordain the specifics of the political regimes human beings should live under; the people have to make those choices themselves. However, if we mean *democracy* in the most original sense of the term—that is, as the original authority of the community of people as a whole to exercise sovereignty over their own affairs under God—then the answer is yes. The people as a whole indeed possess authority, and this without any special act of will or disposition; the community possesses the power from the very nature of things by God. The great Thomist political theorist Yves R. Simon is quite clear on this implication of Suárez's theory. The creation of any political regime requires an act of transmission by the people, but democracy, in the specific sense as the natural right of the people as a whole to exercise jurisdiction over their own affairs, "can exist . . . as a result of a merely natural establishment or process, without any addition being required." This is so, Simon writes, because *"the natural reason states that the supreme political power follows upon [the gathering of men into] a perfect community and that, by virtue of this same reason, it belongs to the whole community."*[45]

Bergoglio is aware that the Jesuit missions in Argentina were deeply influenced by the Suarezian theory of popular sovereignty; they were the culmination of Suárez's ideal. Bergoglio refers to the time of the missions (1545–1750) as "the great moment of Suárez" and posits that some of the original Jesuit missionaries were probably Suárez's students. He underlines accordingly that the original deposit of power is with the people, who then delegate it.[46] Based on this ideal, the Jesuits had worked to create a sovereign people, with their own culture, history, and economy. This warranted the respect of the European powers, but, tragically, the Suarezian ideal would not prevail. The Jesuit missions would be destroyed via the machinations of powerful interests and ideologies in Europe. As we will see, the demise of the work of God embodied in the missions becomes a paradigmatic event in the mind of Jorge Mario Bergoglio, a tragedy that is etched in his mind, important not only for its specific repercussions in history but, for him, a permanent model of wrong ways of thinking and acting.

The background to the eventual destruction of the missions lies with the enlightened policies of the French Bourbons, who acceded to the Crown of Spain after the War of Succession at the start of the eighteenth century. This is the early-modern period in Europe when the new nation-states were emerging in a process that led to great concentrations of power in the state, in contrast to the medieval period when authority was more diffuse. The European monarchs had no love for the missions or the work of the Jesuits in general. For them the missions represented two trends they most sought to reverse: successful economies and civilizations increasingly independent of centralized power, and the embodiment of the Jesuit theory of popular sovereignty, which was the polar opposite of their desire to centralize power in the state generally and the Crown in particular. The beginning of the end of the missions was in 1750, with the signing of the Treaty of Permuta, which resulted in the handing over of seven of the Spanish-held reductions to Portugal. The Portuguese had no interest in the project of the missions either. In the ensuing years the entire work of the Jesuits in the region would be destroyed. More than ten thousand Guaraní were killed or enslaved and the Jesuits ordered to leave.[47] For their assertion of the right of popular sovereignty and an independent Catholic Church, both of which were in conflict with the European monarch's dreams of consolidation and centralization, the Jesuits were disbanded as an order in 1773.

After the expulsion of the Jesuits from the region, the Bourbons sought to accelerate the economic and political integration of Latin America into the empire. As part of their modernizing, centralizing tendencies, the Bourbons sought to make the colonies "more efficient" economically, by which they meant to eliminate competition and force the region to specialize more in extractive industries and agricultural production, all oriented toward export and satisfying the needs of the European center. This was accompanied by a major shift in favor of trade via the Atlantic coast rather than the Pacific. Politically, the movement was away from autonomy, self-subsistence, and local political participation. After the initial period of the conquest, when power had been highly centralized in the Crown, native-born Americans, the *criollos*, had in the latter part of the seventeenth century come to participate in local positions of political leadership.[48] However, the Bourbons saw the native-born Americans and the Catholic Church they belonged to as a source of independence and, therefore, a threat. They removed many criollos from positions and sought to harness the Church to the power of the Crown. The fact that the Bourbons were of French origin only heightened the sense of resentment and the impression that these "Bourbon Reforms" amounted to an imperial invasion more than a mere shift in policies. Reaction to the Bourbon Reforms would, within a matter of decades, fuel the fires of the independence movement.

The tragedy of the Jesuit reductions and the history that ensued left an indelible imprint on the soul of the man who would become Pope. It would not be an exaggeration to say that the destruction of the Jesuit missions conditioned Bergoglio's thinking in determinate ways. For Bergoglio, what happened here is far more than a historical injustice; it is a paradigmatic event in which played out a pattern that continues to the present day. Abstract theories, rooted in Enlightenment rationalism, mostly or totally abstract from historical context, are taken up by elites in the centers of power and imposed on people without the means to resist. These impositions invariably ignore the history, culture, economics, and politics of the people upon whom they are imposed. When the people impacted are Christian, as they were in Latin America, the impositions systematically destroy the work of inculturation of the Gospel. In fact it is their very intention to do so, as the work of the Gospel and its associated developments—the dignity of peoples, popular sovereignty, human rights, and all the ways the faith has been incarnated in the life of a people—are inevitably in conflict with the intended imposition.

Imperial invasions, rooted in Enlightenment abstractions and related ideologies, served then and have always served to justify various forms of absolutism. What we have in the destruction of the missions and afterward is enlightened absolutism versus the Catholic and Hispanic roots of Latin America. Moreover, these are by no means mere historical concerns but ever-present realities.[49] This is necessarily so because Gospel inculturation in any place and at any time is the opposite of absolutism and the surest guarantee against it. Those who fancy themselves enlightened, and, hence, superior to the benighted people living under the influence of historical Christianity, tend more easily to rely on rationalist constructs, which inevitably lead to ideology and factions. As disengaged rationalists, they often fail to see that their ideas benefit some but harm others.[50] The common good as the end of political activity is either thrown aside or simply redefined to suit the interests of those making the imposition. "In the Treaty of Permuta," Bergoglio writes, "America would witness the total disruption of this right: the ruler will not seek the common good, and—from the spheres of the Enlightenment—the life of the culture and people will be betrayed."[51]

Absolutism in political and economic practice is rooted in a convergence of thought, which Bergoglio terms *uniform thinking* ("pensamiento único"), having a global diffusion and projection in the dominant culture. This thinking has "a gnostic structure: it is inhuman; it is a reediting of various forms of rationalist absolutism."[52] The deeper point undergirding his rejection of enlightened absolutism is that "intelligence is fundamentally historical." In much of modern thought, starting with the Enlightenment, there is a divorce between *ratio* and intelligence. "*Ratio*," he writes, "is instrumental to intelligence, but, when it makes itself independent, it seeks support in ideology or social science as autonomous pillars."[53] The Incarnate Word, the Truth, is cast aside. Yet, intelligence needs the love of God present in the Incarnate Word to fulfill its purpose. "Only the heart," he writes, "unites and integrates." Intellect without the heart tends to divide. "The heart unites the idea with reality, time with space, life with death and eternity," Bergoglio writes:

> The temptation is to dislocate the understanding from the place where God . . . placed it. . . . God did not create human intelligence to constitute itself judge of all things. . . . Our understanding is not the light of the world, simply a spark of light to illuminate our faith.

> The worst thing that can happen to a human being is to allow himself to be swept away by the "lights" of reason. He will become an ignorant intellectual or rootless intellectual. Rather, the mission of our mind is *to discover the seeds of the Word in our humanity, the logos spermatikoi.*[54]

This passage helps us grasp the full significance of what the destruction of the Jesuit missions means to Bergoglio. The work of the Incarnate Word in shaping a new creation—a people with a way of life, history, culture, and economy rooted in the Gospel—is destroyed by an imperial invasion justified in terms of an abstract rationality, completely disincarnated from the actual life of the people. This is a way of thinking rooted no longer in love but in the desire to subjugate. Bergoglio confirms that "the universal fecundity that integrates and respects differences and idiosyncrasies is replaced by an absorbent metropolitan hegemony of a dominating type. These lands, which had been 'provinces' of the Kingdom passed [with the Bourbon Reforms] to be 'colonies.' Here there was no place for projects of the heart: it was the epoch of the enlightenment of the mind."[55]

Bergoglio's reaction to the tragedy of the Jesuit missions, the tragedy of the Jesuits themselves, has made him permanently suspicious of abstract theories as the bases of any dimension of social life: cultural, political, or economic. In fact his thinking is historically based. All communities, and all persons, for that matter, have a past, present, and future.[56] The absence of a sense of historical roots leads to a pervasive sense of orphanhood for so many today. The absence of a sense of links with the past contributes to a broader experience of fragmentation and lack of ties, since significant social bonds and roots are generated over time. The sense of discontinuity in time is in itself harmful, generating other social ruptures, as the orphaned lack a sense of how to live in family.[57] A people seeking to better themselves must look to their roots, the lessons learned from their history, where wisdom is found, particularly when the Gospel has been inculturated. He contrasts the person of wisdom with the "enlightened" person—one who has intellectual capacity but remains distanced from the people and their faith and therefore lacks historical, spiritual wisdom. The latter, whether in Jesus's time or ours, tends to reject the Gospel. For this reason the enlightened elites do not learn the lessons of history, and think very little of the past, believing they can reconstruct everything from the beginning as though the past either did not exist or counts for nothing. Bergoglio often calls this "adolescent progressivism."[58] In Argentina, for example, it is an attitude that prompts people to, symbolically speaking, throw great people from the past, such as the country's founders, over the cliff.[59] On the other hand, there is the temptation, in the face of the difficult challenges of today, simply to take refuge in the past. Memory is indeed important, but we should remember the path already trod to open spaces for the future. The faith is perhaps the best example of the point. We do not remember what Jesus did or what the saints did simply to fill our consciousness with them but to provide the basis for the way forward. To fail to do this is the root of fundamentalism.[60] Healthy thinking, whether concerning religious or social topics, is always a product of the unity among past, present, and future.

It is apropos at this time to mention that Calvinism shared many of the same features of the Enlightenment, particularly in that it separated reason from the heart and was also a project with imperialist bent, designed to destroy the unity of the people and their culture and separate them from their history.[61] Calvinism brought three splits, and it was the Jesuit mission to restore the three unities. The first was the division within human beings, separating the heart from the head, or reason from the emotions. Calvinism imposed a rigid discipline hostile to all that was rooted in human sentiments. A related division occurred alongside between positive and speculative reason, leading to the absolutism of science that would fracture the unity of metaphysics. By way of contrast, the Ignatian Rule preserved the unities. "The Rule," Bergoglio writes, "is a marvel of fusion between the emotive and the speculative, and all inserted in the living tradition of the Church."[62]

The second split was in society, as Calvin made the bourgeois class the true evangelizers. The bourgeois were set in opposition to the nobility, but Bergoglio emphasizes that Calvin also opposed the nobility of work and hence associations of people who worked, artisans, and craftsmen. As a result Calvinism depreciated the people, their history, and their culture. Bergoglio thinks the point is better understood in the subsequent developments in Locke (1632–1704), who held that a man could possess the fruit of his work but needs money to render this fruit incorruptible. Bergoglio sees in this the "monetarist" attitude of liberalism. What is more, this modern version of liberal reason introduces the notion that one can purchase the work of another. This divides society into two classes: those who have accumulated money (much of which comes from the purchased labor) and those who do not. Bergoglio sees the liberal, Lockean state as one that protects the moneyed class from those who have to sell their labor to live. Calvinism, for Bergoglio, was like a reverse of Marx's dictum: "Workers of the world, unite," became "Bourgeoisie of the world, unite." He further posits that this "Calvinist—schismatic—liberal" ideal, having fractured the unity of society, pushes the workers to rebellion. Marxism becomes the necessary consequence ("hijo obligado") of liberalism.[63] The Jesuits fought this through the inculturation previously discussed, making the evangelized a people with their own dignity, their own polity, economy, culture, and history. Economically they emphasized work not so much as a method of collecting monetary wealth but as an activity of a man's deepest interiority, expressed in all the works and creations of the people.

Calvinism occasioned a third split—that within the Church. As social and economic class becomes real and primary, the Church fades to more of an abstraction. No more are the "pueblo fiel de Dios" (faithful people of God). The ecclesial community is reduced to separate social classes. The international bourgeoisie replaces the unified Church. The bourgeoisie attack the united syndicates, the fraternities of working people, and the artisans. Finally, the people are deprived of the Eucharist and thereby of the mediation of Christ. The Jesuits, on the other hand, fought to preserve the Church's unity, in its inculturated economic and political forms but also as a strong affirmation of the popular religious traditions of the people, wherein love and the unity of people and Church were expressed.[64] Bergoglio, following Saint Ignatius, will always resist what he sees as the temptation to reject "the institutional Church" in favor of some ahistorical vision of a "pure" Gospel.[65] Bergoglio's understanding of Saint Ignatius's view of the Church *contra* Calvinism can be well summarized when he writes, "Saint Ignatius and his first companions . . . taught us that the project of the evil spirit divides because it guarantees the progress of individualism and terminates institutional mediations; moreover, it suffocates religiosity in the horizon of the state. In the face of this, the mission of the Company was simple but conclusive: (1) the consolidation of the institutional Church (the principle and foundation of which is the fourth vow to the Pope); [2] . . . initiate an evangelization of real inculturation in America and Asia that [in opposition to Calvinism] offers the real sense of universality."[66]

The way Bergoglio appropriates Saint Ignatius's understanding of inculturated evangelization, rooted in the practices of the first Jesuits in Argentina, conditions his entire interpretation of Latin American history in ways that even today determine his views on politics, culture, and economics in the region. The stark contrast between the project of the heart, the inculturation of the Gospel for a people conceived as sovereign, and the project of domination by the metropolitan center in Europe will continue to play out in the region's history. Notwithstanding, and not denying the reality of subordination, Bergoglio clings to his conviction that the history of the Latin American people remains inseparable from the original evangelization. Latin American history remains a history of inculturated faith. As evidence of this, he cites the depth of the evangelization of the native peoples. Far from what liberal historiography would claim, the Guaraní had a depth of faith and spirituality that easily rivaled and in many cases surpassed that of typical European Christians. In a 1977 discourse Bergoglio quotes from historical record numerous accounts of converted natives who spoke eloquently and movingly on a variety of themes: a depth of desire to be baptized, conviction that they have immortal souls, faith that God is truly Creator and Father and all are brothers, and the profundity of love of neighbor and confession of sins.[67]

One of the most lamentable impacts of the impositions on Latin America by Europe was the way elites within the region would ape the European patterns of thought and action, further imposing enlightened projects of domination in Bergoglio's native country. He believes European attitudes were in many ways imposed on Argentina in opposition to its Catholic and Hispanic roots.[68] Although the population was overwhelmingly Catholic, the Church in Argentina was actually weak. Living under the old Spanish nationalist policy, the Patronato, the state had to approve episcopal appointments. Although originally implemented as something of a privilege for Spanish monarchs, in a more secular age it would be an instrument of limiting the Church's independence. The Church would become significantly more of an independent force in the twentieth century, with an impressive growth of Catholic institutions and expansion of dioceses and parishes. Nonetheless, the dominant political forces were not interested in Gospel inculturation or a vibrant, independent Church. On the one hand was the older, landed oligarchy who saw the Church as a bulwark of the kind of society they wanted—that is, as a socially conservative force that would support their dominance. On the other hand, there was a self-styled reformist element, more intellectual in nature, that embraced European liberalism. They were suspicious when not hostile to the Church, seeing it as tied to the conservative agenda. In Latin America, enlightened reformism would in many ways be in distressing continuity with the enlightened absolutism that undermined the cause of evangelization in the first place. Postindependence liberals, like the absolute monarchs who preceded them, wanted to enlighten a society imbued with what they saw as backward Catholic and Hispanic roots, maintain the Church within limits determined by the state, and promote economic freedom for a burgeoning domestic bourgeoisie. They wanted to privatize land held by communities or associations of the people, particularly Church land, and eliminate the autonomy of local communities, including associations of workers, producers, and artisans.[69] The economic centralization carried out by the Bourbons would be replaced throughout the region by a new centralization among various combinations of landed elites, foreign industrializers, or domestic corporations, often in league with a centralized state bureaucracy. The dominant agenda would remain elitist and exclusionary. Argentina would not have a free and fair election prior to 1916. Even when the elections were not fraudulent, the economic and political agenda would originate with the privileged few. Although the Catholic Church would certainly find its voice in the twentieth century, it would be kept away from the centers of political and economic power.

The predominant trends in historiography would be decidedly liberal, in contrast with Bergoglio's insistence on a Latin America grounded in an evangelized people with their own history and culture meriting respect.[70] Bergoglio sees in much of the development of modern history a true "disincarnation," whereby God is removed—or, if not removed, separated—from the historical Church and Christ. Of course, in the enlightened and liberal view the Catholic Church as an independent factor was always something to be eliminated. Going back to the censure of Suárez's writings by European despots in the preindependence period, what emerged by the time of the centennial of American independence was a standard interpretation of Latin American history. This rendering would emphasize the importance of the centralized, self-sufficient modern state, answering to no external power, formed by a lay, secular nation, in accord with European models, replete with enlightened stereotypes of Hispanic culture and traditions; the role of the Catholic Church is radically reduced, insignificant in the march toward progress.[71]

Along the same line but worthy of separate mention has been the role of the Black Legend in Latin American historiography. The Black Legend began with the decidedly negative view of Spain propagated by its sixteenth and seventeenth century rivals, the English. Originally, it underlined and exaggerated the excesses of the conquistadores in the New World, their violence and mistreatment of the native peoples. Ironically, the English were fond of quoting some of the Spaniards who protested mistreatment at the time it occurred, most notably the extended treatment of the subject by the Dominican Bartolomé de Las Casas. In the context of the New World, the legend broadens into a completely negative view of the people and civilization that emerged from the Spanish colonizers. In this denigrated history, the entire roots of Latin American civilization appear rotten: backward people, a viciously exploitative colonial state, a hypocritical and compliant Church. Backward, unenlightened, mired in ignorance and despotism, completely lacking in the virtues of the modernizing European civilization—this is the Latin America that accompanies the Black Legend. Moreover, as authors such as Guzmán Carriquiry and Alberto Methol Ferré have pointed out, this rendering of Latin America's origins continues to impact the region in a negative way. Today blowback from the legend is somewhat more directed against the Catholic Church and Latin America itself, discouraging the region's coming of age through economic, political, and cultural integration. One of the worst effects that emerged over time has been the decided tendency to distort the way the history of Latin America is appropriated, even by its own people.[72] Methol Ferré describes in forceful terms the worst results of the intellectual and cultural imperialism discussed here. "The black legend," he writes, "leaves us with rotten roots. We are sons of bitches. Our history is worthless. It is the mere history of infamy. What are we? What can we be with such a birth? Nothing, simply nothing. We remain divided among ourselves. Neither indigenous, nor *criollos*, nor mestizos, nothing. And from nothing, what can come? Only a new destiny as a colony."[73]

In opposition to this intellectual component of the project of domination, Bergoglio has persisted in his historically grounded convictions that reverence the heroic work of the early Jesuit evangelizers. He continues to believe that what the world truly needs is the inculturation of the Gospel. Despite the errors and injustices of many Spaniards of the colonial period, Bergoglio in no way views the history of Latin America as all black. More specifically, two convictions continue to surface: First is the belief that the history of Latin America is the history of a real people who are a true subject, a communal "who" extant for over five hundred years. For Bergoglio, that is real history, ideological readings notwithstanding. Second—and related—history, as previously indicated, can only be validly seen in the context of a tension among the memory of real past, commitment to the reality of the present, and projection toward the future. The people have a real heritage of which the Catholic faith is a constitutive part. The identity of the people is an ongoing construction, yes, but one defined by what they have received from their fathers, a history not simply to be idealized but reverently sifted, realizing that there is good in the present that was transmitted from the past, good that in wisdom should be preserved. The future of the people will be a product both of what has been bequeathed to them and what they will make of that inheritance. Ideologies and imperial projects that seek to distort this process, distorting the past for the purpose of distorting the present and molding the future in the long-standing interests of the powerful—these remain for Bergoglio, now Pope Francis, projects to be defeated. As he said many decades ago, following Saint Ignatius, our faith is a combat.

In conclusion, we can see that evangelization through inculturation, as practiced by the original Jesuit missionaries in Argentina, remains for Bergoglio the fundamental paradigm. For him the Word of God intends to penetrate the entire life of the people, transforming them both interiorly and through the creation of new social institutions reflective of Gospel values. The people become a veritable Incarnation of the Word and hence themselves a source of ongoing theological and pastoral reflection. The sense of the Latin American people as an evangelized people, a new creation, and for all that people with their own rich and distinct history, remains fundamental in Bergoglio's social thought. These people, conceived as being in the image and likeness of God, come to recognize in their personhood the basis of their own sovereignty. In the time of the missions, the Jesuits sought to create a vibrant and reasonably independent political economy. Tragically, this success aroused the ire of the "countermission," that which emerged originally from the Enlightenment and its related theories of state sovereignty, particularly in the power of the monarch. In the ensuing destruction of the missions, Bergoglio sees the paradigm of the conflict that for him remains relevant to our own time. The historically constituted people, with their own unique histories and cultures informed by the Gospel, are threatened by imperial projects from the outside. A true culture and politics of resistance is needed.

NOTES

1. Francis, *Evangelii gaudium*, The Holy See (Vatican website), November 24, 2013, http://w2.vatican.va/content/francesco/en/apost_exhortations/documents/papa-francesco_esortazione-ap_20131124_evangelii-gaudium.html, 20–24, 27 (hereafter *EG*). For more on this theme, see also the chapters "Being with Christ," 15–20, and "To the Outskirts of Existence," 99–101, both found in Francis, *Church of Mercy: A Vision for the Church* (Chicago: Loyola Press, 2014).

2. This is from the chapter "Historia y presencia de la Compañía de Jesús en nuestra tierra," found in Jorge Mario Bergoglio, *Reflexiones espirituales sobre la vida apostólica* (Bilbao: Ediciones Mensajero, 2013), 248.

3. Jorge Mario Bergoglio, *Mente abierta, corazón creyente* (Buenos Aires: Editorial Claretiana, 2012), 218.

4. My discussion of the Jesuit missions is drawn from the following sources: Jorge Mario Bergoglio's chapter "Proyección cultural y evangelizadora de los mártires rioplatenses" in his *Reflexiones en esperanza*, 1st ed. (Madrid: Romana Editorial, 2013), 289–317; and also his chapters "¿Qué son los jesuitas?," 229–45, and "Historia y presencia de la Compañía de Jesús en nuestra tierra," 246–63, both found in Bergoglio, *Reflexiones espirituales*, 229–45. Unless otherwise noted, all translations in this book from the original Spanish are mine, in conjunction with Rosita A. Chazarreta Rourke.

5. From the chapter "¿Qué son los jesuitas?" in Bergoglio, *Reflexiones espirituales*, 236–37.

6. During the colonial period, an *encomendero* was a person granted an *encomienda*, which, in turn, was a tract of land, understood to include the right to the labor of the native peoples who lived on it. When in the hands of the

unscrupulous, encomiendas were the source of many injustices committed against the native peoples.

7. Bergoglio, *Reflexiones espirituales*, 251.

8. A *reduction* was "a type of particular indigenous community: the Indians were organized by family groups, the [accompanying] land common or collective property[;] the work was freely done in different shifts; [the reductions] gave birth to an economic system of communitarian type." They were "relatively administratively independent" and "were led by an official who fulfilled a guardian function." Carlos A. Loprete, *Iberoamerica: Historia de su civilización y cultura* (Upper Saddle River, NJ: Prentice Hall, 1995), 82. In this book, the terms *reductions* and *missions* are used interchangeably.

9. A good summary of the culture developed by the Jesuits via the missions is Guillermo Fúrlong Cárdiff, *Los jesuitas y la cultura rioplatense* (Buenos Aires: Editorial Biblos, 1994).

10. It is essential to note that many would certainly reject Bergoglio's reading of the missions. In fact, criticism of the missions was constitutive of Enlightenment and Protestant thought. I will not go into these debates in any detail here. For the purposes of this book, which is to explain Bergoglio's thinking, I follow his reading of the missions as essentially positive. There can be no question that hostility to the missions was closely related to broader anti-Catholic perspectives energetically propagated by proponents of Protestantism and the Enlightenment. At times these narratives were clearly ahistorical and propagandistic in nature. It must always be recalled that the Black Legend was invented by the Anglo-American world precisely to diminish Spain and the entire Hispanic tradition by underlining and exaggerating the misdeeds of the Spaniards. Hostility to the missions in the Anglo-American world must always be seen in relation to the Black Legend and England's hostility toward and rivalry with Spain. As famous Argentine writer Leopoldo Lugones succinctly put it, "This economic system [in the missions] based on [community] was antagonistic to the independence of individualistic character that the eighteenth century initiated" (quoted in Loprete, *Iberoamerica*, 85). The Black Legend was first discussed in the 1913 work by Julián Jederías y Loyot, *La leyenda negra y la verdad histórica*, Clásicos de Historia 65, available online at https://www.dropbox.com/s/4ce6qljbyxg3giq/Juderias.pdf?dl=0. See also the discussion of the Black Legend later in this chapter.

11. Pope Francis, quoted in Elisabetta Piqué, "Francisco, contra las ideologías: 'Siempre terminan mal, no sirven,'" *La Nación* (Buenos Aires), July 12, 2015, http://www.lanacion.com.ar/1809765-francisco-contra-las-ideologias; emphasis mine.

12. Austen Ivereigh, *The Great Reformer: Francis and the Making of a Radical Pope* (New York: Henry Holt, 2014), 177.

13. Bergoglio, *Reflexiones en esperanza*, 289–317. Bergoglio gave the conference on May 27, 1988, on the occasion of the canonization of the martyrs of Río de la Plata. Fathers Roque González, Alfonso Rodríguez, and Juan del Castillo—all Jesuit priests—worked in the Jesuit reductions in Paraguay, evangelizing the native Guaraní. They were put to death at the bidding of an angry native shaman; the first two were martyred on November 15, 1658, and del Castillo two days later. John Paul II canonized them in Paraguay in 1988.

14. Ibid., 302.

15. Ibid., 305.

16. In Argentina, "una promesa"—a promise—is made to God to do something specific, usually involving self-sacrifice, if a prayer request is granted. I spoke with a man who rode his bicycle three days to the shrine of La Virgen del Valle (the Virgin of the Valley) in the Argentine Province of Catamarca in thanksgiving for an answer to a prayer. Since a promise is seen as sacred, people often think they should not alter its terms without first consulting a priest.

17. From the chapter "El Reino de Cristo," in Jorge Mario Bergoglio, *Meditaciones para religiosos* (Ediciones Mensajero: Bilbao, España, 2014), 153–54.

18. This is found in the prologue Bergoglio write to Guzmán Carriquiry, *El bicentenario de la independencia de los países latinoamericanos* (Ediciones Encuentro: Madrid, 2011), 5–9.

19. Jorge Mario Bergoglio, *Diálogos entre Juan Pablo II y Fidel Castro* (Buenos Aires: Editorial di Ciencia y Cultura, 1998), 54.

20. Romans 13:1. All biblical citations in the text are taken from the sources as indicated. Scriptural quotations contained within ecclesiastical documents are from the documents as cited. In the very few cases where there is no source indicated, all scriptural references are to the Revised Standard Version, Catholic Edition (San Francisco: Ignatius Press, 2006).

21. Francis, *Only Love Can Save Us: Letters Homilies and Talks of Cardinal Jorge Bergoglio*, trans. Gerard Seramik (Huntington, IN: Our Sunday Visitor, Inc., 2013), 41.

22. Francis, *Only Love Can Save Us*, 42.

23. Bergoglio, *Meditaciones para religiosos*, 137n1.

24. Bergoglio, *Reflexiones en esperanza*, 217.

25. Jorge Mario Bergoglio, *La nación por construir: Utopía, pensamiento y compromiso* (Buenos Aires: Editorial Claretiana, 2005), 24.

26. Bergoglio, "Esperanza e institución," in Bergoglio, *Reflexiones en esperanza*, 218–19.

27. "Esperanza e institución," found in Bergoglio, *Reflexiones en esperanza*, 218–19.

28. Ibid., 220–21.

29. The following is drawn from "Una institución que vive su carisma," in Bergoglio, *Meditaciones para religiosos*, 49–60.

30. Ibid., 50.

31. Austen Ivereigh, *Catholicism and Politics in Argentina: 1810–1960* (New York: St. Martin's Press, 1996), 3–11. Francisco Suárez's major work on political theory is *"De legibus, ac deo legislatore"* (Of the Law, and God the Lawgiver), found in *The Classics of International Law*, Vol. II, ed. James Scott Brown (London: Clarendon Press, 1949). Hereafter Suárez's chapter will be referred to as *"De legibus."*

32. Suárez, *"De legibus,"* 364–65.

33. Ibid.

34. Ibid., 367.

35. Ibid., 48–49.

36. Ibid., 90.

37. Ibid., 113.

38. Ibid., 379.

39. Ibid., 379.

40. Ibid., 373.

41. Ibid., 373–74.

42. Ibid., 375.

43. See Francisco Suárez's *Defensio fidei catholicae adversus anglicanae sectae errors*—specifically, volume 3: *De summi pontificis supra temporalis reges excellentia, et potestate*, chapter 2, *"Utrum principatius politicus immediate a deo sit, seu ex divina institutione"* (Works, XXI), as quoted in Yves R. Simon, *Philosophy of Democratic Government* (Notre Dame, IN: University of Notre Dame Press, 1993), 172.

44. Suárez, *"De legibus,"* 375.

45. Suárez quoted in Simon, *Philosophy of Democratic Government*, 173; emphasis mine.

46. Bergoglio, *Reflexiones en esperanza*, 293.

47. Ivereigh, *Great Reformer*, 62. The tragedy is well captured in the final scenes of the historically based film *The Mission*.

48. Carriquiry, *El bicentenario*, 29–32. *Criollos* originally referred to Spanish-born people in the New World. Later the term was applied to their descendants, even when they were not born in the Old World. Today its use in Argentina often refers more broadly to pride in local Latin American roots.

49. A striking recent example of this, which was not well understood by commentators, was Bergoglio's reference to "ideological colonization" in the context of discussing contraception and gay marriage. This exemplifies his

worldview—noting foreign ways of thinking that have been imposed by various kinds of coercion.

50. See more on this theme in, for example, Jorge Mario Bergoglio, *Ponerse la patria al hombre: Memoria y camino de esperanza*, corrected and updated (Buenos Aires: Editorial Claretiana, 2013), 82–83.

51. Bergoglio, *Reflexiones en esperanza*, 293. The Treaty of Permuta was an accord signed in 1750 that handed over seven of the Spanish-held reductions to Portugal. The natives fought to protect their territory, but over the years the reductions were destroyed.

52. Bergoglio's prologue to Carriquiry, *El bicentenario*, 7.

53. Ibid.

54. Bergoglio, *Mente abierta*, 28–29; emphasis mine.

55. Bergoglio, *Reflexiones en esperanza*, 315.

56. Ibid., 33–34.

57. Bergoglio, *La nación por construir*, 19–20.

58. For example, in Bergoglio, *La nación por construir*, 75.

59. Bergoglio, *Ponerse la patria al hombre*, 85.

60. Bergoglio, *La nación por construir*, 27–28.

61. The discussion of Calvinism is from Bergoglio, *Reflexiones espirituales*, 231–39. As with the case of the missions, many would of course take issue with Bergoglio's assessment, but my exposition will simply follow Bergoglio closely in matters of interpretation.

62. Bergoglio, *Reflexiones espirituales*, 233. Bergoglio notes that the Rule particularly praises Saint Thomas, Saint Bonaventure, and the "Master of *The Sentences*" (Peter Lombard).

63. Bergoglio, *Reflexiones espirituales*, 234–35.

64. Bergoglio, *Reflexiones espirituales*, 238–39.

65. Bergoglio, *Meditaciones para religiosos*, 149–50.

66. Bergoglio, *Mente abierta*, 33n4.

67. Bergoglio, *Reflexiones espirituales*, 258–61.

68. See Ivereigh, *Great Reformer*, 5–9, 18–22. Also see my previous note 31 in this chapter for a relevant summary of the Argentine history referenced here.

69. Carriquiry, *El bicentanario*, 57.

70. Bergoglio's views on these matters are found in the prologue he wrote to Carriquiry, *El bicentanario*, 5–9.

71. Carriquiry, *El bicentenario*, 24–25.

72. Ibid., 82–83.

73. Alberto Methol Ferré, quoted in Carriquiry, *El bicentenario*, 83–84. Methol Ferré is an old friend of Bergoglio, going back to the organization of the Third General Conference of Latin American Bishops, held in Puebla,

Mexico, in 1979. They share the inculturated Catholic understanding of Latin American history with an emphasis on cultural roots.

3

HISTORICAL-THEOLOGICAL ROOTS II

From Vatican II to the Theology of Liberation
and the Vatican Response

In this chapter we move to consider the more proximate influences and development of Bergoglio's thought, beginning with the Second Vatican Council. It is not possible to understand the social thought of any Latin American prelate from the 1970s onward without reference to a considerable number of ecclesiastical documents that emanated from both the universal and Latin American Church. In considering these documents, we will stick to the elements relevant to Bergoglio's social thought. We will begin with the seminal documents from Vatican II—*Lumen gentium* (1964) and, of the greatest significance, *Gaudium et spes* (1965).[1] Because of their particular influence on Bergoglio, we will also need to summarize Paul VI's great encyclical on development, *Populorum progressio* (1967), as well as what Bergoglio himself has cited as his favorite pastoral document, Paul VI's apostolic exhortation *Evangelii nuntiandi* (1975).[2] From here we shift scenes to examine how these developments in social and pastoral thinking play out in Bergoglio's world, Latin America. Of particular interest will be the monumental Second General Conference of Latin American Bishops, held in Medellín, Colombia, in 1968. This conference paralleled the development of the new theology of liberation, which would sweep through the entire region. Its influence would come to impact the entire Latin American Church. The radicalism it spawned would force a confrontation with the Church's more established body of reformist social thought. Eleven years later the Third General Conference of Latin American Bishops, held in Puebla, Mexico, in 1979, would develop important ideas about the social order, giving more emphasis to the history and culture of the region as sources for social thinking. This modified line parallels Bergoglio's own thinking.

We begin with some of the shifts in emphasis that occurred in the Church universal, focusing on those that would come to bear in significant ways on Church and society in Latin America. Four themes are central to the discourse: (1) the definition of the Catholic Church as the "people of God," (2) the renewed emphasis on collegiality among bishops, (3) the increased emphasis on the promotion of social justice, and (4) renewal of the laity generally and particularly with respect to the pursuit of (3).

Lumen gentium (*LG*), the "Dogmatic Constitution on the Church," although not introducing any doctrinal changes in ecclesiology, did introduce a shift in emphasis. Certainly, as the document points out (*LG*, 18–29), the Catholic Church is hierarchical. Nevertheless, *Lumen gentium* underlines the Church as "the people of God" (*LG*, 9–17). This term underlines the equality of the Church's members under Christ the King, as it also points out that the Church is, to a limited degree in history, "the kingdom of heaven on earth" (*LG*, 3). The Church is no collection of individuals but a people raised up by God to serve Him in holiness (*LG*, 9). *Lumen gentium* affirms that the call to holiness is universal and that there is "a true equality between all with regard to the dignity and to the activity which is common to all the faithful in building up the Body of Christ" (*LG*, 32). In what would be among the most frequently discussed themes of the Second Vatican Council, the document devotes an entire chapter to "The Call to Holiness" (*LG*, 39–42), clarifying that there is no distinction with respect to this call, that it is in the strictest sense universal and incumbent on all of God's people. The document affirms "the special vocation" of the laity "to seek the kingdom of God by engaging in temporal affairs and directing them according to God's will" (*LG*, 31). In fact there are "places and circumstances" where it is through the laity alone that the Catholic Church "can become the salt of the earth" (*LG*, 33). Additionally, *Lumen gentium* states that, because of their "knowledge, competence or pre-eminence," the laity are "empowered . . . to manifest their opinion on those things that pertain to the good of the Church" (*LG*, 37).

Lumen gentium also launched a second theme that would be particularly important for the Church in Latin America after Vatican II: collegiality among the bishops. Since the time of the Reformation, the Catholic Church had been emphasizing its oneness under the unique authority of the Pope, reacting in a variety of ways to Protestant rejection of the Petrine ministry (the papacy). There had been some decided tendency to deemphasize the authority of bishops either as individual leaders in their respective dioceses or, collectively, as Church leaders in different regions of the world. *Lumen gentium* sought to rebalance this by getting back to a vision of the role of bishops inspired by New Testament sources and the practices of ancient Christianity. *Lumen gentium* refers to the bishops collectively as "a college or permanent assembly" (*LG*, 19). Each bishop is a teacher of doctrine and holds an office of real authority granted by Christ Himself (*LG*, 20). In union with the Bishop of Rome, they have "supreme and full authority over the universal Church" (*LG*, 22). In their particular local churches they are ordained to govern (*LG*, 23). Moreover, the constitution acknowledges that "through divine providence . . . different churches [were] set up in various places by the apostles and their successors [the bishops]." Hence, "episcopal conferences at the present time are in a position to contribute in many and fruitful ways to the concrete realization of the collegial spirit" (*LG*, 23).

The shifts in emphasis to the roles of the bishops and the laity were to have a profound impact in postconciliar developments, motivating the Latin American Bishops Conference to teach with more specific reference to the social problems besetting the region. In addition, *Lumen gentium* encouraged the laity to become more involved, which would take the form of popular movements for social justice from the 1960s onward.

The most important statement from Vatican II concerning social justice was *Gaudium et spes*, the council's longest and last document. It was designated "Pastoral Constitution on the Church in the Modern World." As the council will be remembered for its "opening to the modern world," *Gaudium et spes* is in a very real sense Vatican II's signature document. Prior to becoming Pope Benedict XVI, Joseph Ratzinger—one of the *periti*, or theological experts, at the council—

addressed in depth what the council fathers were trying to accomplish with the document.³ The Catholic Church was trying to move away from the hostile stance it had taken toward the modern world from the time of the French Revolution. The Church sought to redefine its relationship with the modern world as one of dialogue and mutual cooperation. This was accompanied by a thoroughgoing examination of conscience whereby the Church acknowledged its own flaws and sought to avoid making new ones. For this reason the document tended to emphasize positive features in the modern world without at the same time neglecting the Church's commitment to permanent beliefs in the reality of sin reflected in that same world. The Church was announcing its desire to be a partner with modernity for the purpose of making the world better and more just. Six years later, the bishops of the world would give perhaps their clearest statement ever on the subject, writing that "action on behalf of justice and transformation of the world fully appear to us as a constitutive dimension of the Gospel . . . of the Church's mission for the redemption of the human race and its liberation from every oppressive situation."⁴ *Gaudium et spes* (*GS*) begins with the bold reminder that the "joys and hopes" as well as the "griefs and agonies" of the people of our time are the same as those of the followers of Christ, emphasizing the essential unity of the human experience (*GS*, 1). The document then links this commonality to the uniqueness of Christ, declaring that "in reality it is only in the mystery of the Word made flesh that the mystery of man becomes clear. . . . Christ the Lord . . . in the very revelation of the mystery of the Father and of his love, fully reveals man to himself and reveals to him his most high calling" (*GS*, 22). Therefore, there is no contradiction between the commitment to Christ and to the world. Indeed, Christ shines light on all human problems and guides us to their proper solution.

A number of *Gaudium et spes*'s themes guide the Catholic Church in its social dimension in the post–Vatican II world. Among the most important is the dignity of the human person, which keeps the Church on the forefront of the struggle for human rights around the world (*GS*, 47–52, 73–76).⁵ The faith demands such commitments, as it provides the basis for the dignity of the person created in the image and likeness of God. Second, *Gaudium et spes* emphasizes the human community as ultimately one, affirming that "God has willed that all men should constitute one family and treat one another in a spirit of brotherhood" (*GS*,

24). From this flows the Church's commitment to work for peace in an increasingly dangerous world, in accord with the beatitude, "Blessed are the peacemakers" (*GS*, 79). The faith's contribution is to reiterate Christ's deeper command to love all, which raises up justice and, via forgiveness, brings justice to a new and higher level in God. Third, the document discusses needed improvements in the economic, political, and cultural arenas, particularly for people in the developing world who suffer the absence of basic goods, are deprived of access to political participation, and need to live under governments that genuinely pursue the common good (*GS*, 60–63, 73–76). The Catholic Church has "no proper mission in the political, economic, or social order" (*GS*, 42). Nonetheless, as it is a place where "the earthly and heavenly city penetrate each other," the Church, in the pursuit of its proper mission "contribute[s] greatly towards making the family of man and its history more human" (*GS*, 40). The promotion of unity among people does pertain to the Church's mission from Christ (*GS*, 42). There can be no shirking of these temporal responsibilities. Rather, "let there be no false opposition between professional and social activities on the one hand, and religious life on the other" (*GS*, 43). Moreover, despite the fact that the Church does not have the role to implement political or economic solutions, "the Christian view of things will itself suggest some specific solution in certain circumstances" (*LG*, 43).

The theme of the development of peoples would come to acquire renewed emphasis with Paul VI's publication of *Populorum progressio* (The Development of Peoples) in 1967. Alongside Leo XIII's *Rerum novarum* (1891), it would become a foundational document in the Church's social teaching, as indicated by two subsequent documents published in commemoration—John Paul II's *Sollicitudo rei socialis* (1987) and Benedict XVI's *Caritas in veritate* (2007).[6] Although of great significance in the universal Church, *Populorum progressio* was inevitably of the greatest significance for the part of the developing world that was most Catholic, Bergoglio's home, Latin America.

Populorum progressio (*PP*) begins by asserting the Catholic Church's "deep interest and concern" for the "progressive development of peoples" (*PP*, 1), a situation demanding an urgent response. The hungry cry out to those blessed with abundance, and the Church "asks each and every man to hear his brother's plea and answer it lovingly" (*PP*, 3). Paul VI outlines the problems of the underdeveloped nations, such as staggering inequality and lack of food, employment, and health care (*PP*, 6–13). He references remnant colonial structures that "are no match for the harsh economic realties of today" (*PP*, 8). He strongly affirms the Catholic Church's belief that "created goods should flow fairly to all" (*PP*, 22) and that the realization of this end is no mere suggestion but a moral imperative: private property rights and free trade principles are subordinate to the demand that the needs of all be met (*PP*, 22–23). He specifically criticizes certain practices widespread in Latin America, such as large estates (*latifundia*) that are "extensive, unused or poorly used" and the practice of exporting capital, money gained from investment in a poor country then exported out of it for private gain. In both cases, Pope Paul VI opens the door to defining possible remedies (*PP*, 24). He reiterates the Church's longstanding rejection of economic liberalism, which places the pursuit of profit, in a context of private property and competition, in the absence of "concomitant social obligations" (*PP*, 26). Moreover, in such a context, technology threatens to become technocracy (*PP*, 34), by which technological developments simply accelerate the processes of inequality—that is, economic development for some and poverty for others. In response to these pressing, often tragic, circumstances, Paul VI lays on the wealthy and the developed countries a threefold obligation: mutual solidarity, social justice, and universal charity (*PP*, 43–53). Amid the treatment of the material components of development, Paul VI expresses what would fundamentally come to underpin Bergoglio's thought: that development must be "of the whole man and every man" (*PP*, 14, 42). Social sciences had and often continue to exhibit a tendency toward reductionism in the discussion of development, reducing it to the realization of particular empirical results in the economic and social field. Here Paul VI makes a particularly important contribution rooted in the Catholic tradition, insisting on a holistic, integrated, or "full-bodied" humanism" (*PP*, 42). Paul VI specifically talks about the importance of cultural development and the maintenance of traditional cultural values, particularly the family. Modern culture threatens to undermine important moral values and leave people without the cultural heritage they need to sustain human development. Attitudes of solidarity and dialogue, particularly when motivated by authentic love of others, will be absolutely necessary for the authentic development of peoples (*PP*, 73). These insights will become cornerstones for Bergoglio's thinking.

Two years later, Paul VI issued what is arguably Bergoglio's favorite ecclesiastical document, *Evangelii nuntiandi* (*EN*), which he has described as "the greatest pastoral document ever written."[7] Although the document's focus is on evangelization, not social justice, Paul VI does here address the relationship between the two in decisive terms. Furthermore, as we have seen repeatedly, Bergoglio links evangelization always with inculturation in the broader social order. No reader of Bergoglio could fail to miss the influence of this most important document.

Evangelii nuntiandi goes to the very identity of the Church and of its various dimensions. Evangelization is "the duty incumbent on [the Church] by the command of the Lord Jesus.... This message is necessary. It is unique. It cannot be replaced" (*EN*, 5). It is in a real sense the Church's "deepest identity," strikingly evident in the Gospels themselves. The Catholic Church is "linked to evangelization in her most intimate being" (*EN*, 14–15) and itself is the "most immediate and visible fruit" of evangelization, the product of the activity of Jesus Himself and the first apostles. The Church "remains in the world . . . as a sign. . . . She prolongs and continues Him" (*EN*, 15). The document clearly underlines the "profound link between Christ, the Church and evangelization" (*EN*, 16). Paul makes specific reference with sorrow to the situation, already widely present in 1975, whereby people will claim to love Jesus but not the Church, who claim to listen to Christ but not the Church, and who claim to belong to Christ but not the Church. Without denying the good intentions of these people, he calls these dichotomies "absurd," in conflict with the Lord's own dictum that "Anyone who rejects you, rejects me" (Luke 10:16, in *EN*, 16). Such attitudes equally ignore Saint Paul's statement that "Christ loved the Church and sacrificed himself for her" (Ephesians 5:25, in *EN*, 16). Love for the Church means love of and participation in one's local church in the context of the Church universal. In contrast to divisive tendencies in the Church justified by appeals to the particularities of local churches, Paul VI is careful to hold the many together in the one. The universal Church is not a sum "of essentially different individual Churches" (*EN*, 62). It is essential to the Church that it truly be one, professing one faith with one baptism. Nonetheless, Paul VI is profoundly aware that the "pole" of the universal exists in conjunction with a second pole, the local church (*EN*, 62). A church not inculturated locally would be an ineffective evangelizer. He is not proposing a universalism truly at the expense of the local. Yet, even while protecting the value of the particular and the local, he issues the concomitant warning that evangelization "risks losing its power and disappearing altogether if one empties it or adulterates its content under the pretext of translating it" (*EN*, 63).

The relationship between evangelization and culture is taken up explicitly. The Catholic Church indeed seeks to convert, but in a profound and all-encompassing way. Evangelization intends to impact "the personal and collective consciences of people, the activities in which they engage, and the lives and concrete milieu which are theirs" (*EN*, 18). This includes "mankind's criteria of judgment, determining values, points of interest, lines of thought, sources of inspiration and models of life," whenever the former conflict with the "plan of salvation" (*EN*, 18). In other words, "what matters is to evangelize man's culture . . . in the wide and rich sense which these terms have in *Gaudium et spes*, always taking the person as one's starting-point and always coming back to the relationships of people among themselves and with God" (*EN*, 20). Paul VI is careful to distinguish between the Gospel and any particular culture, emphasizing the former's radical independence. On the other hand, as an incarnate faith embedded in the exigencies of time and place, the Gospel must be lived by people who inhabit a particular culture, which necessitates the employment, in a discerning way, of various components of human culture. He references the split between the Gospel and culture in our time, noting that such a situation is not historically unique. Certainly today cultures need again to be evangelized, "regenerated by an encounter with the Gospel" (*EN*, 20). This is only going to happen, however, if the Gospel is proclaimed. Undoubtedly, especially today, the work of evangelization requires effective witness, to which all Christians are called (*EN*, 20–21).

As important as witness is, it is insufficient. It must be supplemented by explanation and justification. There must be a clear proclamation of the fullness of the message of Christ. "There is no true evangelization," Paul VI writes, "if the name, the teaching, the life, the promises, the kingdom and the mystery of Jesus of Nazareth, the Son of God are not proclaimed" (*EN*, 22). The proclamation consists of the original announcement—or *kerygma*—of the saving knowledge of Jesus Christ. The foundation and center of evangelization is the "clear proclamation that, in Jesus Christ, the Son of God made man, who died and rose from the dead, salvation is offered to all men, as a gift of God's grace and mercy" (*EN*, 27). The original proclamation is supplemented by the more lengthy work of catechesis. The evangelized are brought into the life of the community, the Church. Their lives become characterized, among other things, by "adherence to the Church," and "acceptance of the sacraments" as instruments of grace to transform their lives (*EN*, 23). Finally, the evangelized will move forward with their own "apostolic initiative[s]" to evangelize others (*EN*, 24). The totality of evangelization "consists in the implantation of the Church, which does not exist without the driving force which is the sacramental life culminating in the Eucharist" (*EN*, 28).

In a discussion that would come to have the greatest repercussions for the Catholic Church in Latin America, Paul VI takes up the difficult topic of "liberation" from many distressing problems of this world—such as dire poverty, inequality, lack of food, disease, illiteracy, injustices in the economic dimension, and structures of domination in international economic and political arrangements (*EN*, 30). He notes that this was widely discussed in the preceding synod by Third World bishops (*EN*, 37–38). In an approach that Church authority will continue to follow, Paul tries to steer between two temptations: First, he strongly states that there are indeed "profound links" between "evangelization and human advancement" or "development and liberation" (*EN*, 31). The links between the two are deep. They are anthropological, as evangelization occurs in a world where there are political, economic, and social questions. They are also evangelical, touching biblical themes of love, justice, and response to the suffering Christ in the world (*EN*, 31). Hence, one cannot proclaim evangelization and ignore the very real problems of poverty, injustice, development, and imminent threats to peace in the world. There can be no retreat from these problems, as *Gaudium et spes* had already clarified. There is, however, a second temptation, one that the Latin American Church will grapple with for decades, and that is that those working in the liberation effort in the social sense are frequently "tempted to reduce [the Catholic Church's] mission to the dimensions of a simply temporal project. They would reduce her aims to a man-centered goal; the salvation of which [the Church] is messenger would be reduced to material well-being. Her activity, forgetful of all spiritual and religious preoccupation, would become initiatives of the political or social order" (*EN*, 32). He insists that in such a projection the Church loses her identity. As a result, Paul VI used *Evangelii nuntiandi* to reaffirm strongly that there is a fundamental distinction between human liberation and salvation. Therefore, he reasserts forcefully that the Catholic Church has a properly religious, transcendent vocation (*EN*, 31–33). In this world, temporal liberation will always fall short to the degree that the properly spiritual dimension, "salvation and happiness in God," is lacking. Moreover, although it is surely important to build more just structures in economic and political life, efforts for reform will always fall short to the degree that there is not the kind of conversion of heart and mind that is the focus of the Gospel (*EN*, 35). Therefore, the Church, while not in any way eschewing the need for social action, must maintain its self-understanding, not to be replaced by a socioeconomic project. Witness, preaching, and catechesis are needed every bit as much today, and they cannot be reduced to a social and political project (*EN*, 38–47).

Evangelii nuntiandi discusses two elements concerning local churches that would come to be of profound significance in the coming years and in the thinking of Bergoglio: popular religiosity and ecclesial base communities. *Popular religiosity* refers to religious practices that have a particular appeal to the people in a specific location, particularly in parts of the world long evangelized, where particular practices have become lasting components of the local culture. Latin America is replete with such traditions, most often focused on devotion to the Eucharist, the Blessed Mother, or particular saints. Untethered from the fuller context of authentic evangelization, Paul VI acknowledges that such religious expressions can lead to theological distortions, take on superstitious elements, or become sectarian (*EN*, 48). However, his emphasis is on the positive dimension so long as popular religion remains tied to a genuine "pedagogy of evangelization" (*EN*, 48). He notes its richness in values, the way it manifests desire for God in the hearts of simple people, the "awareness of profound attributes of God: fatherhood, providence, loving and constant presence." Furthermore, "it engenders attitudes rarely observed to the same degree elsewhere: patience, the sense of the cross in daily life, detachment, openness to others, devotion" (*EN*, 48). Aware of the decided tendency in the Catholic Church since Vatican II to diminish, even despise, popular religion, often in the name of restoring the centrality of the liturgy, Paul VI clearly seeks to preserve its important place in the life of local churches where it has thrived.

A similar set of concerns surrounded the issue of ecclesial base communities, particularly in Latin America. A base community is a small community of people who gather voluntarily, often responding to the need for more intimacy than can usually be found in large urban parishes or isolated rural communities where there is no regular priest. Again Paul VI notes positive and negative tendencies to be avoided. Much good can result from such associations. There can be a deeper experience of community prayer, more intense evangelization, focus on particular local ministries, or linking together people of particular demographic characteristics who share common challenges and experiences. However, he notes that in many places these communities are rooted in a divisive spirit, in opposition to what they term "the institutional Church." They want to be free from structural restraints. They often reject the Church's hierarchical dimension and even the sacraments. Paul VI terminates the discussion by issuing a series of guidelines for base communities—namely, that they (1) be fed by the Word of God, carefully avoiding political polarization and ideologies, (2) integrate into and stay attached to the local church, remaining in union with the local church leadership, (3) never look on themselves as the sole beneficiaries or sole agents of evangelization, and (4) reflect the Catholic Church's universality, avoiding all sectarianism (*EN*, 58).

Vatican II and *Populorum progressio* set in motion a number of trends that would bring profound changes in the Latin American Church and ultimately to society at large. Arguably the greatest impact would be the renewed emphasis on social justice and development combined with the principle of collegiality and the understanding of the laity as the principal subjects for the renewal of the temporal order. Bishops, theologians, and lay people would find in the developing Church doctrine a new emphasis and fervor to fight for social justice in the region, to eliminate the scourge of poverty brought about by human choices, and to reform the economic, political, and social orders so that they would be more reflective of a truly evangelized society. As the world's most Catholic region, and among the poorest, Latin America seemed destined by providence to be the place where the themes of social justice and development would get the most attention and encounter the greatest reaction. As we will explore later, Bergoglio's entire life and thinking have come to be defined in the midst of these conflicts.

Although interpretations of this period of Catholic Church history will always be divided, few would deny the seminal significance of the Second General Conference of Latin American Bishops, held in Medellín, Colombia, from August 24 to September 6, 1968. One could argue that there has never been in the history of the Catholic Church a regional conference of bishops that had a greater subsequent importance. Although the conference produced documents from sixteen committees, three stood out and continue to be most identified with it: *Justice*, *Peace*, and *Poverty of the Church*.[8] Perhaps the most striking feature of the documents emerging from the Medellín Conference, as it has come to be called, was their tone, particularly the prophetic and forceful language used to discuss poverty and injustice. There is a strong emphasis throughout that the existence of poverty in Latin America, far from being acceptable to God, is "a dehumanizing and debilitating scourge," producing "a deafening cry . . . from the throats of millions asking their pastors for a liberation that reaches them from nowhere else," which imposes an obligation on the Church to opt always with preference for the "poorest and most needy sectors" (*Poverty of the Church*, 1, 2, 8). Although greed is frequently named as a fundamental source of the problem, Medellín would emphasize that sin is not only personal but also embodied in structures and, in various ways, institutionalized. At the top of the list of the "sinful structures" are "dependence on an economic power"—the industrialized developed nations in the northern hemisphere. "Our nations," the bishops write, "do not frequently own their own goods or have a say in economic decisions affecting them" (*Peace*, 8). Furthermore, "the principal guilt for the economic dependence of our countries rests with powers inspired by uncontrolled desire for gain" (*Peace*, 8). In order to overcome dependence, the document repeatedly uses the term *liberation*, by which the bishops mean an "integral" process, both personal and structural. In one sense the use of *liberation* was quite traditional, in that one must be liberated from sin. Without discarding that traditional dimension, however, Medellín rarely focuses on liberation from personal sin alone, shifting to a focus on the unity between personal liberation from sin and liberation from institutionalized oppression (*Justice*, 3, 7). The work of the Gospel in Latin America is described as "an action of integral human development and liberation" (*Justice*, 4). The establishment and the fruits of ecclesial base communities are explicitly endorsed, as they counterbalance powerful political and economic interests. They are places where the poor can learn about their rights and how to become participants in the processes of liberation (*Justice*, 20).

Finally, Medellín addressed what was becoming a central ethical and religious issue: the use of violence to bring about social change. More than any particular turn of phrase, Medellín prompted a shift in worldview on the topic. Prior to Medellín, condemnations of political violence generally provided no justification for the violence associated with political uprisings. Criticism of violence was widely understood to mean violence by political rebels. On the other hand, although there had been criticism of the excessive use of force by governments, the evil in such cases was viewed as a certain excess; the legitimacy of the right of governments to use force was less questioned. Medellín turns the tables somewhat. When the status quo has been flatly described as a set of unjust structures, which cry out to heaven for redress, then force by the state is seen more as an institutionalization of injustice, hence an "institutionalized violence." Specifically, the violence used against the poor is often employed to defend combined results of (1) the very organization of agriculture and industry, (2) the international economic and political framework, and (3) the typical workings of the entire social order. So, when an entire town lacks necessities, for example, and is left without recourse to bring about peaceful changes through the people's own initiatives, "this itself is a situation of . . . institutional violence," even if no shots are fired or no riots are erupting (*Peace*, 16). Of course, this raises the question of whether or not recourse to violence might be justified. The bishops note that, given the injustices involved, there should be no surprise that people turn to violence. Although they do not condone violence, readers of the document are left with the impression that when violence erupts it is the rich and powerful who are to blame. Not excluding recourse to violence in cases where all else fails, Medellín nevertheless teaches that "violent changes in structures would be fallacious, ineffectual in themselves and not conforming to the dignity of man, which demands that the necessary changes take place from within, through a fitting awakening of conscience" (*Peace*, 16).

At the same time as Medellín was underway, a number of theologians from Latin America—most notably Peru's Gustavo Gutiérrez—

were developing a theology along similar lines. One might say that this developing "theology of liberation" fed into the Medellín Conference and vice versa; the new theologians received a great deal of impetus from Medellín as they saw in it an essential validation of the line they were taking. Rooted in Vatican II and the renewed emphasis on social justice, this new line of theology made what Medellín termed *integral liberation* its central motif. Although there was a real diversity among the authors associated with this school, common themes emerged. First, the liberation theologians saw temporal liberation in the same light that the 1971 synod of bishops came to endorse it—that is, as "a constitutive dimension of the Gospel."[9] The emphasis on temporal liberation often involved rethinking and reformulation of traditional theological themes and has since its inception been a matter of profound controversy.[10] For example, Jon Sobrino developed the argument that traditional Christology underemphasized the historical and political dimension of the life, and particularly the Passion of Christ, as a confrontation between Jesus and the forces of evil of His time.[11] This changes how one understands the Cross in our existence today. Discipleship must participate in the same conflicts that Jesus did, and this means conflicts with the powers that be in our time. This kind of political rereading of the life of Jesus and the Cross would be a constant in the theology of liberation. In some crude, populist versions Jesus would be portrayed as a revolutionary, but theologians of liberation mostly claimed that the renewed focus on temporal liberation did not negate the traditional eschatological components of the faith. Hence, the term *integral liberation* (encompassing worldly and transcendent dimensions) became commonplace. For example, liberation theologians often turned to the book of Exodus for a paradigm, wherein God, in the process of calling His people into a sacred covenant, initiates a process of political liberation from oppression in Egypt. In a sense, Christians in Latin America have been likened to the Jews in Egypt. In a related argument, these theologians criticized what they saw as a "dualism" implied by the "distinction of planes"—that is, between the temporal and the eternal. Gutiérrez would call it a "burned-out model," but not because the distinction affirmed transcendence. Rather, the problem was that the theory encouraged complacency with respect to injustice in opposition to the spirit of the Gospel and failed to recognize the salvific dimension of struggling for justice in this world. In accord with the "preferential option for the poor," endorsed by Medellín, theologians of liberation insisted that all political, economic, and social options had to be weighed in the light of this overriding commitment.

Base communities, or *comunidades eclesiales de base*, would become the movement's predominant institutional form, often called "the popular church." Although one must be careful not to overgeneralize the diversity of situations, it would be fair to say that these communities were generally bases for consciousness raising, attempts to bring the people involved to see their lives in light of the movement's focus on social and political change. The biblical message was discussed with an emphasis on social themes. It is a fair criticism to note that these communities often did not meet the criteria Paul VI laid out in *Evangelii nuntiandi* in that broader catechesis, attachment to the local and universal Church, and the sacramental life received less emphasis than did longed-for social transformation. In their worst manifestations, the base communities seemed to function mostly as centers of ideological formation. In a number of cases, particularly where violence broke out on a large scale, they were often politicized in opposition to the political right and clearly identified with the left. In all fairness to the base communities, however, whatever lack of integration they may have had with their local bishops was not all their own fault. Many bishops did not like them, discouraged them, and made few efforts in their direction. In situations such as in El Salvador under Archbishop Romero, when the bishop made efforts to work with the base communities and maintain them in the shepherd's fold, the results were often much better in terms of the maintenance of Catholic identity.

The most significant debate—and one that will probably never be resolved to the satisfaction of all sides—concerned the extent to which this burgeoning theology relied on Marxist or more broadly radical social and political categories and analysis. Given the vast number of authors who eventually came to be associated with this school, clearly nuance is necessary. Ultimately, the conflict would be between two paradigmatic positions. The "conservative" position sees in liberation theology nothing more than Marxism dressed up in Christian garb, a theology that would quote the Bible frequently but essentially twist the biblical hermeneutic to come up with a Marxist reading. It must be said surely that one can find examples of this in certain populist expressions wherein Christian identity became indistinguishable from being a good revolutionary. Liberation theologians themselves always countered that the Marxist element was secondary to the theology, although many would claim that Marxist analysis helped in the interpretation of the social reality. They thought the attacks were largely motivated by attempts to maintain the status quo and avoid Christian social responsibilities. As we shall see, it is perhaps the case that time had a way of permitting a certain development in the theology of liberation that rendered it incompatible with either of these polarized positions.

There certainly was no question that the early expressions of the theology of liberation relied heavily on social sciences from the ideological left. Particularly frequent were *radical dependency theory* and *Marxist class analysis*. Dependency theory was based on the conviction that capitalism is a world system in which there is a "center" or "metropole" that has a hegemonic relationship with a "periphery." Of course, the center is Europe and the United States—and later Japan—while most of Asia, Africa, and Latin America constitute the periphery. Even with the end of formal colonialism, dependency theorists contended that the global political economy is essentially a structure of domination wherein Third World nations mostly export relatively cheap primary products and have to import either the products of modern industrialization or the very expensive technologies needed to produce the formerly imported products themselves. At all points of interaction—be it trade, foreign investment, credit, or employment of people and resources—the entire system has a decided tendency to solidify, perpetuate, and even amplify the differences in wealth and power. The more radical expressions of this theory suggest very strongly that there is no way out by means of a process of development within the system. On the contrary, radicals believed that the existing system pointed in the direction of revolutionary disengagement from the system and the reestablishment of a new political economy along nationalist lines, much the way that Cuba would eventually go after 1959. Additionally, Marxist class analysis often appeared central in this theology. Liberation theologians often defended themselves by claiming that, in speaking of the class struggle, they were in no way advocating a theory, merely describing a reality they witnessed. Although the developments defy facile generalization, there was no question that many bishops, priests, and lay people were concerned that liberation theology often became troublingly indistinguishable from Marxism and that the eschatological components of the faith, even the Resurrection itself, seemed to lose their traditional sense. Yet, in all fairness to the theologians of liberation, one very valid criticism was that, "aside from evincing a common opposition to capitalism and all structures of domination, nearly all the liberation theologians speak in such general terms that it is difficult to derive any concrete proposals of a positive nature from their writings."[12] Additionally, the theology of liberation in varying degrees was quite critical of the Catholic Church, emphasizing its links to oligarchies both old and new. The institutional Church often seems to be a part of the oppressive order, prompting a divisive preference for the "popular Church." Ironically, it is not an exaggeration even to say that at times the image of the historical Church that emerges in liberation theology seems to be along lines inspired by the Black Legend.

A turning point in the history of the theology of liberation came in 1984 and 1986, when the Congregation for the Doctrine of the Faith issued two documents concerning the theology of liberation and the movement it had inspired. The first, *Libertatis nuntius* (1984), was largely seen as a criticism of both the theology and the movement, although it fell short of a condemnation.[13] The document critiqued some of the predominant trends: the tendency to borrow uncritically from Marxist social analysis; the use of rationalist biblical hermeneutics that gave Scripture a more politicized meaning; the acceptance of class struggle as a given for the Christian; a reductionism of theology to political radicalism, even messianism; the failure to link the struggle for social justice with the broader content of the faith; encouraging the creation of a "church of the people" in opposition to the Church's hierarchical structure; and the overemphasis on structural sin to the neglect of the primary and original sense of sin as personal. Although *Libertatis nuntius* recognizes diversity, the reader gets the sense that what is being criticized are predominant trends, not the direction of a few aberrant elements. Liberation theologians generally believed that the Congregation's instruction lacked nuance and overemphasized the Marxist and ideological elements in the theory and movement. In all fairness to the Vatican, however, the initial instruction was never intended to be a simple rejection of the theology of liberation. A second instruction, *Libertatis conscientia* (1986), focused on the theme of liberation and can be seen as an attempt to dialogue with the movement in the sense of clarifying what a valid approach to liberation would be from a biblical and Catholic perspective.[14] Although it reiterates some of the original criticisms, the document did provide support for some of the themes of liberation theology. Confirming the primary sense of sin as personal, the document does accept that one can speak of "structural sin" in a secondary but real sense. It also concedes that the improvement of unjust social structures should be part of conversion. Strong enforcement was given to the "preferential option for the poor," and it would not be an exaggeration to say that the theme became completely mainstream in Catholic social teaching, an undoubted contribution that this theology made to the Church's theological patrimony. However, this commitment had to distance itself from any ideological element that would deny love to others. Finally, echoing Paul VI in *Evangelii nuntiandi*, the document approved of base communities so long as they were integrated into the Church and provided sound catechesis. A statement made by John Paul II in a letter dated only one week after the second instruction seemed to best underline the Vatican's desire to integrate liberation theology into the Church so long as the criticisms made of its earlier expressions were taken seriously. Beginning with the proviso that their response as bishops to the problems of injustice must conform to the Gospel, the Church's tradition, and the teaching authority of the Church, John Paul II writes that "we are convinced that the theology of liberation is not only timely but useful and necessary. . . . It should constitute a new stage . . . of the theological reflection initiated with the apostolic tradition . . . by the rich patrimony of the Church's social doctrine."[15]

Similar to every other Jesuit priest in Latin America, Jorge Mario Bergoglio's thinking and pastoral practice could not help but be defined by the way he responded to these developments, whose impacts were felt like shockwaves throughout the region, including Argentina. Moreover, in 1973, Bergoglio, at the unusually young age of thirty-six, was named Provincial of the Jesuit Province centered in Buenos Aires. The Jesuits, perhaps as much or more than any other order, were at the time fully caught up in the whirlwinds of controversy and suffering polarization internally. To this day this period is controversial and Bergoglio's handling of his mission as Provincial subject to criticism.[16] At this time, with the Jesuits under the leadership of Father Pedro Arrupe—a Spaniard of Basque origin, elected in 1965—the Jesuit mission was redefined from "defense and propagation of the faith" to "service of the faith, of which the promotion of justice is an absolute requirement."[17] A significant element within the young Provincial's area of responsibility gravitated to the more-radical expressions of liberation theology, while another faction strongly opposed it. In the early 1970s the Movimiento de Sacerdotes del Tercer Mundo (or the Movement of Third World Priests, as they were called in English) would claim as members perhaps as many as one-fourth of young priests in the nation. The movement took a socialist bent while identifying as well with traditional Argentine Peronism. Socialist discourse was coupled with a call for changes in Church doctrine and discipline, most notably the obligation of celibacy for priests. In the broader society, the polarizing tensions had already broken out into violence. By the time Bergoglio became Provincial, the Trotskyite ERP (Ejército Revolucionario del Pueblo), and the left Peronist MPM (Movimiento Peronista Montonero) were already engaging in acts of murder and kidnappings to raise money on a national scale. Within his Province, Bergoglio's election was arguably due to his ability to speak to people on both sides while not being identified with either. It is abundantly clear that Bergoglio never accepted the radical line of the theology of liberation, leading to his permanent branding by many on the left, including members of his own order, as "a conservative." Yet, it is equally clear that Bergoglio did not embrace a simply conservative stance in that he was from the beginning a reformer, not a revolutionary.

Three dimensions would remain central to Bergoglio's approach. He would always distance himself from any theology that would (1) place political and social change on its own terms in the center of Jesuit life, (2) discount the value of the tradition, or (3) overemphasize ideological elements drawn from outside. First, Bergoglio, prior to being Provincial, was a member of the group that formed around Father Miguel Angel Fiorito, whose principal concern was to renew Jesuit spirituality by going back to Saint Ignatius's emphasis on the discernment of spirits in the context of guided retreats. Second, as we have already seen, Bergoglio's approach to Jesuit reform and reform in the Church generally is to go back to the original charism and sources. For Bergoglio this would always mean returning to the work of the early Jesuits in Argentina to consider how that approach might be adapted to the contemporary period. Third, Bergoglio would always prioritize direct service to the ordinary, poor, and faithful people.[18] For him, this could not be replaced by the pursuit of any social program, no matter how justified; authentic reform can only be rooted in this kind of direct pastoral concern. He saw in much of the liberationist approach a kind of vanguardism wherein the pastors are more involved in imposing a program on the people in their name than truly walking with them, accompanying them on their journey. He will never lose his suspicion that the radical approaches shared in the imperialism, the "metropolitan hegemony," that had beset the Church's missionary efforts in the region going back to the Enlightenment.

In this chapter we have begun to trace the more proximate roots and developments relative to Bergoglio's social thought beginning with the epochal Vatican II documents *Lumen gentium* and *Gaudium et spes*. These signaled important developments in the Church's pastoral approach that will echo throughout the Catholic Church. The former document emphasizes the Church as the people of God, underlining the true apostolic role of the laity and the universal call to holiness. The latter reorients the Church to a deeper engagement with the modern world in a spirit of dialogue with it. From here Paul VI's *Populorum progressio* brought the theme of development to the fore, yet with a distinctively Christian anthropology, stressing that development had to be "for every man and the whole man." From *Evangelii nuntiandi*, Bergoglio's favorite pastoral document, we find the roots of three of his most longstanding beliefs: (1) evangelization is key to the Church's very identity, (2) popular religion remains, even in our time, an important source of values that ought not be ignored, even though it must always be guided by sound catechesis from the Church's broader doctrine, and (3) it is a mistake to reduce the Gospel to a worldly project, even in the midst of powerful and legitimate demands the vicissitudes of history may present. The Gospel is a message of salvation that always transcends and can never be reduced to a temporal project, no matter how seemingly noble.

Switching to the Latin American context, we saw that the Latin American bishops, in their attempts to implement the conciliar documents, prophetically addressed the themes of development and social injustice at the Medellín Conference in 1968, with a clarion call for the Catholic Church to recognize the need for decisive action to promote development and to end the scourge of poverty. This paralleled the development of the theology of liberation, which, in its call to make social justice the central focus of pastoral work, became a source of controversy in the region from the 1960s through the 1990s. Ultimately the Vatican would intervene, trying to purify the theology of liberation of ideological elements, yet insisting on the calls for change flowing from *Gaudium et spes* and *Populorum progressio*.

Finally, we situated Bergoglio with respect to these developments. Drawing on his oldest roots as an Argentine Jesuit and the teaching of Paul VI in *Evangelii nuntiandi*, Bergoglio was inoculated against ideological encroachments, maintaining his focus on serving the poor in their concrete, daily needs, respecting their history and culture, and avoiding the imposition of projects defined from Enlightenment influences. He tried to steer a path between the more-radical expressions of liberation theology, on the one hand, and reactive restorationism, on the other. In the next chapter we will see how his thinking dovetails with other developments in theology in Argentina and, later, the broader direction of the Latin American bishops generally. This will catapult Bergoglio into a position of regional, then global, leadership in the Catholic Church.

NOTES

1. Paul VI, *Lumen gentium*, The Holy See (Vatican website), November 21, 1964, http://www.vatican.va/archive/hist_councils/ii_vatican_council/documents/vat-ii_const_19641121_lumen-gentium_en.html; and Paul VI, *Gaudium et spes*, The Holy See (Vatican website), December 7, 1965, http://www.vatican.va/archive/hist_councils/ii_vatican_council/documents/vat-ii_const_19651207_gaudium-et-spes_en.html. As a reminder, all documents from Vatican II or authored by Popes, with the documents' paragraph numbers, can be found online at http://w2.vatican.va/content/vatican/en.html.

2. Paul VI, *Evangelii nuntiandi*, The Holy See (Vatican website), December 8, 1975, http://w2.vatican.va/content/paul-vi/en/apost_exhortations/documents/hf_p-vi_exh_19751208_evangelii-nuntiandi.html.

3. The two extended treatments of *Gaudium et spes* are found in Joseph Ratzinger, *Theological Highlights of Vatican II* (New York: Paulist Press, 1966), 147–71; and Joseph Ratzinger, *Principles of Catholic Theology* (San Francisco: Ignatius Press, 1987), 367–93. Ratzinger is critical of what he came to see as the overly optimistic attitude of the council fathers, an insufficiently skeptical attitude toward the modern world, and the document's inadequate

focus on Christology and the doctrine of salvation, but he does not reject it. He believes its overly optimistic attitude was destined for disappointment as the hoped-for collaboration between the church and the modern state fell short of expectations.

4. Synod of Bishops, *Justice in the World*, The Holy See (Vatican website), November 30, 1971, http://www.vatican.va/roman_curia/synod/documents/rc_synod_doc_19711130_giustizia_po.html (available here only in Portuguese), 6 (available online in English at http://www.shc.edu/theolibrary/resources/synodjw.htm).

5. Although *Gaudium et spes* as a council document gave the theme of rights special impetus, Pope John XXIII had developed many of the constitution's themes in his two social encyclicals prior to the council—*Mater et magistra* (The Holy See, May 15, 1961, http://w2.vatican.va/content/john-xxiii/en/encyclicals/documents/hf_j-xxiii_enc_15051961_mater.html) and *Pacem in terris* (The Holy See, April 11, 1963, http://w2.vatican.va/content/john-xxiii/en/encyclicals/documents/hf_j-xxiii_enc_11041963_pacem.html). The latter gives the more-detailed list of rights the church supports (paragraphs 11–27).

6. Leo XIII, *Rerum novarum*, The Holy See (Vatican website), May 15, 1891, http://w2.vatican.va/content/leo-xiii/en/encyclicals/documents/hf_l-xiii_enc_15051891_rerum-novarum.html; John Paul II, *Sollicitudo rei socialis*, The Holy See (Vatican website), December 30, 1987, http://w2.vatican.va/content/john-paul-ii/en/encyclicals/documents/hf_jp-ii_enc_30121987_sollicitudo-rei-socialis.html; and Benedict XVI, *Caritas in veritate*, The Holy See (Vatican website), June 29, 2009, http://w2.vatican.va/content/benedict-xvi/en/encyclicals/documents/hf_ben-xvi_enc_20090629_caritas-in-veritate.html.

7. Austen Ivereigh, *Great Reformer*, 122.

8. Excerpts from the Medellín Documents are in Joseph Gremillion, *The Gospel of Peace and Justice* (Maryknoll, NY: Orbis Books, 1976), 445–76. As previously indicated, in this one case the name of the document will be cited in the text with the corresponding paragraph number(s). See also the following: Latin American Bishops, *Justice*, from the Medellín Documents, Second General Conference of Latin American Bishops, Medellín, Colombia, September 6, 1968, text found online at http://www.shc.edu/theolibrary/resources/medjust.htm; Latin American Bishops, *Peace*, from the Medellín Documents, Second General Conference of Latin American Bishops, Medellín, Colombia, September 6, 1968, text found online at http://www.shc.edu/theolibrary/resources/medpeace.htm; and, finally, Latin American Bishops, *Poverty of the Church*, from the Medellín Documents, Second General Conference of Latin American Bishops, Medellín, Colombia, September 6, 1968; text found online at http://www.shc.edu/theolibrary/resources/medpov.htm.

9. Synod of Bishops, *Justice in the World*, 6.

10. The literature on liberation theology is vast and far beyond the scope of this work. The following summary is largely taken from my entry, "Liberation Theology," in *The Encyclopedia of Catholic Social Thought, Social Sciences and Social Policy*, vol. 2, ed. Michael L. Coulter, Stephen M. Krason, Richard S. Myers, and Joseph A. Varacalli, 629–32 (Lanham, MD: Scarecrow Press, 2007). The most influential text at the time on the then-burgeoning topic of liberation theology was Gustavo Gutiérrez, *A Theology of Liberation*, rev. ed. (Maryknoll: Orbis Books, 1988). Other central sources used were Ignacio Ellacuría and Jon Sobrino, eds., *Mysterium Liberationis: Fundamental Concepts of Liberation Theology* (Maryknoll: Orbis Books, 1993); Jon Sobrino, *Christology at the Crossroads* (Maryknoll, NY: Orbis Books, 1978); Leonardo Boff and Clodovis Boff, *Introducing Liberation Theology* (Maryknoll, NY: Orbis Books, 1987); Paul Sigmund, *Liberation Theology at the Crossroads: Democracy or Revolution?* (New York and Oxford: Oxford University Press, 1990). To my mind, Sigmund's work remains a balanced reading—sympathetic but critical.

11. Sobrino, *Christology at the Crossroads*.

12. Sigmund, *Liberation Theology at the Crossroads*, 70.

13. Congregation for the Doctrine of the Faith, *Libertatis nuntius*, The Holy See (Vatican website), August 6, 1984, http://www.vatican.va/roman_curia/congregations/cfaith/documents/rc_con_cfaith_doc_19840806_theology-liberation_en.html.

14. Congregation for the Doctrine of the Faith, *Libertatis conscientia*, The Holy See (Vatican website), March 22, 1986, http://www.vatican.va/roman_curia/congregations/cfaith/documents/rc_con_cfaith_doc_19860322_freedom-liberation_en.html.

15. John Paul II, quoted in Sigmund, *Liberation Theology at the Crossroads*, 168–69.

16. The criticism from the left is that Bergoglio was a conservative who aided and abetted the crackdown on liberation theology. Some, such as Horacio Verbitsky, claim that Bergoglio was responsible for the arrest and torture of two fellow Jesuits—Franz Jalics and Orlando Yorio. I strongly disagree with such readings. Bergoglio has conceded that as a young and inexperienced Provincial he made errors and was overly rigid. However, he denies that he was ever on the right politically or ecclesiastically. Certainly with respect to the themes of this book I see an essential continuity in his thought. I reject Paul Vallely's thesis that Bergoglio was a conservative traditionalist who repented of his actions during the dictatorship on his way to becoming some essentially distinct man who emerged thereafter. See Paul Vallely, *Untying the Knots* (London: Bloomsbury, 2013). On biographical matters, I concur with the interpretations of Austen Ivereigh (*The Great Reformer*) and Elisabetta Piqué

(*Pope Francis: Life and Revolution* [London: Darton, Longman and Todd, 2014]), both of whom see Bergoglio's thinking and pastoral leanings in essential continuity over time.

17. Austen Ivereigh, *Great Reformer*, 120–21.

18. Ivereigh claims the influence of French theologian Yves Congar here, particularly his 1950 text, *True and False Reform in the Church*, trans. Paul Philibert (Collegeville, MD: Liturgical Press, 2011). Congar believes that true reform has always been based on service to the ordinary faithful who tend to embody tradition, whereas false reform tends to be based on trying to make links with elite projects originating in the milieu of the time outside the Church. See also Austen Ivereigh, *Great Reformer*, 93–94.

4

HISTORICAL-THEOLOGICAL ROOTS III

From the Theology of the People to Pope Francis's Vision for the Church Today

At the end of the last chapter, we saw that Bergoglio did not follow the radical expressions of the theology of liberation and how this refusal reflected a deep consistency in his thinking. However much he would concur with the criticisms of the existing social injustices, Bergoglio saw elements of ideological invasion in much of the theology of liberation. He preferred to look to the people's own roots. In section I of this chapter we will begin by discussing an alternative to the theology of liberation, known as the theology of the people, which developed in Argentina and is closer in spirit to Bergoglio's own thought. This theology takes the struggle for social justice seriously but relies more on the actual history and existing culture of the people as sources, avoiding the emphasis on social class; the expositors of this theology saw such emphasis as a flaw in the theology of liberation. Lucio Gera, Rafael Tello, and Juan Carlos Scannone will receive treatment here as important contributors. Central to both the theology of liberation and Bergoglio's own thinking is a positive appropriation of the role of popular religiosity for pastoral and social matters. Developments in thinking after the Puebla conference dovetail with Bergoglio's own thinking, most evident in the Fifth General Conference of Latin American Bishops, in Aparecida, Brazil, in 2007.[1] Bergoglio served as redactor of the final document. Finally, the section concludes with later developments in the thought of liberation theology's most famous expositor, Gustavo Gutiérrez, in tandem with the current Prefect of the Congregation for the Doctrine of the Faith, Gerhard Müller. This is for the purpose of demonstrating how the correctives coming from the Congregation show a way forward for the theology of liberation in tandem with Pope Francis's own thinking.

Section II of this chapter provides a brief summary of the thinking of Bergoglio's longtime friend from the Río de la Plata, Alberto Methol Ferré, who influenced his thinking on a range of issues from Christian anthropology to politics.

In section III we conclude with a summary of Bergoglio's current vision for the Catholic Church, as no understanding of his social thought and its likely development can be separate from his broader ecclesial vision.

I. THE THEOLOGY OF THE PEOPLE IN ARGENTINA

Concurrent with the development of the theology of liberation was a second, related, strain of thought, the beginning of which can be traced to the Argentine bishops' formation of the Comisión Episcopal para la Pastoral (COEPAL), founded in 1968 to chart the course for the Argentine Church in the spirit of the Second General Conference of Latin American Bishops at Medellín. One of the presiders, Bishop Enrique Angelelli, would later be put to death under highly suspicious circumstances during the period of military rule. From 1968 to 1973, COEPAL was the principal source for this new theology, most often called *la teología del pueblo*—or "the theology of the people." Its influence is seen in part of the document that the Argentine bishops put forth in 1969 in their attempt to apply the conclusions of Medellín, the Declaration of San Miguel. Echoing Medellín throughout, the declaration nonetheless had a very distinct feature, which came from the pen of Argentine priest Father Lucio Gera, the originator of the new theological current. There is a very clear statement in the declaration that Marxism "is alien not only to Christianity but also to the spirit of our people."[2] It is in understanding what Gera meant by *the spirit of our people* that this theology finds its distinctive element. Gera reminds theologians and prelates of the uniquely Gospel insight that in so many cases the poor and simple people—shepherds, people pulling carts—immediately grasped the mystery of God[3] while the intellectuals and professionally religious did not. In Latin America, despite the negative dimensions of colonization, the simple faithful had in many ways throughout their history incarnated the Gospel in their culture.[4] This reverential attitude toward the people prompted Gera and those who would follow this approach to focus theologically on culture, seeing in it a rich resource for both theological reflection and pastoral direction. In the same vein, Gera saw that in order best to comprehend culture as embodying elements of incarnate faith, the historical approach would be far superior to the ahistorical approaches of the social sciences. Theologian Sebastián Politi says, "The living substance of the real, of the people, of men and women and their struggles and hopes, can only be perceived in its own dynamism and the concrete becoming of their aspirations, realizations and failures."[5] Therefore, in the words of Gera, quoted in the San Miguel Declaration, what theology calls "the world" or "the temporal dimension" must focus not on the state but on "the Argentine people." Following this line of thought, Gera writes that the Church in Argentina "must involve and incarnate itself in the national experience of the Argentine people," always drawing near "to the poor, the oppressed, and those in need." To strengthen the religious expressions of the people as historically manifest and to evangelize among the poor would remain characteristic of the pastoral line that would develop from this theology.[6]

Gera underlined a crucial distinction between pastoral activity that would focus on the poor or be devoted to their problems and one that would truly come *from* the people. The people are to be active agents of their own history. Therefore, "the Church must exercise discernment about its liberative or salvific activity from the viewpoint of the people and their interests." In discerning what the Gospel calls "the signs of the times," they are to be found "in the happenings the people perform or which affect them." Again, this is done best by adopting the perspective of the history of the people.[7] Gera was saying that the people themselves had a rationality of their own from which they derive their own projects. Gera writes, "Either theology is the expression of the People of God or it is nothing."[8] It was principally in this sense of the people themselves and their role that made the theology of the people unique. In this conception, "the people" could not be translated by reference to categories alien to the people's own historical experience. Marxist or any properly sociological categories could not define the people. For this reason, Gera and Tello would never join the Movement of Third World Priests, although they remained in dialogue with its members.

Father Rafael Tello was perhaps the second-most important figure in the development of the theology of the people. Tello emphasizes that his theology begins with the Vatican II call to return to the focus on the human person in the concrete. Universality would still be preserved in understanding the equality of each person as created by God. Nonetheless, the focus would be on the particular. As Tello saw it, there was no better way to get to the depth of people in the particular than to emphasize the specificity of their culture. For Tello culture is "the quality, disposition, accustomed ways of using and disposing of things, of self-expression, of style, the entire conception of life within which every human activity has its place, that conforms to and proceeds from a communal environment historically constituted."[9] In Latin America this culture was formed in significant ways by faith and baptism. Everyone had an identity in this new order and a fundamental dignity and equality as sons and daughters of God. To this culture belonged most of the common people, and many of the indigenous were incorporated as well.[10] Concerning this Tello said in 1977:

> In the faith announced to him, the Indian will encounter these elements: he . . . forms part of a new society. . . . He is a living member of a new society. . . . The baptized Indian is a Christian; and in a Christian society this means a lot. Here are the roots of liberty, the Indian baptized knows he is a son of God exactly equal to the noble or the viceroy. . . . Here is born the feeling of equality and liberty that remains in our people. He enters as a member of a society, and in this society the Indian acquires a name, he is someone . . . because he is a son of God.[11]

Two related features of this popular culture are key to understanding it as an interpretive factor in Latin America, theologically and historically. First, the culture coexists in the region with a second culture present in the same space—that is, the modern, and now postmodern, culture. Second, the popular culture exists in perpetual tension with this postmodern global culture. Tello explains in detail that the popular culture is characterized by its resistance to secularism; it affirms God and life in God as the supreme reality and sees temporal life as the necessary means to reach God. Moreover, in a second contrast, the popular culture is not individualistic; one seeks perfection not in oneself but in God and in communion with others. Finally, the popular culture, in contrast to the modern, seeks a common good to be shared by the entire community and by each member, again in contrast to individualism.[12] What emerges from these cultural roots is a distinctive way of viewing the contemporary conflicts. The predominant struggle is neither exactly (1) capitalism versus socialism nor (2) capitalism versus the popular culture nor (3) Marxism versus the traditional culture. The struggle is really the authentic, historically based Latin American culture versus the modern culture. Both individualistic capitalism and Marxism in this account are alien impositions not rooted in the culture and life of the people. This obviously will set the theology of the people apart from the sociopolitical focus of the theology of liberation, which accepts the assumptions of modern culture. However, it is equally important to understand that the theology of the people did embrace the social-justice component of liberation theology and was in no way a simple throwback to a restorationist role for the Catholic Church.[13] To see the cultural emphasis as "conservative" would only be valid if these theologians appealed to the predominant culture; but they did not. The affirmation of the historical culture of the people in no way affirms any kind of domination—cultural, economic, or political. It was perfectly consistent with the premises of the theology of the people to criticize the same structures of domination that the liberation theologians did. What differed was the point of departure. Whereas the liberationists were struggling for a liberation defined largely in purely modern terms, the theology of the people would keep the historically constituted people with their culture at the center of the analysis and the pastoral approach proceeding from it.

Juan Carlos Scannone, another significant figure in the movement, elaborates further on the breach between the two schools of thought. Careful to point out that there were in fact overlapping concerns for the poor, he, nevertheless, sees five major contrasts in emphasis. The first distinction lies in interpreting what exactly was meant by the theology of liberation's expression—originally formulated by Gustavo Gutiérrez—that faith is a critical reflection on historical praxis. Scannone raises the question of *whose* historical praxis is to be critically reflected on. Is it the praxis of the Latin American peoples themselves or the group of people committed to the theology of liberation? Moreover, is it the faith praxis of the people of God that is to be critically reflected on, or is it historical praxis generally? If the latter, then it would not be specific to faith praxis but praxis itself, which would not be unique to the people of God and might reduce to what unites the practitioners of the theology of liberation with other groups who shared the same political goals. Second, the theologians of liberation tended to accept the mediating role of dependency theory and Marxist social science, whereas the theology of the people awarded the predominant place to the historical experience of the people. This leads to a third division in which the theology of the people saw the praxis of liberation already present in the history of the people, whereas liberation theology tended to emphasize history as simply the history of oppression. While the theology of the people values the popular culture and sees a wisdom in it that must inform reflection on praxis, the theology of liberation tended not to see the same culture as a valuable source for reflection or praxis. Fourth, these distinctions will issue in different assessments of the popular religious culture in Latin America. The theology of the people will have a predominantly positive view, seeing in it a source of wisdom and theology. The theology of liberation, on the other hand, will tend to see it as inadequate, itself a reflection of domination and alienation, in need of the enlightenment that the theology of liberation could provide. Fifth, and finally, this reflected a deeper division over the Enlightenment. The theology of the people was suspicious of the Enlightenment rationality that seemed to be behind both liberal modernist approaches to development and the Marxist alternatives; these seemed to be two branches of the same rationality that held the unenlightened culture of the people in a critical light. Hence the theology of the people saw in the theology of liberation elements of yet another alien imposition.[14]

It is important to situate Bergoglio in the midst of these developments. In a 2015 discourse in Paraguay, we witness Bergoglio's ongoing, distinctive focus on the problems of modern ideologies generally. His words this day reflect longstanding themes in his thinking about evangelization and inculturation in the context of poverty and inequality in Latin America.[15] He says that ideologies do not have a full relationship with the people but a sick or evil one. They do not begin with the people. They are stuck in the last century and always lead to the same result: dictatorships of one kind or other. Ideological viewpoints, he insists, always serve the interests of other political or personal interests other than those of the people themselves. Ideologies always claim to think on behalf of the people, but they do not allow the people to think. As he has frequently said, these ideologies "act for the people but never with the people." By way of contrast, "in order to seek effectively the true good of the people, the first thing is to have a true preoccupation for them as people, to value them in their own respective good. This entails a disposition to learn from them. The poor have much to teach humanity concerning goodness and sacrifice." Lest anyone conclude from this that Bergoglio intends to negate the material dimension of life, he emphasizes that work "is a right that gives dignity to people. To bring bread to the house, to offer one's children a roof, health, and education are essential aspects of human dignity, and business people, politicians, economists must fight for them." "I ask you," he continues, "not to cede to an idolatrous economic model that needs to sacrifice humans on the altar of money and profitability. In the economy . . . in politics . . . first is the person." Referencing the "enormous social inequality and alarming indexes of poverty in Paraguay," he pleads for the need to respect the poor person and not "use him to wash away our own sins."[16]

With reference to the theology of liberation, there is nothing in Bergoglio's writings suggesting his adaptation of the principal line taken by these theologians in the earlier, radical stages of its development. On the other hand, all the evidence suggests his identification with the main lines of the theology of the people. Bergoglio had long been struck by the traditional teaching that the "pueblo fiel" (faithful people) was infallible in its belief. From this he derived a second formula: "When you want to know *what* to believe, go to the Magisterium; when you want to know *how* to believe, go to the faithful people. The Magisterium will teach you who Mary is, but the faithful people will teach you how to love Mary."[17] As far back as 1970 and 1971, Cardinal Bergoglio would later recount, there was much talk about "el pueblo" (the people), but in senses not always clear. Leaders had long referred to "the people," but often with a populist political overtone, and, of course the intellectuals and Marxists employed it in various senses tied to class and sociological categories. Bergoglio wanted to use it in the pastoral sense of the "people who follow Jesus [and] look to Jesus, and the Virgin, and have a basic fidelity pointing in that direction. . . . I started to talk about the holy people of God, the faithful people . . . the santo pueblo fiel de Dios" (the holy, faithful people).[18] Moreover, Bergoglio shared the anti-elitism of this burgeoning "teología del pueblo" (theology of the people), respecting the historical presence of the Incarnate Word already in the people, and distanced himself from both the clerical right and revolutionary left. Again underlining the connection between the Incarnate God and His people, Bergoglio quotes Dostoevsky: "He who does not believe in God does not believe in the people of God. However, the one who does not doubt God's people will also see the holiness of the soul of the people, even when up to this time he had not believed in it. Only the people and their future spiritual strength will convert our atheists, cut off from their own roots."[19]

Bergoglio himself was not an academic theologian and so could not be considered a participant in the development of this theology himself. Nonetheless, the record shows many signs of support. As Provincial, he tried always to steer away from both the radical left and the clerical, restorationist right, pursuing what he saw as the Jesuit mission as he had always understood it: a mission to the periphery with a special focus on the poor, evangelizing and inculturating the faith in the life of the people, in a way always respecting their existing traditions. In an interview Father Juan Carlos Scannone states that Bergoglio's pastoral work at this divisive time is best understood in light of the theology of the people. At a time of polarization when this theology was itself often held in suspicion, even inside the Catholic Church, Bergoglio provided Scannone ongoing support and advice, even advising him to mail articles from alternative post offices in Buenos Aires to avoid being censored. In 1985, Bergoglio organized a conference focusing on inculturation of the Gospel, which featured Lucio Gera. Soon after Bergoglio became bishop, Gera died, and Bergoglio had him buried in Buenos Aires Metropolitan Cathedral with a special plaque, clearly an honor. Moreover, although Cardinal Aramburu had largely ostracized Rafael Tello in the '70s, Bergoglio made a point later of participating in the presentation of a book about Tello, vindicating him in a public way.[20]

Understanding Bergoglio as a social thinker is enhanced by brief consideration of how this line of theological reflection influenced both the universal and Latin American Church. Lucio Gera influenced Paul VI's *Evangelii nuntiandi*. The mediation was through Bishop Eduardo Pironio, former bishop of Mar del Plata, who, interestingly, was confessor to Paul VI and also chaired the synod of bishops that immediately preceded the issuance of that Pope's document. Of even greater significance was that this synod marked the beginning of a turn for the Latin American Church toward a more historical-cultural approach associated with the theology of the people. A few years later, Bergoglio participated in the preparations for the Third General Conference of Latin American bishops, to be held in Puebla, Mexico, in 1979.[21] Puebla represented an important breakthrough for those who wanted the Latin American Church to look more to its own history and culture. Although it did affirm the preferential option for the poor, and certainly did not downplay the importance of the struggle for justice, the conference's issued document did not place socioeconomic liberation at the center. Although liberation theologians were thankful that the document did not move in a restorationist direction, it seems fair to say that they did not celebrate the shifts in focus either.[22]

The document that emerged from the Puebla conference (hereafter *Puebla*) shows the influence of the historical-cultural approach and *Evangelii nuntiandi* throughout. It begins with the assertion that "evangelization is the very mission of the Church." The Church's history in the region is "fundamentally the history of the evangelization of a people that lives through an ongoing process of gestation;" it is a history where the faith has been continually "incarnated." In this way, the Church contributed "to the birth of nationalities and deeply imprints a particular character on them. Evangelization was deeply present in the origins of the region and remains so, leaving the region with a 'radical Catholic substrate'" (*Puebla*, 4, 7).[23] Although making clear reference to the failures of the initial evangelization, including "weakness and cowardice," the bishops self-consciously affirm the authentically positive elements, including "the labor of our saints," such as Saint Rosa of Lima and Saint Martin de Porres, and "the intrepid champions of justice and proponents of the gospel message of peace," including Bartolomé de Las Casas (*Puebla*, 7,8). Underlining the existence of a real people with a historical identity, characterized by their commitment to the faith, the document asserts that "the living presence of Jesus Christ in the history, culture, and real life of Latin America is plain to see . . .[a] presence . . .

inseparably bound up with that of the Church; for it is through the Church that Christ's Gospel has resounded in our lands" (*Puebla*, 221). Echoing *Evangelii nuntiandi* throughout, *Puebla* asserts that "the Church cannot be separated from Christ because he himself was its founder." Therefore, one cannot accept Christ without accepting the Church, which is one (*Puebla*, 222, 225), a renewed affirmation against those who were propagating the existence of a "popular Church" in opposition to the "institutional." Nonetheless, "a false triumphalist outlook" is to be avoided (*Puebla*, 231). In a revealing passage, the document underlines both the depth of the popular spirituality and its connection with the Church's emphasis today. The bishops write, "Our people love pilgrimages. In them the simple Christian celebrates the joy of feeling immersed in a multitude of brothers and sisters journeying together toward the God who is waiting for them. This action is a splendid sign and sacramental of the great vision of the Church offered to us by Vatican II . . . the People of God on pilgrimage throughout history" (*Puebla*, 232).

Concerning the evangelization of culture, *Puebla* takes its cues from *Evangelii nuntiandi*, paying a great deal of attention to the importance of inculturation. When people accept the Gospel, "it becomes incarnate among them and assumes their culture," giving rise "to a close bond between them"—that is, between faith and culture (*Puebla*, 400). Historically in Latin America "evangelization was deep enough for the faith to become a constitutive part of Latin America's life and identity. It provided Latin America with a spiritual unity that still persists" (*Puebla*, 412). Of great significance is the assertion that devotion to Mary is "part of the innermost 'identity' of the Latin American peoples . . . [and] shrines to Mary on our continent are signs of the encounter between the faith of the Church and [our] history" (*Puebla*, 282).

Puebla discusses concretely the various challenges to evangelizing the culture today (*Puebla*, 420–43). Yet none of this is intended to negate the strong affirmations of the Medellín conference in favor of liberation and social justice, which also merits an entire section (*Puebla*, 470–506). It also warns against ideologies, particularly "capitalist liberalism" and "Marxist collectivism" (*Puebla*, 542–43). Of great significance is the strong reaffirmation of the preferential option for the poor (*Puebla*, 1134–65). The focus is not exclusive, expressed alongside an equal concern to embrace a preferential option for young people. The latter certainly incorporates the material dimension but also speaks to cultural concerns, such as the variety of modern influences in the region (*Puebla*, 1166–1205). Finally, Puebla affirms base communities but is careful to situate that affirmation along the clear guidelines Paul VI had laid out in *Evangelii nuntiandi* (*Puebla*, 648).

It is fair to say, in summary, that the conclusions of the Puebla conference represent a shift in the direction of a greater focus on evangelization and culture, a clearer distancing of the Catholic Church's pastoral activity from political radicalism linked to Marxism—reaffirming strongly the preferential option for the poor and social justice in the region. These developments dovetail with Bergoglio's own thinking, which would culminate later in the Fifth General Conference of Latin American Bishops, held in Aparecida, Brazil, in 2007, where Bergoglio served as redactor for the final document.[24]

Although a full treatment of the developments in liberation theology after the Puebla conference is beyond the scope of this book, it helps us situate Bergoglio in the context of Latin American theological developments to take note of some of the shifts that occur in liberation theology. This can perhaps be done in no better way than to consider briefly two works from the 1980s by the most famous theologian of liberation—Gustavo Gutiérrez's *On Job: God-Talk and the Suffering of the Innocent* and *We Drink from Our Own Wells: The Spiritual Journey of a People*.[25] In both works Marxist social science and the Enlightenment framework are absent. Both works are predominantly biblical reflections. In *On Job*, perhaps the most striking themes are that, in light of reflecting on Job's experience, God criticizes "every theology that presumes to pigeonhole the divine action in history and gives the illusory impression of knowing it in advance."[26] God is free and His love gratuitous, which has consequences for all human pursuits, however noble, including the struggle for justice. In truth, "justice alone does not have the final say about how we are to speak of God."[27] There are two languages corresponding to two dimensions of our relationship with God: The first, perhaps more easily identified with the theology of liberation, is the prophetic. Here Gutiérrez explains that, in the midst of his own suffering, Job is called to recognize the pain of others and to commit himself to serving those who suffer. In a second phase, Job must acknowledge that he cannot impose his version of justice on God but must accept God's freedom and His gratuitous love. Therefore a second language of contemplation and worship must supplement the prophetic language, which rails against injustice and cries out to God. God cannot be reduced to "the guardian of a rigid moral order," no matter how just that order might seem.[28] There is nothing in Gutiérrez's book suggesting any reduced imperative to strive for justice, but it clearly puts that struggle under an equally firm commitment to the transcendence of the Gospel over any kind of social or political program. God's hand cannot be forced, and the kingdom is not here.

In *We Drink from Our Own Wells* Gutiérrez attempts to provide a framework for a spirituality of liberation, beginning with an acknowledgment of the plight of millions of poor in the world, leading to solidarity with them. This entails for many a moving out of their own particular experience to make the way of the poor their own. The spirituality of liberation is a new way of following Jesus. In the spiritual life, one must be in relation to the Word of the Lord, consider the signs of one's own time, and be aware of other ways of following the Lord. Gutiérrez sees such a process in the historical spiritualities of the Dominicans, Franciscans, and Carmelites and notes that these orders have much to teach even today.[29] The new spirituality developing in Latin America has distinctive characteristics. First, there is an emphasis on conversion in the sense of taking to heart the social mechanisms that cause marginalization, examining our own participation in them, and consciously moving to an attitude of solidarity with the marginalized, taking seriously Christ's claim that the way we treat the poor is the way we treat him.[30] Second, there is the element of gratuitousness—first in the sense of the recognition that the backdrop of all struggles for justice is a God who loves us and loves the poor not because of our merit or theirs but simply because it is His nature to do so. This realization opens us to the kind of radical self-giving that transcends every obstacle.[31] Third is the element of joy, even in the midst of the most discouraging situations, the experience of Easter joy even in the midst of suffering and death.[32] Fourth is the element of spiritual childhood, which goes hand in hand with the humility that permits one truly to open oneself up to God and acknowledge one's dependence on him. The simple people accept God's gift of childhood and respond with attitudes and acts of solidarity.[33] Fifth is the element of community in the midst of experiences of painful solitude and difficulty. This necessarily flows from the commitment to justice in the midst of conflict. The experience of community sustains the disciple. Gutiérrez notes the depth of the sense of celebration in the people and that the Church is the context in which those committed to justice live.[34] Throughout, as the title of the book implies, this spirituality draws from the well of the Latin American experience.

Perhaps the best way of summarizing the journey of the theology of liberation is to say that it began in many cases with an uncritical appropriation of radical social science and Marxism, which compromised its integrity as theology in many cases. However, after the Puebla conference and the Vatican correctives, it has in some ways been integrated into the larger body of theology in ways that have still not been completely worked out.

In order to illustrate this last point, we will close this discussion with a consideration of a work that Gustavo Gutiérrez wrote with Gerhard Müller, who replaced Cardinal Levada as Prefect of the Congregation for the Doctrine of the Faith, the symbol of theological orthodoxy.[35] This work, stripped of Marxist social science and accepting the corrections given by the Vatican instructions as givens, recapitulates the theological vision of liberation for our time. As Müller puts it, the purpose of the joint book is "to support . . . overcoming . . . indifference in the face of the suffering and poverty of our brothers and sisters, but also [to construct] a system of coordinates to situate the theology of liberation."[36] In many ways the work reminds us of the degree to which many of the major lines of thinking and concepts from this theology have been mainstreamed in the Church universal. Among these are (1) the commitment to justice as part and parcel of the Gospel commitment, (2) the language and theology of "integral liberation," understood as liberation from personal sin as traditionally conceived and liberation from political, economic, and social oppression, (3) the understanding of poverty as having different senses theologically, with the absence of human necessities associated with human sin, and (4) the preferential option for the poor as a constitutive dimension of the Catholic Church's social doctrine. Most significantly, both Gutiérrez and Müller underline the themes of evangelization and inculturation, echoing the Puebla conference.[37] Liberation from oppression is integrated into the interpretation of both of these themes, but not in an exclusive way so as to redefine either. Müller emphasizes that the theology of liberation is in continuity with *Gaudium et spes*, *Lumen Gentium*, and Paul VI's *Popul-*

orum progressio. The Word of God is transmitted for the purpose of a transformation that is to begin now. Müller believes that at this point in time the theology of liberation is part of the universal theology of the Church. The more important point of the work is not simply to revindicate the past and remind readers that there was no blanket condemnation of this theology but to underline its relevance for today. Notwithstanding the dizzying levels of progress brought about by technology, the century to come will be, in the words of the president of the World Bank, Enrique V. Iglesias, both "fascinating and cruel." It will be fascinating for those who participate in the progress of science and technology but cruel for those who are left out, the "insignificant." Poverty and marginalization will increase for them as the gap widens between the two groups.[38] Therefore, all of the prophetic denunciations that came from the theology of liberation remain relevant, particularly the criticism of "market idolatry" and the tremendous social debt it leaves behind. In the 1990s, with the end of the Cold War, economic liberalism had a resurgence in Latin America, dubbed *neoliberalism*. It would be fair to say that much of the critical language about it, the way it put profits first and placed economic value over broader human values, was very much in line with the theology of liberation. John Paul II wrote that, "more and more, in many countries of America, a system known as 'neoliberalism' prevails; based on a purely economic conception of man, this system considers profit and the law of the market as its only parameters, to the detriment of the dignity of and the respect due to individuals and peoples. At times this system has become the ideological justification for certain attitudes and behavior in the social and political spheres leading to the neglect of the weaker members of society. Indeed, the poor are becoming ever more numerous, victims of specific policies and structures which are often unjust."[39] So long as such approaches prevail and there remains so much poverty in the midst of plenty, there will remain a need for a theology that proceeds along these lines, even if the theology of liberation, considered in itself as a school of thought, does not perdure.[40]

In conclusion, we have seen that the theology of the people, which developed in Bergoglio's native Argentina, shared his longstanding commitments to the incarnated presence of the Gospel in the culture and history of the Latin American people. Bergoglio's own thinking developed along a similar line. This parallels developments that take place in the Latin American episcopate more broadly. When the bishops gathered in Puebla, Mexico, in 1979, they, too, gave renewed emphasis to the people's own history and culture as a source for pastoral and social action. We saw that the bishops, while not renouncing the prophetic call at Medellín, shifted emphasis somewhat eleven years later at Puebla. This was to clarify where the Latin American Church needed to be concerning developments fueled by liberation theology since Medellín. Countering the tendencies to rely on ideological interpretations of the region emanating ultimately from European Enlightenment influences—Marxism in particular—Puebla speaks more positively of the historical reality of an incarnated faith in the region and sees Latin American history and culture as a source for true development and the way forward. One can also see the influences of Paul VI's *Populorum progressio* and *Evangelii nuntiandi* particularly in the calls to see development in broader human terms informed by Christian anthropology, the value of popular religion, and the warnings against ideological interpretations of the Gospel. In line with these developments, in light of his own Jesuit influences, with the experiences of the missions always in mind, Bergoglio continues to steer an independent path, with his characteristic passion for justice and love of the poor. This puts him on course to assume a major role of leadership in the Latin American Church by the end of the century.

II. THE INFLUENCE OF ALBERTO METHOL FERRÉ

One thinker deserves individual attention in considering influences on Bergoglio: Alberto Methol Ferré, the Uruguayan autodidact from the other side of the Río de la Plata. Cardinal Bergoglio eulogizes him as "a great man" who "helped us to think."[41] Bergoglio had been familiar with Methol Ferré's writings for some years before their first encounter, leading up to the Puebla Conference, in 1978, at which Methol Ferré played a significant role. Their friendship was rooted in similarity of perspective. They shared (1) common affinities for Latin America, (2) the conviction that it was time for Latin America to play a larger role in the Catholic Church, (3) the conviction that theology and pastoral practice should be oriented to inculturation, and (4) a conviction that ideologies both left and right were the problems. Nonetheless, Methol

Ferré was more the intellectual, and even though it is not really possible to pinpoint where the influence begins, it seems fair to say that Methol Ferré's work in three areas impacted Bergoglio. The first was the political conviction—originally expressed at the time of independence by great liberators Simón Bolívar and José de San Martín—that America should be united, a *patria grande*, one nation. Bergoglio speaks of the need to "walk again the paths of integration toward the configuration of the South American Union and the great Latin American nation." "Alone," he continues, "we will go nowhere." Such a path is "a street with no exit that would condemn us to be marginated segments, impoverished and dependent on the great world powers."[42] Bergoglio came to share the conviction that globalization would open the doors to this possibility and that it would be necessary for Latin America to pursue this integration. Methol Ferré had long pronounced political integration to be "the profound logic of the twentieth century, that continues in the twenty-first. One who does not form a state-continent will terminate, and more than ever in a globalized world, at the margin of history, constrained to express itself in terms of lament, fury and silence."[43] However, Bergoglio was aware, along with Methol Ferré, that the result was not guaranteed to be a good one and, harkening back to his rejection of Enlightenment projects, remains concerned about an "imperial conception of globalization."[44] Integration must proceed in ways that recognize the role of the faith in creating Latin America's common culture, the true basis of any unification that will produce healthy results.

In his growing conviction that now is the time of the Latin American Church, beginning with the Puebla conference, recognizing itself as the region where the Gospel has been inculturated for five hundred years, Bergoglio was deeply impacted by this longstanding theme in Methol Ferré's writings. Methol Ferré had borrowed an expression from Brazilian theologian Henrique de Lima Vaz, who distinguishes between "source churches" and "reflection churches," as we first discussed in chapter 1. Source churches have the springs of their own renovation and impart influence on the Church elsewhere, while reflection churches rely more on what goes on in the source churches. It is not an easy or perfect dichotomy, but Methol Ferré believed the distinction was visible in Catholic Church history. What is important for today was that, at the time of his death in 2005, Methol Ferré believed Latin

America was transitioning into a source church.⁴⁵ Interestingly, perhaps prophetically, his death came a few short years before the Fifth General Conference of Latin American Bishops, held in Aparecida, Brazil. Bergoglio would play an important role in it, redacting the final document. In an interview conducted in the last year of his life, when asked whether Latin America was now a source church, Methol Ferré responded that the next Latin American bishops' conference would answer the question.⁴⁶ 2007's Aparecida conference, followed by Bergoglio's 2013 election to the papacy, plausibly mark the fulfillment of Methol Ferré's prediction. One can certainly see in the particular themes shared by the Aparecida document and Pope Francis's papacy the true ascension of a five-hundred-year-old Church to a leadership role in the universal Church, just as Methol Ferré had predicted: a Church that goes out from itself, evangelizing and inculturating, aware that the people of God have a history and a culture of their own, a Church of the poor and for the poor, pursuing justice while eschewing ideology.⁴⁷

The third clear influence is evident in Bergoglio's praise of Methol Ferré for bringing to life the best traditions of Christian anthropology. "The subject of his metaphysics," Bergoglio wrote, "is the real being as such—determinate and limited—who opens the door to the concrete universal" in opposition to the "imported ideologies that generate abstract universals;" the latter have obscured modern anthropology. With this deeper perspective, Methol Ferré was able to see beyond the appearances of the opposition between the Marxist "East" and the democratic capitalist "West." On the one hand, there was the dialectical materialism associated with the "atheistic messianism" of Marxism; on the other was the "vulgar materialism" that spread in the West, associated with modern capitalism. In the latter developed a more implicit "libertine atheism," which came to prevail at the end of the Cold War.⁴⁸ This atheistic libertinism of the consumer society is the root of the new opium of the people, a pattern of uniform thinking now spread all over the world through television and the new technologies. Its ethos, for those who can afford it, is a life of imminent satisfaction excluding references to any real transcendence, a "permissive cornucopia."⁴⁹ This ethos is embodied in the consumerism and relativism of modern culture, which features go hand in hand. What is often missed in this society of alleged liberal neutrality and egalitarianism is the absence of any real or permanent source of value. The only value left is simply the law of the strongest: power. As we will see, this insight is decisive for Bergoglio's developing views of political and economic developments in Latin America and the world.

III. BERGOGLIO'S VISION FOR THE CHURCH TODAY

To conclude this discussion of the historical and theological backdrop to Pope Francis as a social thinker, we have now to summarize his vision for the Catholic Church. This is laid out clearly in his first apostolic exhortation, issued November 24, 2013, titled *Evangelii gaudium* (*EG*).[50] It is not our purpose here to discuss Pope Francis's entire vision for the Church—merely those aspects relevant to understanding his social thought. However, as we have seen already, with his emphasis on inculturated evangelization, social thinking goes to the very core of his vision of what the Church is. Hence the reader will indeed see in the following what have become the signature themes of his papacy. Also worthy of initial note is the very high degree to which the vision outlined in *Evangelii gaudium* echoes his thinking as it has developed over decades. One could rewrite most of the document using his prepapal writings without missing very much.

We begin with his emphasis—echoing Paul VI's *Evangelii nuntiandi*—on evangelization as the "grace and vocation proper to the Church, her deepest identity."[51] Although the Catholic Church over the centuries has taken a kind of permanent residence in many places, cultures, and social locations, Francis now wants to renew the Church with this evangelical focus. "Missionary outreach," he writes, "is paradigmatic for all the Church's activity" (*EG*, 15). From this source flows some of the rhetoric with which his papacy is most associated—that is, to go out "to the streets," "to the outskirts," "to the existential peripheries." Because whoever or wherever is considered marginal can and does change with the times, the Church needs to be on the margins at all times and places to be faithful to Jesus.[52] In his characteristically exhortative tone, he enjoins priests to "Get out of the sacristy! Get out of the parish secretariat! Get out of the VIP rooms! Do the pastoral work of the patio, the doors, homes and streets. Don't wait, go out!"[53] With the joy of the Gospel in our hearts, Pope Francis calls us to create "the new years of justice and holiness . . . [to be] the Church of open doors, to go out and fill with the gospel the streets and the life of people of our time, a Church that lives, prays and works in missionary key."[54] This means going back to the Gospel itself, the principal source of all authentic renewal. In it we recover the original spirituality and audacity of the Christian. Again, this manner of appropriating the Church's missionary thrust is characteristically Ignatian.

Long before assuming the Chair of Saint Peter, Bergoglio was equally clear as to what needs to be overcome. As the Catholic Church has become large and entrenched as an institution in so many places, there is the need to resist the temptation to be a "self-referential Church." Even Catholics who are faithful to their identity run the risk of congregating only among themselves, profoundly distanced from people outside. In the context of secularization, which the Pope clearly recognizes, the Church runs the risk of becoming "paranoid" in its self-enclosure. He writes that "what happens to a self-referential Church is the same as what happens to a self-referential person: it becomes paranoid, autistic. Surely, if one goes out the street, one can get hurt like any other child in the neighborhood. But I prefer a thousand times a wounded Church to a sick Church."[55] At the individual level, to be self-sufficient, to believe, one "has all the answers to the questions, is proof that God is not with him." It is an attitude "seen in all the false prophets, in all mistaken religious leaders, who use religion for their own ego. It is the posture of religious hypocrites, because they talk of God . . . but do not practice His mandates."[56] Moreover, even in absence of hypocrisy, the worst we can do is "entrench ourselves and bitterly lament the state of the world." In this way we become overly suspicious of the world outside and "congratulate ourselves, in our little enclosed world, for our doctrinal clarity and our steadfast defense of truths . . . defenses that end by serving our own satisfaction."[57] We have to reach out to that world outside in the manner that Christ did, making efforts to understand it on its own terms so as to be able to communicate and dialogue with it. The pastor of today has to face the fact, as he humorously relates, that he is often in a situation quite different than that of the shepherd in the parable who had ninety-nine sheep but goes out in search of one. In many cases, the pastor has one in the corral and has to go out and seek ninety-nine.[58]

The Church faces temptations in our time, not unlike the past, concerning both the pole of interiority and the pole of reaching out to the world. On the one hand, some would cultivate an inward piety of one kind or another, emphasizing the subjective dimension. It is a kind of "elitism of the spirit," wherein one element considers itself above those who have not had the same kind of inner experiences. These spiritual elites in a real sense distance themselves from the people of God. At its worst, this imbalanced immanentism loses sight of the central truth of the faith that the Word became flesh. Therefore, there is among the adherents a related lack of commitment to moral and social obligations, to the practical daily demands of the Gospel in one's situation. Bergoglio offers the community in Corinth, described by Paul in I Corinthians, as an example.[59] Such attitudes inevitably divide the Church and cause it to lose the sense of love as the predominant Christian virtue. On the other hand, there are those who are tempted to overemphasize the historical and objective dimension to the point that they wish to identify the Kingdom of Christ with an observable, humanly definable political order. Not content with the Christ who has not yet definitively separated the wheat from the chaff, in a history always imperfect as a result of sin, these people seek to impose a social order while ignoring that their own authoritarianism separates them from the true love of Christ. In both cases the source of the problem is discontent with the true Christ—the life of self-renunciation and the Cross—in favor of one or another kind of self-sufficiency, an egoistic human "triumphalism, a true caricature of the real triumph of Christ over sin and death."[60] Bergoglio is, moreover, emphatic as to the depth of the problem here, because, as he has long emphasized, self-sufficiency is the germ of the genuine corruption that is beyond the sinfulness that can be forgiven and is the lot of all. The self-sufficient have grown weary of the transcendent God; they are self-contained, enslaved to themselves. Their hearts become truly paralyzed, closed to God.[61]

Pope Francis's vision for the Catholic Church is not one within which there is no conflict. His understanding of unity within conflict derives from the Ignatian vision discussed in chapter 2. In this world there are irreducible antinomies and inevitable tensions: (1) universality versus particularity, (2) the traditional versus the new, (3) unity versus multiplicity, (4) interiority versus the apostolate. We recall also Bergoglio's belief that in prayerful commitment to Christ, who holds all the valid elements together, new syntheses can be found to preserve what is valuable on both sides. This Pope is not one to forestall discussion, debate, even strong disagreement, believing it is part of growth in individuals, communities, and the Church universal. What is to be avoided are what he terms "sterile" and "infecund" conflicts that many times predominate. The latter exist when one faction or another in the Church clings to some part of the Church's truth or mission in an exclusive and ultimately self-centered fashion. Sometimes these are related to one or another of the tensions and antinomies just cited. This tendency to factionalism is inherent in human nature, and Paul had to address it in Corinth during the Church's foundational period. Perhaps the most obvious example is the fruitless fight among "traditionalists" versus "progressives."[62] Both sides have an element of truth but hold onto it in an exclusive way that walls out the Holy Spirit, leading to the dangerous attitudes of self-enclosure and self-sufficiency outlined above.

In proclaiming the Gospel, Pope Francis has long been of the conviction that a definitive order and balancing of themes over time is important. We know that the Church began with a very simple message, captured in the New Testament. Paul captured what appears to be a formula from the ancient Church—that "Christ died for our sins in accordance with the Scriptures, that he was buried, that he was raised to life on the third day . . . that he appeared to Cephas, and secondly to the Twelve" (I Corinthians 15:3–5). Christ, Who has risen, now calls all men to Himself, to share in His victory over death and have eternal life (I Corinthians 15: 20–22). This is what theologians have always called the *kerygma*, the announcement of the Gospel in its original form. Whatever legitimate concerns the local or universal Church may have at any time and place, it must prioritize this kerygma, the saving love of God in Jesus Christ.[63] Of course, as Bergoglio has also long taught, the Catholic Church must give instruction—catechize the convert and the young. It also must develop doctrine in many areas in its sojourn through history. But it remains essential that first things be kept first, and he makes reference to problems related to the failure to keep this proper order in the Church today. Particularly, some largely bypass the kerygma to focus on the Church's moral teachings and, even there, to centralize the Church's teaching in the area of sexual morality. He gives the example of a newly ordained priest presiding over First Communion for a group of girls. Prior to giving them Communion, he first emphasized the conditions the Catholic Church requires for receiving

Communion and the need to avoid using contraceptives! Nothing about the beauty of receiving Jesus![64] This is obviously an extreme example, but it underlines a problem in some quarters today. In the preaching of the Gospel "a fitting sense of proportion has to be maintained." Christ, grace, and God's Word should get more attention than the Church, law, and the Pope (*EG*, 38). Moreover, "pastoral ministry in a missionary style is not obsessed with the disjointed transmission of a multitude of doctrines to be insistently imposed" (*EG*, 35).

As one would expect from a grasp of his roots, the new Pope gives strong emphasis to the need for a missionary Church to be a Church of inculturation. He reminds us that "God's project" is "the Holy City . . . God's dwelling among men. He shall dwell with them and they shall be his people and he shall be their God who is always with them." Of course, in its plentitude this project is in the future, but it is in another real sense already realized in Jesus Christ. "The Catholic Church," the Pope writes, "is at the service of the realization of this city . . . and proceeds transforming in Christ, as ferment of the Reign, the actual city. . . . The destiny of the Church's evangelical activity is communitarian, in the peoples and their cultures. Life is full life when its personal, familial and social dimensions become culture: which is to say inheritable and transmissible from generation to generation."[65] This is why, in another of his most frequently quoted phrases, neither the Church itself nor any of its agents or ministries can be reduced to the status of a nongovernmental organization. Holiness is a necessary characteristic in all the Church does and all it seeks to transmit and bequeath, "like a trampoline toward the transcendent."[66] Without it, not only is the Church corrupted, but broader society as well, for social corruption has its roots in the human heart, and no city or set of institutions can prevent corruption once the latter is rooted in the hearts of the people who dwell therein.[67]

What has the appearance of a teaching fresh and new for many today is actually the fruit of one of the most well-established foundations of Bergoglio's thought: the Ignatian method of contemplating the Incarnation. With our eyes fixed on Christ, we do His work: preaching the Good News, finding Him everywhere—but most especially in the poor and those who suffer—and making His Kingdom present in all dimensions of life, an "integral liberation." This is what the first Jesuits did in Argentina in the 1500s. Times have changed, but the nature and the demands of the mission have not. The Pope's blueprint for the Catholic Church comes directly out of the Jesuit missions of old. It is accompanied by a depth of Christian conviction and Christian anthropology that the faith is necessary for the betterment of the city. Faith frees us from the endless pattern of "generalizations and abstractions" that help no one in the end. Faith propels us to the needed "closeness, involvement, and feeling as though we are the leaven that makes the dough grow," to improve the earthly city. Faith knows that by knowing Christ we see others in their fullness and integrity, making us best equipped for the work of transformation lying before us.[68]

It is necessary to add that the Pope's vision is consistent with the Catholic Church's tradition. Since Francis has been elected Pope, the media has often emphasized the element of newness in his teaching. However, a full reading of the Pope's writings reveals that, similar to Popes who preceded him, he fully understands that "the truths of the faith revealed and transmitted are not negotiable." They are "an inheritance that is not negotiated."[69] Moreover Pope Francis teaches that the same love that is inclusive, that refuses to discriminate, does not relativize either. Precisely because love is personal, it respects differences and creates "welcoming and inclusive structures" incompatible with an "anything goes" relativistic mentality. Dressed in the love and truth that come down from Christ through the apostolic tradition of the Church, we neither discriminate nor relativize in our love.[70]

In *Evangelii gaudium* Pope Francis highlights some particular aspects of the social dimension that necessarily accompanies the social dimension of evangelization today, in three areas: (1) inclusion of the poor in society, (2) the common good, and (3) social peace and the need for social dialogue. First, echoing decades of theological development, the Pope reminds his readers that the now-proverbial "option for the poor" is primarily theological and Christological, based on Christ's claim that He Himself is in the poor. In the final analysis, all love given or refused them is given or refused Christ Himself (*EG*, 197–98). He is especially concerned with demonstrating the scriptural basis of this teaching in both the Old and New Testaments (*EG*, 187). Aware that poverty is no given from God, Pope Francis discusses the inadequacies of simple reliance on market mechanisms, which in many cases have only exacerbated inequalities. The structural causes of poverty must be resolved (*EG*, 202–4).

In the second area, the search for "the common good and peace," longstanding concerns in the Catholic Church's social teaching remain of primary concern. He does, however, add a very original dimension to this teaching by enunciating four principles he had often repeated in Argentina in a variety of contexts: First, time is greater than space. By this he means that a long-term perspective must prevail over the search for immediate results. God's best results are to be given "in the fullness of time," necessitating a certain patience in all apostolic activity. Space refers more to the here and now, often resulting in the desire for power to occupy ground. This principle calls us to think in terms of initiating healthy processes and projects for the long run (*EG*, 222–25). A second principle Francis has long held is that unity prevails over conflict. Whether we are thinking in terms of the Catholic Church or broader civil society, we must recall our common filiation in God. Without ignoring the reality of conflict, and its healthy aspects, perpetual divisiveness in the Church or civil society is ultimately destructive. One must be willing to see the truth in the other. Diversities can be harmonized where there is goodwill and openness to the unifying action of the Holy Spirit (*EG*, 226–30). Third, Francis has long taught that realities are more important than ideas. This, as we have seen, goes to the very origins of Pope Francis's social thinking. Only in Christ do we see the fullness of reality, and this can never be encapsulated by any mere idea. Ideas are not inherently evil but become so when they become more important than reality, particularly when we are talking about the reality that is people. Millions have been sacrificed in the modern world under the pretext of a conquering idea. The primacy of the real over any abstraction goes back to the "Incarnation of the Word and its being put into practice" (*EG*, 233). Fourth, and finally, Francis has long emphasized that the whole is greater than the part. This important principle comes into play when we consider globalization in relation to the local and also between the totality of the Gospel and its more specific incarnations in people and places. We need to pay attention to both the whole and the part in ways that preserve the integrity of each. When the whole is overemphasized, the integrity of the local and particular can be obscured or destroyed. The global economy can eliminate important components of a local economy. On the other hand, overemphasis on the part undermines the integrity of the whole, as when, for instance, local church movements begin to pull away from the universal Church (*EG*, 234–37).

The third area the Pope discusses under the social dimension of the Gospel is the need for social dialogue. Again, the Pope has become known for yet another characteristic phrase that represents a pastoral direction—that is, the need for "a culture of encounter." Rooted in his Christian anthropology, the Pope rejects any defensive or aggressive proclamation of the truth the Church has to offer. Just as the Master mostly taught through the encounters He pursued with people, so the Church must, filled with faith and confidence, proclaim its truth in a context of dialogue, not imposition. He specifically references the need for dialogue today (1) between faith, reason, and science (*EG*, 242–43), (2) among Christian churches (*EG*, 244–46), (3) with Judaism (*EG*, 247–49), and (4) with other religions (*EG*, 250–54). He reaffirms the importance of religious liberty in the world today (*EG*, 255–58).

The Catholic Church's work today faces challenges particular to the vicissitudes of our time in two particular areas: (1) those emanating from the world of global political economy and (2) those originating in the cultural changes of our time. He echoes longstanding concerns on the part of the Church on behalf of those excluded from political and economic progress. "Such an economy kills," he wrote in an uncompromising tone (*EG*, 53). The economy of exclusion is part and parcel of the "throwaway" or "disposable" culture he has long criticized. Its regularity in the world is leading to an attitude he terms "the globalization of indifference" (*EG*, 54). He makes more explicit reference to the financial sector, which he believes is governed by a truly idolatrous economy focused on money above the human person. He mentions "financial speculation" as a good example, where money seems to operate in a manner independent of any conception of the common good. These problems, too, flow from an absolutization of material and market values above properly ethical limitations. The resulting inequality is likely to spawn more and more political violence (*EG*, 52–60).The second area where the Pope sees challenges is in cultural developments. He reiterates the historical reality of inculturation of the faith in many regions of the world and praises popular piety for its contributions to many cultures. At the same time, he points to growing deficiencies—such as expressions of the faith that lack a commitment to social improvement and the breakdown of the process of intergenerational transmission of the faith. Today a process of secularization tends to relegate the faith to the realm of the private and subjective, at the same time generating a public square rife with relativism, materialism, and social anomie. Finally, there are today many challenges emerging from the new urban cultures. Aware that these very often are not connected to historical processes by which the faith was inculturated in many ways, the Catholic Church must creatively find ways to engage these cultures and penetrate them with the message of the Gospel (*EG*, 64–65, 67–75).

NOTES

1. I will reserve treatment of the content of the Aparecida conference for chapter 5.

2. Ivereigh, *Great Reformer*, 95.

3. Lucio Gera, in Juan Antonio Presas, *Luján: La ciudad mariana del país* (Buenos Aires: Editorial Claretiana, 1982), 13.

4. Juan Carlos Scannone, in Alejandro Bermúdez, ed., *Pope Francis: Our Brother, Our Friend* (San Francisco: Ignatius Press, 2013), 66.

5. Sebastián Politi, quoted in Omar César Albado, "La pastoral popular en el pensamiento del padre Rafael Tello: Una contribución desde la Argentina a la teologia latinoamericana," in *Franciscanum* 55, no. 160 (December 2013), http://revistas.usbbog.edu.co/index.php/Franciscanum/article/view/443/344, 221.

6. Rafael Tello (1917–2002), probably the most important theologian of this school after Gera, created the Cofradía de Luján (Brotherhood of Luján), with which he was involved for the rest of his life. This association was dedicated to supporting the popular expressions of the people's religiosity—most notably the popular youth pilgrimages to the national shrine of Our Lady of Luján. See Tello's prologue in *Puebla y cultura I* (Buenos Aires: Editorial Patria Grande, 2011), 7–9.

7. Lucio Gera, quoted in Juan Carlos Scannone, "Theology, Popular Culture, and Discernment," in *Frontiers of Theology in Latin America*, ed. Rosino Gibellini, trans. John Drury, 222 (Maryknoll, NY: Orbis Books, 1979).

8. Lucio Gera, quoted in Austen Ivereigh, *Great Reformer*, 112.

9. Tello, *Puebla y cultura*, 147. He cites here *GS*, 53; and John Paul II, *Centesimus annus*, 51 (The Holy See, May 1, 1991, http://w2.vatican.va/content/john-paul-ii/en/encyclicals/documents/hf_jp-ii_enc_01051991_centesimus-annus.html).

10. Tello, *Puebla y cultura*, 115.

11. Tello, quoted in Albado, "La pastoral popular," 232. The passage cited here of course is not intended either by Tello or me to deny the significant historical injustices committed against the indigenous peoples by encomenderos. Rather the purpose is to underline an evangelical and historical truth, which was realized to a considerable degree where evangelization truly occurred, as in the case of the Jesuit reductions and under the aegis of Our Lady of Guadalupe.

12. Tello, *Puebla y cultura*, 128–37.

13. Ibid., 146–48.

14. Scannone, "Theology, Popular Culture, and Discernment," 215–22.

15. The summary of the Pope's talk is from Elisabetta Piqué, "Francisco, contra las ideologías: 'Siempre terminan mal, no sirven,'" *La Nacion*, July 12, 2015, http://www.lanacion.com.ar/1809765-francisco-contra-las-ideologias. I will alternate between paraphrasing and direct quotation to best translate into English.

16. Ibid.

17. Bergoglio, *Meditaciones para religiosos*, 46–47.

18. Quoted in Ivereigh, *Great Reformer*, 110–11.

19. Bergoglio, *Reflexiones en esperanza*, 287–88.

20. Juan Carlos Scannone, in Bermúdez, *Pope Francis*, 64–67.

21. Ivereigh, *Great Reformer*, 122.

22. See, for example, Eagleson and Scharper, *Puebla and Beyond*. The volume has contributions by five commentators—Penny Lernoux, Moises Sandoval, Jon Sobrino, Joseph Gremillion, and Robert McAfee Brown—none of whom reference the important shifts in language in the historical-cultural direction in a positive way. They mostly bypass the theme altogether; Lernoux references it in a negative way. Particularly striking in the essays of Lernoux and Brown is the completely negative view of the Catholic Church in its historical role. Lernoux's essay is directly out of the Black Legend—such as suggesting that the Spaniards and the Church had nothing but contempt for the people or, in fact, that the Spaniards who came to the New World were "failures" and "twisted spirits" (quoting Bishop Pedro Casaldáliga), their Church nothing but "a tool of conquest" (4–5). One can search the volume in vain for positive references to missionary activity with respect to evangelization and inculturation of the faith.

23. All numbered references to the *Final Document from Puebla* (*Puebla*) are from Eagleson and Scharper, eds., *Puebla and Beyond*.

24. The Aparecida conference is referenced in section II of this chapter, though its content has been reserved for the discussion of culture in chapter 5.

25. Gustavo Gutiérrez, *On Job: God-Talk and the Suffering of the Innocent*, trans. Matthew J. O'Connell (Maryknoll, NY: Orbis Books, 1987); and Gustavo Gutiérrez, *We Drink from Our Own Wells: The Spiritual Journey of a People*, trans. Matthew J. O'Connell (Maryknoll, NY: Orbis Books, 1984).

26. Gutiérrez, *On Job*, 72.

27. Ibid., 87.

28. Ibid., 72–75, 87–92.

29. Gutiérrez, *We Drink from Our Own Wells*, 19–32, 52–53.

30. Ibid., 95–106.

31. Ibid., 107–13.

32. Ibid., 114–21.

33. Ibid., 122–27.

34. Ibid., 128–35.

35. Gustavo Gutiérrez and Gerhard Müller, *Del lado de los pobres: Teología de la liberación* (Madrid: San Pablo, 2013).

36. Ibid., 180.

37. Ibid., 25–26, 52–53.

38. Ibid., 126–35.

39. John Paul II, *Ecclesia in America*, The Holy See (Vatican website), January 22, 1999, http://w2.vatican.va/content/john-paul-ii/en/apost_exhortations/documents/hf_jp-ii_exh_22011999_ecclesia-in-america.html, 56.

40. Gustavo Gutiérrez, in Gutiérrez and Müller, *Del lado de los pobres*, 173.

41. From Alver Metalli's "Jorge Bergoglio y Alberto Methol Ferré: Afinidades de un papa y un filósofo del Río de la Plata," found in Methol Ferré and Metalli, *El papa y el filósofo*, 34. Metalli's chapter is the best available treatment of the Methol Ferré–Bergoglio relationship and is relied on here. With the exception of the book's introduction and epilogue, *El papa y el filósofo* was originally published in 2006 in Buenos Aires by Edhasa under the title *La America Latina del siglo XXI*.

42. The quotations are from the prologue Bergoglio wrote for Carriquiry, *Una apuesta por America Latina*, which in turn is quoted in Methol Ferré and Alver Metalli, *El papa y el filósofo*, 28–29.

43. Metho Ferré and Metalli, *El papa y el filósofo*, 29.

44. Quoted in Ibid.

45. Ibid., 79–80.

46. Ibid., 80.

47. The Aparecida conference, as I have before noted, will be more fully examined in chapter 5. As its conclusions reflect more Bergoglio's own thought, it seems best to not discuss it in this chapter on influences and background.

48. Methol Ferré discusses Augusto del Noce as an important influence on his own thinking. Methol Ferré's discussion of atheism is more nuanced than what can be presented here; those interested should consult Methol Ferré and Metalli, *El papa y el filósofo*, 127–49.

49. Methold Ferré notes that this term comes from Zbigniew Brzezinski, cited in Methol Ferré and Metalli, *El papa y el filósofo*, 149.

50. Francis, *Evangelii gaudium*. As a reminder, all references herein are to the document's numbered paragraphs, which can be found at http://w2.vatican.va/content/francesco/en/apost_exhortations/documents/papa-francesco_esortazione-ap_20131124_evangelii-gaudium.html.

51. One can see the union of Francis's Ignatian roots and *Evangelii nuntiandi* in a retreat then-Provincial Bergoglio gave to fellow bishops, based on the spiritual exercises of Saint Ignatius. See Bergoglio's chapter "The Lord Who Founds Us" in Jorge Mario Bergoglio, *In Him Alone Is Our Hope: Spiritual Exercises Given to His Brother Bishops in the Manner of Saint Ignatius of Loyola*, trans. Vincent Capuano and Andrew Matt (New York: Magnificat, 2013), 15–28.

52. For example, see Francis, *Evangelii gaudium*, 20–24, 27; "Being with Christ," 15–20, and "To the Outskirts of Existence," 99–101, both in Francis, *Church of Mercy*; Jorge Mario Bergoglio, *El verdadero poder es el servicio* (Buenos Aires: Editorial Claretiana, 2013), 40–41, 57; and also Francis, *Que no les roben la esperanza: Catequésis durante las audiencias de los miércoles* (Buenos Aires: Agape Libros, 2013), 11–12.

53. Bergoglio, *El verdadero*, 40.

54. Francis, in Virginia Bonard, ed. *Nuestra fe es revolucionaria* (Buenos Aires: Grupo Editorial Prensa, 2013), 159.

55. Sergio Rubín and Francesca Ambrogetti, eds. *El jesuita: La historia de Francisco, el papa argentino* (Buenos Aires: Vergara Editor, 2010), 76.

56. Jorge Mario Bergoglio and Abraham Skorka, *Sobre el cielo y la tierra* (New York: Vintage Español, 2013).

57. Bergoglio, *El verdadero poder*, 125.

58. Rubín and Ambrogetti, *El jesuita*, 77.

59. Jorge Mario Bergoglio, *Educar, elegir la vida: Propuestas para tiempos difíciles*, 2nd ed., corrected and updated (Buenos Aires: Editorial Claretiana, 2013), 71–73.

60. Ibid., 75–77.

61. See Bergoglio's chapter "Corruption and Sin," found in Jorge Mario Bergoglio, *The Way of Humility: Corruption and Sin; On Self-Accusation*, trans. Helena Scott (San Francisco: Ignatius Press, 2014), 22–25.

62. Bergoglio, *Meditaciones para religiosos*, 44–45.

63. Bergoglio, in Rubín and Ambrogetti, *El jesuita*, 88–89.

64. Bergoglio in ibid., 90–91.
65. Francis, *Enviados a hacer el bien: Reflexiones y meditaciones* (Buenos Aires: Agape Libros, 2013), 109–11.
66. Bergoglio and Skorka, *Sobre el cielo*, 47.
67. From Bergoglio's chapter "Corruption and Sin," found in Bergoglio, *Way of Humility*, 18–19.
68. From the chapter "God Lives in the City," found in Francis, *Only Love Can Save Us*, 44.
69. Bergoglio and Skorka, *Sobre el cielo*, 37.
70. From Francis's chapter "God Lives in the City," found in Francis, *Only Love Can Save Us*, 44–45.

5

CULTURE AND ITS RELIGIOUS ROOTS

In chapters 2, 3, and 4 we saw that inculturation of the faith is central to Pope Francis's social vision, principally because it is integral to his understanding of the Catholic Church's mission, which is evangelization. In this chapter we develop this understanding further, particularly by way of Pope Francis's understanding of popular religion. Moreover, we explore the theme of historical realism, how necessary it is to have a culturally rooted understanding of the unity among past, present, and future, and how the faith itself contributes greatly to grasping this real unity. We proceed to examine the Pope's vision of a "culture of encounter" and dialogue today, a vision that flows from the faith but is also well suited to the pluralistic world of our time. Then we follow his discussion of the threats to culture today: first we consider the cultural challenge posed by globalization; then, following Pope Francis, we analyze in depth the ways contemporary patterns of living and thinking further undermine the life of the people, who are left bereft of the cultural resources needed to develop "every man and the whole man," to repeat Paul VI's formulation.

I. RELIGION'S CONTRIBUTION TO CULTURE

We have already explored in chapter 2 how the historical inculturation of faith was part and parcel of the Ignatian vision, needed to ward off the destructive impacts of enlightened rationalism and Calvinism, which fragmented the religious and social unity of the people in order to impose a hegemonic and absolutist vision. In the Pope's alternative, Ignatian understanding, authentic inculturation of the faith serves as a kind of inoculation against false visions that deliver domination in the name of emancipation. This vision informs the document that Cardinal Bergoglio redacted at the conclusion of the Fifth General Conference of Latin American Bishops, held in Aparecida, Brazil, in 2007. The Aparecida document (*Aparecida*) clearly echoes then-Cardinal Bergoglio's thinking as we saw it in the preceding chapters.[1] "Faith is only adequately professed, understood, and lived," the document says, "when it makes its way deeply into the cultural substrate of a people. Thus the full importance of culture for evangelization becomes plain. For the salvation brought by Jesus Christ must be light and strength for all the yearnings, joyful or painful situations, and questions present in the respective cultures of peoples. The encounter of faith with cultures purifies them, enables them to develop their potentialities, and enriches them."[2] Moreover, when the faith is inculturated, he affirms that the Catholic Church is enriched, giving birth to new values and social forms, which bear witness to Christ, revealing Him ever more deeply and connecting the faith with the life of the people (*Aparecida*, 479). In consideration of Latin America's historical uniqueness, *Aparecida* recalls, "Faith in God has animated the life and culture of these nations for more than five centuries. From the encounter between the faith and the indigenous peoples, there has emerged the rich Christian culture of this Continent, expressed in art, music, literature, and above all, in the religious traditions and in the peoples' whole way of being, united as they are by a shared history and a shared creed that gave rise to a great underlying harmony" (*Aparecida*, 477). This faith is the very core of our personal and communal identity, justifying us before the Father who created us, the Son who redeems us and calls us to follow Him, and the Spirit who acts within our hearts.[3] This culture, formed by the faith, with Christ at its center, provides us a synthesis of meaning so important today in the midst of the diverging and fragmented words, signs, and messages the people confront in their increasingly complicated lives (*Aparecida*, 43).

Bergoglio had written years before that we must never forget that the people themselves are among the greatest resources of a culture. It is easy for leaders to slip into an elitist attitude that makes the people objects of the various ministrations of their leaders. The latter cannot adopt an approach of "everything for the people, but nothing with the people."[4] It is the people themselves who are the carriers of their own history and culture. Following the meaning of the Incarnation in its deepest sense, inculturation means that the Gospel is intrinsic to the life of the people and, hence, present in the culture itself.[5]

Bergoglio has long appreciated the significance of popular religiosity as a most meaningful component of Latin American culture. In light of his adoption of the "theology of the people," we can see how popular manifestations of faith in the culture of the people take on a profound significance for him. However, much of post–Vatican II academic theology, in its concern for the centrality of the liturgy and the struggle for social change, tended to put the religion of popular culture in a very negative light, even as an obstacle. Nonetheless, a distinctive feature of the document, long emphasized by Bergoglio, is its affirmation of such expressions, in the context of respecting Latin American culture itself. In 2005, at the Plenary of the Commission for Latin America,[6] Cardinal Bergoglio reiterated the affirmations of the Puebla conference: "The Church," the Puebla document (*Puebla*) contends, "has set its seal on the soul of Latin America. It has left its mark on Latin America's central historical identity." The Church has in many ways given birth to the peoples in the region (*Puebla*, 445). The popular religiosity that has developed over the centuries is no superficial cultural appendage but rather a depository of profound values that provide wisdom to the people in their historical sojourn. This wisdom, embodied in the people, provides the links that enrich life, links between God and human beings, the person and the community, faith and identity. Popular religion affirms human dignity, unites the people with nature, ennobles their labor, and brings the Gospel of joy and life to their daily lives. The wisdom derived from popular culture becomes a principle of discernment by which the people distinguish the wheat from the chaff in their personal and collective lives (*Puebla*, 448). Finally, as the Cardinal and *Puebla* confirm, it is through popular religiosity that the Catholic Church expresses its universality. Echoing Paul VI's *Evangelii nuntiandi*, *Puebla* affirms that popular religion convokes the people in masses and thereby opens up the real possibility that the gospel will have the opportunity to reach their hearts (*Puebla*, 449).

The Puebla conference marked a decisive turn in the direction of emphasizing the historically constituted people and their culture, similar to the line of thought developed in Argentina in the theology of the people. In 2007, the Aparecida conference gave renewed emphasis to these themes. The cultural traditions informed by faith provide a profound reservoir of meaning that integrates the lives and experiences of the people (*Aparecida*, 37). Popular religion points to transcendent reality. It does so in simple and direct ways that the people can spontaneously relate to and embraces to a profound degree the love of God, providing an avenue for the true experience of divine love. Popular religion is also an expression of theological wisdom, because the wisdom of love does not depend directly on the enlightenment of the mind but on the internal action of grace. Popular spirituality, echoing the biblical revelation, is found in the culture of the poor and simple, which in no way compromises its spiritual depth (*Aparecida*, 63). It can only be considered a starting point for any attempt to deepen the people's life of faith (*Aparecida*, 262). Faith has provided the Latin American people their characteristic way of dealing with the profound suffering in the region, the pain that comes from poverty, injustice, and lack of opportunity. The bishops note the depth to which the Cross has penetrated Latin American culture. The people find meaning and direction in their suffering as they contemplate the scourged Christ who gave Himself up for them (*Aparecida*, 265). In the suffering of Christ, they find their true dignity that no injustice or calamity can strip them of. Hence it is equally a part of the Latin American culture to recognize the presence of Christ in the sufferings of one's neighbor. The document reiterates that "we also encounter Him in a special way in the poor, the afflicted, and the sick (cf. Matthew 25:37–40) who reclaim our commitment and give us testimony of faith, patience in suffering, and constant struggle to go on living. How many times do the poor and those who suffer actually evangelize us! In the recognition of this presence and nearness, and in the defense of the rights of the excluded, the Church's faithfulness to Jesus Christ is at stake. The encounter with Jesus Christ in the poor is a constitutive dimension of our faith in Jesus Christ" (*Aparecida*, 267).

The role of the Blessed Virgin Mary merits special emphasis here, both for her profound theological significance and for the special role she plays within popular religiosity. Mary is the first disciple and greatest exemplar of holiness. Through her maternal intercession she continues to transmit the salvation won by Christ. In Mary's maternal glance the people see the love and mercy of God. This is especially true when they contemplate the Virgin of Guadalupe (*Aparecida*, 265–66). In many places devotion to the Mother of Christ declined after Vatican II, often relegated to a mere optional devotion. In Latin America, however, a richer understanding has always prevailed. From its inception in the Guadalupe event, Mary is truly the mother of Latin American culture. Mary asked Juan Diego, "Is it not I, here, who am your Mother? Are you not under my shadow and my gaze? Am I not the source of your joy? Are you not sheltered underneath my mantle?"[7] From the beginning of the new creation in Latin America, Mary the Mother has been present, deeply embedded in the history and fabric of the people, as manifested by the countless shrines and devotions to her throughout the region. She has also been the great evangelizer. She invites the people now to reach out to all, especially those living in darkness, poverty, and closeness to physical and spiritual death (*Aparecida*, 265). For this reason, with roots in a common mother, the history of Latin America merges into a common history where Christ the Lord reigns in the people's hearts (*Aparecida*, 43).

In serving as redactor for the Aparecida conference, Bergoglio was for the most part echoing themes of his own preaching. He recognized the ways the inculturated faith could be a creative force. In 2002, in the midst of Argentina's economic collapse and real threat of breakdown in civil order, Bergoglio worked with the government to create "Argentine Dialogue," a seven-month period of extensive civic dialogue, during which the people rose up in a whirlwind of participation, organizing neighborhood initiatives, mutual-aid societies, transportation, child care, and bartering systems. It was like the beginning of a new, participatory civil order from below. Bergoglio helped facilitate it but wanted neither Church nor state to control it.[8] In the midst of the crisis, he appealed to popular religiosity, among the largest manifestations of which in Argentina is the August 7 Feast of San Cayetano. Known as the "Father of Providence," San Cayetano is the one to whom one prays for bread and work, but Bergoglio used the popular feast day as an opportunity for nationwide catechesis. The homilies over the years came to encompass a wide range of Gospel themes: the value of small gestures, the need for hope, making sure that the request for bread is accompanied by solidarity with others, following the example of the

Good Samaritan, understanding that true power is service. The "bread and work" theme expands to the broader social themes of bread and work as rights, for which the people must struggle and which those with means must do more to provide.[9] On May 8, Feast of Our Lady of Luján, Patroness of Argentina, Bergoglio always reminded the people that God needed a mother to enter history, that Mary is with Christ and with the people today, bearing all their crosses. He likened the throngs of people who come to the shrine to Mary and Joseph—parents come to the shrine to consecrate themselves and their children. The faithful people are frowned on, viewed by the left as alienated and by the right as superstitious. Yet, for Mary, they are the faithful she embraces. The nation has a blessing here because it has a mother. "We have no right," he says, "to cower, to lower our hands in loss of hope. We recoup the memory that this nation has a mother. We recoup the memory of our mother!"[10]

In his meditation "El Señor del Milagro" (The Lord of the Miracle), we see another example of the way Bergoglio would use an already-existing popular devotion, connect it to the deepest themes of the faith, and impart a social message as well.[11] This particular devotion is central to the spiritual identity of the people in the northwestern Province of Salta, who commemorate a feast in honor of the image of El Señor del Milagro each September. The icon is a large crucifix with rays that project outward. Bergoglio reminds the people that the Cross encompasses the entire history of salvation that God brings to his people—but not only in a universal sense. Rather, he says, to look at this Cross prompts us to recall the arrival of the Lord here in our lands. Keeping the meaning of the devotion alive, Bergoglio reiterates that the Lord comes again and again in the life of the people. He speaks of a special and singular love for the people of Salta expressed through the image. The image is miraculous, but that does not mean magical. The grace of God must be sought. He underlines the need for patience, gratitude linked to the generosity of the widow's mite, and penance as important dispositions to prepare for the reception of God's grace. Through these we must unite ourselves to Christ on the Cross so that Christ will remain in Salta in the depth of the people's heart. The grace is always available. Finally, Bergoglio asks the people what response they will make to the grace of God in their midst, reminding them they must go forth to bring about the reign of justice, love, and peace. This meditation exemplifies Bergoglio's approach to popular religious devotions: to bring them to life by tying them to essential themes of the Gospel, to challenge the people to grasp the spiritual core of the devotion so it will be no mere memory of what God did in the past but, rather, a renewed source of evangelical fruit and inculturation of the Gospel.

Bergoglio's vision of culture is rooted in a Christian understanding of time and history, which he sees as essential to cultural well-being. The fundamental insight is that life, whether considered at the level of one person or the community, is a unity among past, present, and future. The human person is a historical being for whom life in time is constitutive. History affords us examples of people and communities that have been weighed down by their past. The past becomes a prison wherein people are stuck in historical antipathies or a sense of failure. In our own time, technology and a world of constant flux often separate people from their past to the point that they no longer recognize it or see its significance. Some are tempted by visions of a utopian future in which all their dreams are realized, believing that the past and even the present should be discarded as obstacles. Bergoglio has long believed that the failure to integrate properly past, present, and future is the source of many cultural and political problems today, leading people into dangerous and illusory ways of thinking. Any cultural identity worth having is something that has been constructed over a long time. We need the wisdom and humility to see it for what it is, both the good and the bad. To idealize the past is dangerous, particularly when such visions are used to fuel delusions of grandeur as to today's possibilities. Equally problematic is to throw the proverbial baby out with the bathwater, which is what happens when, due to the weight of historical failures and limitations, we fail to recognize the good, the heroic, and the holy in our past. At its extreme, this leads to the illusion that one can somehow reconstruct reality anew tomorrow. Although fueled at time by idealistic utopianism, it easily degenerates into iconoclastic attitudes fueling violence and intolerance toward those who do not share the utopian vision. In this world there is no escape from the fact that the present is a product of the past and the future a product of the past and the present. The Christian understanding of history prompts us to realize that limitation has always been and will always be the human condition. Yet, equally Christian is to understand that hope is a virtue not restricted to attaining life after death. Memory properly taken opens up possibilities for the future of this world. History tells us holiness and evangelization are possible. Progress in the development of civilization is also possible. We are obliged in hope to seek a better world, cognizant of and guided by the past. There is always continuity and change, and one must strike the appropriate balance. Therefore, Bergoglio has never been captured by restorationist visions, which he sees as idealizing the past and lacking hope for the future. Nor has he succumbed to revolutionary utopianism, which arrogantly pretends to reconstruct everything from a blank slate. Past, present, and future are all related, equally weighed down by human sinfulness, but never in ways that are definitive and final. Christian hope precludes that type of pessimism.

Some passages from his writings help illuminate the vision here: To revitalize social linkages, one must turn to the nation's cultural reserves, which are found in its past. These contain the roots of the national community, embodied in the memory of saints, heroes, and founders. "This cultural reserve," Bergoglio writes, is a "fecund space where the community contemplates and narrates its familial history, where is reaffirmed our sense of belonging, starting with the values incarnate . . . in the collective memory."[12] To remember is much deeper than simply to recall. In the Christian sense it means to remember our history in light of God's revelation and abiding presence. Consider, for example, all that is meant when we "remember" the Lord's Passion at each Mass. Memory stirs us and awakens us to the fuller awareness of our present, to the good left undone, to the evils thoughtlessly committed or acquiesced in. The people have this kind of memory. Bergoglio recalls the story of an old pastor who came upon an Indian man praying with tremendous concentration for a long time. Curious, the priest asked the man what he was reciting. "The catechism," the man answered, by which he meant the catechism of Saint Toribio of Mogrovejo, written four hundred years ago. Bergoglio underlines, "The memory of a people is not a computer but rather a heart."[13] Without memory, people fall prey to idolatry, the cult of new and ephemeral fashions. Bergoglio recalls the biblical understanding of memory here. To forget what the Lord has done, to forget the covenant and Commandments, is the end of the people's blessing and prosperity.[14] People who do not remember their roots lose one of the most important components of their identity. Of equal significance is the importance of a vision for the future, even a utopia, properly understood. A utopia would be something that has its roots within the people, not imported from outside. For the Christian people, the utopia is fueled by the sense that the Incarnation is intended to penetrate every sphere of existence. Even though the faith also tells us this will not be fully realized here on earth, this is no excuse to leave the good undone. Even eschatology itself, the vision of the New Jerusalem, is a foundation of Christian commitment in this world. Authentic hope is, again, an integral hope that believes it is possible to make the world better within history.[15]

Bergoglio draws on Saint Augustine in developing his reflections on past, present, and future. Augustine reflects on how both the past and the future are in the present. The present of the past is memory. The present of the present is vision. The present of the future is waiting. Memory, vision, and waiting are three necessities in our personal and collective life. Without memory, life is meaningless, a never-ending sense of the present from which nothing is learned, reminiscent of the permissive cornucopia of life in the developed world; there are many opportunities but no sense of what is better to choose. Vision and waiting go together, and both presume memory. Vision gives us an understanding of what may be possible, even though it does not exist yet. For its part, waiting is not simply doing nothing but, rather, the work of real hope. We plant the seeds for the future today based on vision, accepting that not all comes to pass today—nor even in many lifetimes, perhaps. Nevertheless, we pursue the project. Maturity consists in the unity of memory, vision, and waiting. Much of Bergoglio's concern about the present is precisely for the lack of this kind of maturity in culture today. Too much of contemporary culture seems to be based on forgetfulness of roots, leading to a lack of vision. Although Bergoglio does not quote him, one thinks here of Andy Warhol's fifteen minutes of fame, which is all that is left in a world somehow too filled with the present to incorporate the past and the future. Like Plato's democratic soul, the modern person often flits from one pursuit to another without any sense of direction. Illusory narratives that come from the worlds of advertising and ideology replace the old narratives of heroes and saints. These are the fodder for totalitarian schemes of one kind or another, structures of domination, contemporary manifestations of the metropolitan hegemony Bergoglio has always opposed.

We proceed to consider the next pillar of Bergoglio's vision of culture: the "culture of encounter" or "culture of dialogue." It is important to understand that this is no mere vague appeal for unity of the kind to which politicians often appeal, an appeal often vacuous because it is not rooted in any proposal for the needed conversion away from divisive dispositions. Rather, the Pope's repeated appeals here have characteristically theological roots, beginning with the Trinity. The Trinity provides the ultimate source of unity for the Catholic Church and the entire human race. The human person, created in the image and likeness of God, in a real though limited sense, is an image and likeness of the divine personhood. The communion among the Father, Son, and Holy Spirit is the ultimate model and end of the human person. This serves as the basis for communion not only within the Church but, to the extent possible, also among all peoples. All are brothers and sisters with a common Father (*Aparecida*, 155, 157). On the Feast of Corpus Christi in 2007 Cardinal Bergoglio reflected on the implications of our common fatherhood when he commented on the narrative of Melchizedek (Genesis 14:17–24). Not a member of the Chosen People, Melchizedek nonetheless gives Abraham a blessing in the name of "God Most High" (Genesis 14:20). Bergoglio interprets this blessing to mean that in Abraham all nations are blessed. The blessing is not only for believers but also extends to all people of faith and goodwill. The blessing unites all humanity, excepting those who embrace violence and injustice.[16]

The Trinitarian depths of the human person root human beings necessarily in the divine. To preserve the transcendent in any adequate human anthropology has always been important to Bergoglio. With his strong sense of the priority of the real over the idea, and his convictions concerning inculturation grounded in the real person in the concrete, transcendence is for him the real core of the person, not some abstract theory to be dithered over. Without transcendence, we do not have the truth of who we are, with disastrous consequences. If we are not transcendent, then our identity is inevitably reduced to what is revealed by the empirical, material facts and statistics. The person without transcendence becomes a mere pawn, a piece of a puzzle, a link in a chain, a number. In such a case people are no different from the material elements in their environment; hence, there is no firm basis for the assertion of human dignity. We cannot be surprised that the world from which transcendence is stripped is the world wherein there is indifference even in the face of the worst injustices and tragedies, such as the killing and abuse of children. An anthropology without transcendence leads us to the view of human beings in terms that no longer distinguish them from objects; we speak today of the death of human beings as "collateral damage" and working people as "factors of production." Human beings are reduced to categories that can be measured and become statistics. This makes it easier to measure people by money. In such a context, ethics as a study of what is good for human beings in the sense of *distinctly* human loses shape and meaning, replaced by various forms of determinism, the products of one or another abstract theory, whether free-market liberalism, collectivism, or materialism. Worst of all, the loss of transcendence leads to the reductionist understandings of the person that cancel the primary moral commitment in the Christian understanding, to love and build the civilization of love.[17]

It is worthwhile to note here that Bergoglio's concern for the preservation of the transcendence of the person is part of a longstanding concern over the loss of identity and invasion of various forms of imperial hegemony. When we lose our religious roots, we lose the meaning of the values rooted in that faith. A veritable "ontological fraud" eventually results, as genuine values used to make important decisions in life become mere cultural adornment, "pretty things," or commonplace expressions speaking for nothing substantive; ultimately, values degenerate to become mere words that mean anything and hence nothing. Fueled by relativism, the classically Christian virtues, such as justice, come to be applied to whatever the speaker desires. An authentic anthropology must face the reality of the Person of God, which grounds the human person and establishes him in relation to the transcendent.[18] Bergoglio references John Paul II's 1988 address to European Parliament to the effect that, in the light of Christ, it is no longer possible to subsume the person in the collective, particularly when it comes to the person's exercise of conscience in search of truth and what is absolute.[19]

Bergoglio has always been aware that the term *transcendence* is subject to the worst misinterpretations when the backdrop of the Incarnation is taken away. In Christian understanding, transcendence of the world is not a separation from the world or some kind of spiritualized hovering above it. Jesus taught us to find the transcendent in the material world, in all dimensions of human life, not by withdrawing from them but by seeing the world and everything and especially everyone in it in their true depths in the God Jesus revealed through his words and actions.[20] Transcendence is recognizing God in the world. Bergoglio gets us back again to his Ignatian roots, wherein we find transcendence in and through the sacred humanity of Christ, who reveals God precisely through His humanity and His historical life.

It is in the Incarnate Word, Jesus Christ, where we find the fullest understanding of what it means to be a person who goes out to encounter others in the world. It begins with our own encounter with the person Jesus. This encounter is the only authentic way to be a Christian, for it is the origin of the faith. Benedict XVI said it at the beginning of the Aparecida conference: to be a Christian is not reducible to a moral choice or even an adhesion to theological precepts. It is the result of an encounter with a person, Jesus Christ, an encounter that invites one to a complete reorientation of mind and heart (*Aparecida*, 243). The Gospels give us the account of this origin, how various men and women encountered Jesus and how the encounter decisively redirected their lives. The encounters are, each in their way, accompanied by a call, which comes whenever and is purely gratuitous. At the same time, the Gospel reveals the necessity of actively seeking the encounter and persevering in it, with heroism and great constancy.[21] This is no mere statement of historical events but an ever-present paradigm, for each Christian today must seek the same encounter with the Person of Jesus Christ. The Catholic Church provides the means to seek and sustain the encounter. One seeks Christ in the Scriptures, in the liturgy, and in the sacraments, especially in the Eucharist. In Latin America, and other places where the faith has been incarnated in popular religion, one can also encounter Christ in the culture (*Aparecida*, 246–65).

The encounter with Christ in one way or other leads us to take on His mission of encountering others. In his homilies on Christmas Eve, Bergoglio was particularly wont to underline the universality of the call of Christ. From the manger, Christ convokes all, especially those most marginalized in the world. The Prince of Peace came into the world to draw people near to Him and to make them brothers and sisters. In the manger, God became and remains God-with-us. We seek Him not in the stars but in the lowliest of guises—in a child, in the poor, the aged, and those who suffer. Despite the simplicity of the manger scene, to which all are called to come and adore, there is a prerequisite: one cannot hold onto one's own self-centered agenda, and one must be humble enough to bend down to worship God who comes in the form of a defenseless child born to people of no worldly position. Christ's call to go out to encounter the world with the Gospel message, with its prerequisites of self-abnegation and humility, abides throughout historical time.[22]

The Eucharist provides the surefooted path to our next theme—solidarity. Cardinal Bergoglio, addressing educators in Buenos Aires, sent the message that in the exercise of our liberty we must never lose sight of our specifically theological motivation—to act "in accord with the Eucharistic model." He quotes John Paul II's *Mane nobiscum domine*, saying that "the Eucharist not only provides the interior strength needed for this mission but is also—in some sense—*its plan*. For the Eucharist is a mode of being, which passes from Jesus into each Christian, through whose testimony it is meant to spread throughout society and culture."[23] The mission is to spread the "fullness of life" that Christ extends. In 2010 Cardinal Bergoglio emphasized that in the Aparecida document the central category illuminating the meaning of "fullness of life" is precisely "interpersonal encounter." Given Bergoglio's anthropological assumptions, this does not refer simply to any kind of encounter but those that bear the marks of true personhood, extending love and communion. Such encounters enrich life.[24] The kind of meeting *Aparecida* refers to is not the kind of superficial and ephemeral encounters that today have so often replaced real communion but the ongoing and permanent ones that lead to inculturation of the Gospel.[25]

When the faithful move out, as the Pope so desires, they must do so in the manner of Christ—that is, by keeping the real people of our time in the center of focus. As we have seen, that means the person in his or her fullness as a corporal yet transcendent being. Two temptations can easily derail the authentic project. The first is to get stuck in today's virtual reality, which underlines images and appearances to manipulate thinking. On the other hand, in going forth believers cannot hang onto the Christian culture of a previous era, for that would be another form of taking "cultural refuge." Discernment is necessary. The core principles of the faith are of course not negotiable, but the inculturated forms of faith can and do change. Clericalism and paternalism should not allow us to forget that the people have always been creative; they can and do find new spaces of encounter. Bergoglio recalls that during the political and economic breakdown of 2002 the Argentine people spontaneously made their own initiatives to weather the crisis in a variety of social forms, such as social-assistance measures and mutual-aid societies. These were not the province of either Church or state, but they were the product of a people with a Christian conscience and sensibilities. In the manner of Christ, the faithful do not go forth with force but with respect for people, hoping to appeal to their minds and hearts with the integrity of their lives and the truth of their proposals. Again, temptations abound, particularly in the way that postmodern culture relativizes and individualizes all messages. The faithful cannot be satisfied by being one more image in the postmodern collage of a "conciliating" syncretism largely devoid of any real union of values. The faithful must respect real differences without compromising their vision of an "integrating universalism." This requires dialogue and, yes, ultimately the exercise of public authority—but a public authority that has itself embraced the conviction that true authority is service on behalf of a common good that is commonly recognized.[26]

One way to characterize the desired result of the "culture of encounter" is a society wherein solidarity reigns. In a culture of relativism and individualism, emphasizing competitiveness and efficiency, nothing less than a new mentality is needed to counteract it. The ethic is embodied in the Catholic Church's social teaching in many ways, particularly in its insistence on the priority of the common good—the "social function of property" and the "universal destination of goods." However, these attitudes no longer reign in the dominant culture. In fact, today the appeal to solidarity is most likely to be appropriated as a mere sentiment or a disposition adopted by an individual. Bergoglio has something much more profound in mind. Solidarity is "a way of understanding and living human society and its activity." It must be reflected in the entire organization of society and the way the parts interact with another. Often the term surfaces as a way of addressing the imbalances, inequalities, and exclusions that exist in the contemporary world. Yet solidarity correctly understood would be present prior to these results, as a way of rethinking the practices and social arrangements that produce them in the first place. So often today solidarity has this minimalistic connotation, a kind of palliative salve put on wounds generated by the daily workings of the political, economic, and social orders. Bergoglio has long sought to raise the bar here, contending that, if we fail to form people with the new mentality of real solidarity, we have simply failed in our mission. Today we use the word *excellence* so frequently to describe what we want from people. Bergoglio suggests that we think in terms of excellence in solidarity and striving for perfection with respect to it. One significant obstacle is that we have come to accept changes in mere attitude to be sufficient, what is said of individuals who are "good" and "generous." In the cultural appropriation of these terms, an actual change of results is not considered necessary. If our attitudes are good, and the results are not forthcoming, then we obviously are not choosing adequate means of achieving ends such as elevating the poor and the uneducated. Solidarity must reconsider the means and be willing to fight for changes in results. We need to elevate our standards with respect to both the ends and the means. We cannot accept that people are left behind simply because we lack the courage and initiative to find ways to include them. Bergoglio sees it as a violation of hope to accept meager results in the field of solidarity.[27]

There are times in the perusal of the Pope's writings when it might appear that in his own way he is stuck in the past. Someone looking at contemporary culture, even in Latin America, cannot fail to note that it is not an inculturation of Christianity; therefore his remarks on this theme might appear somewhat out of touch with the present. But this is not the case. As a pastor he has always been immersed in the actual culture of his time, and no one is more aware of the changes than himself. Often in moments of great disappointment he has called Buenos Aires "pagan," and in the Aparecida document he boldly states that in the present time Christians are no longer the predominant drivers of culture (*Aparecida*, 509). The Christian must be aware of the cultural world into which he or she enters. In the face of the new plurality of cultural influences, dialogue is a necessary component of the culture of encounter.

In the search for the peace of which the Gospel speaks, Bergoglio refers in his first apostolic exhortation, *Evangelii gaudium*, to the importance of dialogue not only among believers but also among faith, reason, and science. He affirms the legitimacy of science and calls for "a synthesis" between it and other legitimate modes of reason—such as philosophy and theology. Following the Catholic Church's traditional teaching on the subject, he insists that faith and reason cannot contradict one another, as they both come from God. Scientific advances are in need of the light the Church sheds on morality so that important values—such as respect for the human person—are maintained (*EG*, 242–43).

Interreligious dialogue is also necessary. It begins with other Christian churches, particularly because disunity among Christians is a serious impediment to evangelization. Such dialogue provides many opportunities for mutual enrichment and learning (*EG*, 244–46). In addition, dialogue is particularly necessary with Jews, from whom Christians have acquired components of their own identity, going back to Abraham and the Old Testament. There is a rich complementarity and opportunities for mutual enrichment through common reflection on the components of Scripture shared with the Jewish people (*EG*, 247–49). Concerning dialogue with religions with which we do not share scriptures, the challenges can be greater. Nonetheless, anthropologically, we all come from the same God and benefit from common religious and human values. We share their "joys and sufferings," as we do with all peoples. In many areas, such as freedom of worship, the search for peace, the recognition of fundamental principles of justice, respect for family and obligation to the poor, Christians can and must enter into fruitful dialogue and collaboration with non-Christians (*EG*, 250–54).

In all cases, dialogue can only take place in a context of liberty of conscience and mutual respect (*EG*, 255–58). One sees traces in the exhortation of the Pope's oldest concern—"the myopia of a certain rationalism," which "descend[s] to crude and superficial generalizations in speaking of the shortcomings of religion." This rationalism also leads to "contempt for writings [that] reflect religious convictions, overlooking the fact that religious classics can prove meaningful in every age. . . . [These writings] have an enduring capacity to open new horizons, to stimulate thought, to expand the mind and the heart" (*EG*, 256). In the background, one can only recall Bergoglio's appreciation for what an inculturated faith has accomplished for the world over time.

Given the degree to which urbanization has become common throughout the world, the Pope has long been aware that urban cultures provide special challenges to the work of inculturation, promotion of solidarity, and dialogue.[28] Today especially, urban life is particularly dynamic, subject to rapid transformation and the development of new cultural forms. The mass migration of poor from impoverished rural areas only intensifies the changes. In such a context, it is accurate to speak of new cultures, with new forms of language and symbols (*Aparecida*, 58, 510). These new urban cultures pose many challenges to those who do pastoral work. It is very easy for the Christian today to feel intimidated by and alienated from these emerging cultures and subcultures. A series of antinomies coexist there—"globality/particularity, inclusion/exclusion, personalization/depersonalization, secular language/religious language, homogeneity/plurality, urban culture/multiculturalism" (*Aparecida*, 512). Nonetheless, the Catholic Church must recall that it formerly inculturated the Gospel in urban centers and took on life there and that it can do so again with a new missionary impulse. Signs of creativity are already present in parish renewal and restructuring, new ministries with a specifically urban focus, and new organizations and movements focused on unique urban populations and issues (*Aparecida*, 513).

Bergoglio emphasizes that, rather than being intimidated by the difficulties and immensity of the tasks ahead, we should consider the phenomenon theologically and proceed on that basis. Two principles are here paramount: First, "God lives in the city." Second, "God's project is 'the Holy City, the new Jerusalem,' coming down from heaven. . . . In its fullness this project is yet to come, but it is being fulfilled in Jesus Christ . . . who tells us 'Behold, I make all things new'" (*Aparecida*, 514–15). In the same vein, in a talk he gave in Buenos Aires in 2011 to the Congress on Urban Ministry, Bergoglio refers to paragraph 514 of the Aparecida document as "a short hymn of faith, somewhat like a psalm where the city shines forth as a meeting place." He writes:

> Faith teaches us that God lives in the city in the midst of its joys, yearnings, and hopes and likewise in its pain and suffering. The shadows that mark everyday life, such as violence, poverty, individualism, and exclusion, cannot prevent us from seeking and contemplating the God of life also in urban environments. Cities are places of freedom and opportunity. In them people seek the possibility of knowing more people and interacting and coexisting with them. Bonds of fraternity, solidarity, and universality can be experienced in cities. In them the human being is constantly called to ever journey toward meeting the other, coexisting with those who are different, accepting them, and being accepted by them.[29]

Christians are to be the heavenly Kingdom's leaven in the midst of today's multidimensional urban cultures. In order to do so, they must always go back to their own roots to connect with what is specifically Christian. Believing that theological imagery can be a fruitful source of social imagery, Bergoglio recalls the images of the Promised Land and the heavenly city from Scripture, noting that they are a source of perpetual hope for urban dwellers. On the other hand, the cities of Babel and Babylon represent the fears and anxieties of city dwellers contemplating social disharmony and even destruction.[30] But the best images of the city are derived from the image of the Kingdom of Heaven, the true reign of God, where every tear is wiped away, where weapons for defense are unnecessary, where life is received as a pure gift in solidarity with others.[31] The true faith perspective avoids the modern temptation to withdraw into abstraction. Recalling his theological and ecclesial roots, Bergoglio insists that the needed perspective is that of a concrete subject, the historically constituted people of God, looking at the concrete realities of the city where the living God already dwells. The authentic faith perspective leads us to go out to encounter our neighbor, seeking relationships of solidarity while avoiding relationships of domination, with ever-renewed hope. Like leaven, faith is alive, seeking nothing temporary but rather involving itself in long-term processes of change by being with the people.[32]

II. CONTEMPORARY CULTURAL CHALLENGES AND OBSTACLES

Globalization in many respects represents a specific contemporary example of Bergoglio's most longstanding concerns about imperial projects imposing their hegemony on weaker nations. With respect to culture, this takes the form of rejecting the culturally uniform feature of globalization with respect to its impacts on particular cultures, particularly in Latin America and other poor nations. Behind the often-accompanying rhetoric of "pluralism" and "multiculturalism" often lies the reality of a uniformity in thought and practice that particularly threatens the developing world. As Bergoglio said bluntly in 2010 in an interview, "the globalization that standardizes is essentially imperialist and instrumentally liberal, but it is not human. Ultimately, it is a way of enslaving people."[33] Increasingly around the world people consume the same cultural products and wear the same clothes. Bergoglio references the cultural anomaly in his homeland, where significant works of culture, literature, and art genuinely reflecting universal values are cast aside. He wonders why there is no insistence on the reading, watching, listening to, and contemplation of these works, "recuperating some of the space hegemonized by empty products imposed by the market."[34] Globalization's unidirectional, homogenizing impacts are largely due to its reliance on the market, wherein value in the monetary sense reigns supreme. In the process, the liberal culture out of which economic globalization flows dominates and undermines the values of local cultures around the world. In the process it contributes to uprooting people's identity, the loss of certainty, "uniform thinking," and the elimination of the true diversity proper to societies. Its disintegrating tendency is to reduce people to consumers, undermining their capacity to transform societies in healthy ways. Its tendency is to promote "a sole line of thinking, a sole line of conduct, a sole line of surviving, behind which there is one cultural direction of existence. . . [a] globalization that, in its negative aspect, strips us of our dignity to make us dance in the capricious, cold, and calculating market economy."[35]

The uniform tendencies of globalization, nonetheless, provide no clear moral norms, replacing the values of the particular cultures with a stultifying relativism. This process is accelerated because the market reduces value to whatever can be marketed successfully, which always appeals to the lower elements in human nature, the sensationalist, the ephemeral, the material, whatever cultural product turns the quickest and largest short-term profit. The globalized culture cannot provide objective ethical norms even with respect to economic matters. In the face of widespread exclusion, evidenced by inhuman levels of inequality, unemployment, and undeveloped and unused human capacity, the globalized culture speaks with no clear voice. In fact, the world seems to find it ever more difficult even to face problems honestly. The globalized culture provides no meaning to life in its deepest sense as a unity of meaning that ties life together in all its dimensions (*Aparecida*, 37). *Aparecida* goes so far as to say that the globalized culture may conceal the meaning of life in Christ (*Aparecida*, 35). In response to the real problems of the world, amid what Bergoglio frequently calls "the globalization of indifference," we often get nothing more than the enunciation of principles that emphasize the formal over the real, which recall Bergoglio's permanent concern that reality is more important than ideas. The corrosive effect of a culture of individualism laden with relativism is a loss of confidence in and a lack of interest in real commitment to the common good, which leads to taking refuge in the culture of immediate satisfactions through the marketplace.[36]

It is equally important to recall that Bergoglio has never suggested that cultures of the poorer nations should hermetically seal themselves off from other cultures. As we have seen, he proposes, rather, a "culture of encounter," or dialogue among peoples, for their mutual enrichment. As peoples become integrated into the global dialogue, they bring the values of their own culture and must defend them against any process of dilution or absorption into an undifferentiated whole. At the same time, they can absorb from other peoples, with full respect, what belongs to them. The result is no mere eclecticism or syncretism, processes that market elements of a culture, often divesting it of its deeper values in the process.[37] Following Jesuit theologian Ismael Quiles, Bergoglio proposes a process of cultural encounter and dialogue, which can only begin when each culture possesses self-knowledge and self-affirmation. Then, in a second movement, people can move on truly to recognize the other culture in all its integrity. Finally, in the process of mutual recognition, an interchange of cultures emerges that can be mutually enriching, rendering each greater than it was before, a "being more" for both.[38] This avoids the false paths of "relativist isolation," being "local hermits in a global world," on the one hand, or, on the other, "brainless and mimetic passengers in the caboose, admiring the fireworks of the world of others, [in awe] with an open mouth and programmed applause."[39] Yet, Bergoglio does not seem convinced that mutually enriching interchange is the predominant way contemporary globalization works with respect to cultural interaction.[40]

Notwithstanding the evils committed by many members of the Catholic Church at the time of the original evangelization of the New World, the inculturated faith in Latin America provides many positive examples of true dialogue among cultures, a "mestizaje." Historically, there was real success in promoting universality along with respect for the identity of the other. Bergoglio believes that Latin America is where this cultural interaction is most demonstrated.[41] He underlines that he is not talking about a superficial collage of cultures that exist alongside one another with little interpenetration nor about a fusion by which one culture is absorbed by another.

Bergoglio's discussion of the challenges of culture may indeed begin with the phenomenon of globalization, but he extends the analysis to look inside the cultures of nations today in order to underline the challenges and destructive tendencies of our time. To these we now direct our attention.

Arguably the biggest influence on the development of the man who would become Pope, concerning the characteristic features of the modern world, was Romano Guardini.[42] In the Pope's recent encyclical *Laudato si'* (*LS*), the influence is clear in his discussion of the predominant culture. In a 2003 discourse Cardinal Bergoglio, citing Guardini, noted that the most encompassing feature of our civilization is that power becomes increasingly anonymous, disconnected from a sense of being exercised with properly moral responsibility. "This is the seed," Bergoglio writes, "of all the dangers and injustices we suffer."[43] It is not that technology itself is an intrinsic evil; Bergoglio is careful to note that we are all beneficiaries of the enormous advances science and technology have brought us, remedying "countless evils [that] used to harm and limit human beings . . . improving the quality of human life" (*LS*, 102, 103). The problem is that, precisely due to its undoubted successes, there is a decided tendency to extend the logic of technology, itself oriented to power and control, to all dimensions of life, directly or indirectly. Citing Guardini, he contends that "contemporary man has not been trained to use power well." This is because development in technology "has not been accompanied by a corresponding development in human responsibility, values, and conscience." Nor does the technological mentality itself in any way encourage such development, as it does not include a sense that power has to answer to any moral criteria external to it, as its "only norms are taken from alleged necessity, from either utility or security" (*LS*, 105). The sense of necessity engendered is not about moral imperatives—dicta that would mandate human action or inaction based on their nature as right or wrong. Rather, the sense of necessity is derived from criteria internal to the desire to exercise control; an example would be the sense of an imperative to fire workers or destroy local economies that fail to meet efficiency criteria.

What makes the problem worse is the influence that technocratic ways of reasoning have on all dimensions of existence. "The basic problem," Bergoglio writes, "goes even deeper: it is the way that humanity has taken up technology and its development *according to an undifferentiated and one-dimensional paradigm*. This paradigm exalts the concept of a subject who, using logical and rational procedures, progressively approaches and gains control over an external object" (*LS*, 106).[44] Based on the scientific method, this paradigm looks at everything in the same way—whether persons or things—as objects to be manipulated according to whatever ends those who control the technology desire (*LS*, 106). The underlying problem is that this technocratic mentality does not recognize human nature as a source of moral norms. Even more fundamental is the negation of nature itself as something that has its own integrity (*LS*, 106). The logic of power and control now supersedes all that. A human person, the air, the water are all essentially the same as objects to be manipulated. None of them has a valid claim that its own nature be respected by the use of technology. This is the ultimate origin of the widespread expression that human beings become "just a number."

Naive assumptions accompany the technocratic mentality. These too derive from a superficial understanding of human beings without considering them in their depth as free and moral. Perhaps the first of these is the myth that technology itself and scientific advances themselves constitute human progress. If scientific and technological changes are by definition advances, it is easy to assume that advance is the model for human affairs generally, that with technology we move always in a progressive direction. Under this assumption, recognition that the power made possible by technology might be used for an evil that undermines progress itself is undermined and not taken seriously. Moreover, since technology has no inherent limits, and the mentality behind it becomes generalized in the culture, it is easy to buy into assumptions of limitless growth and limitless supplies of the raw materials that make that growth possible (*LS*, 104–6).

Insofar as culture today is driven by globalization and the technocratic mentality behind it, it is also a culture that strips culture of its historical context. By separating people from their real history, globalization is a major source of another of the Pope's major cultural concerns: the fragmentation of human bonds. The past is a storehouse of many cultural treasures and wisdom, which serve as a permanent source of values and creativity to respond to the challenges of the present. The past gives people identity and a definite sense of how they are connected to others. People without a past from which to derive wisdom are immature and will tend to live in the moment without direction, easily manipulated by the images and narratives proposed by the consumerist, materialist, and utilitarian elements of the dominant global culture. However, people can bypass neither their history nor the real problems of the present. Bergoglio writes that "postmodern culture, which dilutes everything, has declared old-fashioned every concrete ethical proposal. To present worthy examples of service, struggle for justice, commitment to the community, sanctity, and heroism tends to be seen as a useless or pernicious tunnel vision."[45] Without adequate appropriation of history we repeat the same errors; we are left with "a hollow present, the present of *everything now*, the present of consumerism, squandering, the eagerness for easy money, irresponsibility (anyway, who is going to remember?), or . . . the immediate present of mutual mistrust and skepticism."[46] In a world of disorientation, it is all too easy for the people to be controlled by one-dimensional thinking in whatever guise it might take. Along these lines, Bergoglio frequently critiques "adolescent progressivism," which he says "blocks all real human progress and, in the name of a claim of progress but without the force of memory . . . configures totalitarian schemes of various types but cruel like those of the twentieth century; totalitarianisms led by *democratic gurus* of monolithic thinking. It confuses the process of maturation of people and countries with a canned milk factory. In addition, the digital culture promotes a mentality of speed, immediate responses."[47]

The technology-centered culture of our time generates problems simply emphasizing speed and immediacy. The solution is not to simply forbid access to this world but, rather, to teach young people especially not "to apply uniquely digital speed to all spheres of life." Nevertheless, that seems to be precisely the problem: Technology provides a model that tends to influence thinking generally. In the technological world, the past is useless. Who wants a computer or cell phone made a decade ago? Technology accustoms people to thinking that change is necessary and good, to devaluing the past, and to applying this way of thinking to all areas of life. Bergoglio cites another example in contemporary culture that similarly reflects the mentality of "immediate stimulus response": the ubiquitous use of and reliance on public-opinion polls. People are encouraged to express an opinion on subjects whether they know anything about them or not. They need to take time to learn and dialogue, but how can this be done "when daily we nurse a style of thought that is provisional, shaky, and unconcerned about coherence?"[48] Contemporary culture encourages a superficiality characterized by the lack of adequate reflection that holds together the real unity among past, present, and future.

A very concrete example of the importance of unity among past, present, and future is the need that the generations have for one another. The extremes of the age spectrum underline the importance of what has come before as well as the future. Very often, and in the starkest terms, Bergoglio criticizes a "throwaway culture" that goes so far as to discard people, especially the very young and the old. The Pope has always been a staunch defender of life, refusing to reduce it to some uniquely religious issue. Scientifically we know that human life begins at conception.[49] Additionally Bergoglio is alarmed at the degree to which children die, are abused, or live without the needed guidance of adults. He cites the widespread problems of malnutrition that leads to mental insufficiency and the lack of education among youth. Both prevent children from ever becoming integrated members of society. He has always used the most moving language when discussing these pathologies of contemporary society and links them to the loss of a sense of past, present, and future:

> If there is no past, one does not learn; if there is no future, one does not risk or prepare. We are stuck in a vacuum, in the lying atemporality of the [television and movie] screens. . . . [Many people] wander aimlessly through the streets and no one sees them, like children who in large numbers beg for a coin or hit a telephone booth to extract a few cents. Children without time; children to whom no one has given them the time they need. Or like adolescents who know not what to wait for or from whom to learn, with absent or empty parents in a society that excludes them or expels them and puts them in a place of victims or victimizers . . . instead of recognizing them as subjects full of future.[50]

Lack of appreciation for the past causes disregard for the aged. No longer productive economically and in need of care, they are devalued by a society that thinks only of today. However, the elderly are actually the repository of living wisdom, which comes from a knowledge of the past and the life-giving traditions of a people. A society with no past equally has no future. Speaking of the natural human nostalgia to return home, Bergoglio believes we have lost it. "When we keep the elderly in geriatric wards," he writes, "as if they were an old overcoat with three mothballs in their pockets, we have lost this nostalgic sense, because being with our grandparents means encountering again our past."[51]

The contemporary "culture of shipwreck" is one of orphanhood, experienced as "discontinuity" of memory related to time and history.[52] As the past teaches us how we are related to one another in community, the loss of memory implies a breaking of these important bonds. In this way, the young do not learn the abundant lessons of the past, so we often hear the illusory promise that tomorrow we can start again from zero, which means bereft of historical wisdom. This discontinuity causes other discontinuities—namely, (1) between society and its leadership class, characterized by disinterest and blindness on both sides, and (2) between institutions and personal expectations. Examples abound in the world of these phenomena. The gap between political leadership and a disillusioned people seems to characterize polities throughout the democratic world, both in developed and developing areas, increasingly accompanied by cynicism and lack of political will. Moreover, people come to doubt and even order their lives without reference to social institutions, including those involving education, religion, and society.

Another experience of orphanhood today is uprootedness. One form of this is spatial. The local city and all its dimensions of life are uprooted by the global culture. The global chains, the ubiquitous presence of the mass media, and the ways of thinking associated with them and their cultural products replace local business and institutions. What remains is an economy for exports and the entire litany of modern social problems: homeless people, exploited children, drugs, and violence. This advances to the point of the dissolution of personal and communal identity. We lose the capacity to identify various groups of people in the city according to human categories. Many places become truly "no-places"—that is, "empty spaces wherein reigns only instrumental logic (marketing), bereft of symbols and references that support the makeup of community identity."[53] Even worse, the uprootedness does not end there but extends to existential and spiritual levels. Without past or future to interpret the present, people cannot find the long-term projects that give meaning to personal and communal life. For human beings identity is belonging over time, precisely the sense that is often now lacking. In addition, the loss of transcendence also contributes to the emptying of culture. Some might say that we are simply going through a process whereby the modern media generate new myths and landmarks to replace the old. Bergoglio thinks this is not at all what occurs. To illustrate, he gives the example of an image of the Virgin Mary in a neighborhood club. This image refers to an image in a basilica, which evokes the entire system of meaning found in the Catholic faith and ultimately to a transcendent reality. In the final analysis, then, the image links the person to the absolute, to God. On the contrary, in "the culture of the image," where images are put out through the modern means of communication, the image refers to nothing outside of the circle of meaning created by the media. These images refer only to one another in a self-referential system.[54] One can go from one image to another, but one remains in a circle of interpretation that has no reference point outside the culture of immediacy, gratification, and consumerism. The images do not transmit to their viewers meanings that concern any in-depth journey in life to a transcendent reality. In fact, this culture tends to prevent the cultivation of any deeper sense of reality. One cannot find roots in life by surfing the channels or the Internet.

The fragmenting of human bonds is not surprisingly accompanied by the fragmentation of knowledge. This is due to the modern tendency to place ideas over reality. Clearly science and its applications become the dominant epistemological paradigm. Bergoglio does not question the legitimate autonomy of science. Nevertheless, science cannot provide human beings moral guidance or a broader sense of human meaning. Despite its many achievements, when it comes to dealing with problems in their fullness precisely as human problems, such as poverty, family breakdown, the environment, or various manifestations of social anomie, science is insufficient. We need the assistance of other forms of historically accumulated wisdom that come from philosophy and the world's cultural and religious traditions (*LS*, 110). The lack of any unity of perspective is particularly troubling in modern culture. There is a tremendous increase in knowledge, but mankind needs two other things that science and technology cannot give: the real, concrete ends that need to be achieved and the properly scaled human means to achieving them.[55] Ironically, amid all the scientific and technological achievements, reason is actually being displaced today. With the loss of a sense of an objective moral order, and a corresponding demotion of reason as no longer capable of truly distinguishing right from wrong, what replaces properly moral reasoning is the mere calculation of advantages and disadvantages and the reign of a leveling consensus based on ever-shifting public opinion. Ours is perhaps the first culture in history not based on any sense of certainties concerning human beings, their ends, and purposes as commonly comprehended in a cultural framework providing direction to both the community itself and the individual persons within it. This recalls John Paul II's *Fides et ratio*:

> Since the last century . . . the affirmation of the principle of immanence [rejecting transcendence] has provoked a radical requestioning of claims once thought indisputable. . . . Our age has been termed by some the age of "postmodernity." According to [some interpretations of postmodernity] the time of certainties is irrevocably past, and the human being must now learn to live in a horizon of total absence of meaning, where everything is provisional and ephemeral. . . . This nihilism has been justified in a sense by the terrible experience of evil which has marked our age. . . . [As a result] one of our greatest threats is the temptation to despair.[56]

Using his own terminology, Bergoglio refers to ours as an age of "weak thinking." Nonetheless, it is a weak thinking that silences some voices and permits others. If a word of traditional wisdom is spoken in opposition to the fulfillment of people's desires, the one who speaks it is thrown over the precipice. Truly, to be thrown off the precipice is the fate of a great number of people, whether founders of a nation, great men and women, traditional cultural icons, or artists and religious leaders. On the other hand, this "weak thinking" has no shame in highlighting any perversion, repeated endlessly, nor in embellishing voyeurism where "all is permitted, where the joy of marketing the morbid seems to entrap the senses and submerge them in nothing. Prohibited is to create and to think. Prohibited is courage, heroism, and sanctity."[57]

The current culture renders inconceivable an alternative cultural paradigm. The technological paradigm is such that its "internal logic" dominates wherever its products are utilized. As Guardini long ago noted, people cannot imagine life without their technological devices. As a result, "it has become countercultural to choose a lifestyle whose goals are even partly independent of technology, of its costs and power to globalize and make us all the same. Technology tends to absorb everything into its ironclad logic, and those who are surrounded with technology know" that its tendency is to create a domination over all dimensions of life. Therefore, our ability to reflect, deliberate, and consider alternatives is seriously diminished (*LS*, 108).[58]

In conclusion, we have seen in this chapter that Bergoglio views religion as central to culture, particularly so with respect to Latin America. It is the very dynamic of the Gospel that it become inculturated in society's ethos, customs, and institutions. Despite the legacy of imperialism and sin generally, Latin America remains a region where the Gospel is and has been present, immersed in and informing the culture over centuries. Popular religiosity is one important expression of this inculturation. Moreover, Christian faith has important implications for how a culture understands its identity over time. In the Christian understanding, history is important—and not only because of the historical nature of the definitive content of Revelation itself. Christianity takes time seriously and understands that identity, both individually and communally, is formed over time. In places where the Gospel is present over a long period, wisdom rooted in the faith develops and becomes a central source not only of identity but also of an ever-present source of creativity in the face of historical challenges and vicissitudes. Finally, the principle of the Incarnation mandates that people and cultures reach out in love and solidarity. In so doing they maintain their identity, seeking real bonds and dialogue without abandoning their historically constituted identity, always secure in their conviction that the Gospel destroys nothing of what is good in the other and can only ennoble a people.

Modern culture increasingly presents severe challenges not only to Christian culture but also to all people who have historically constituted identities. Globalization, while not inherently evil and certainly presenting many possibilities for cultural progress, manifests a tendency to promote homogenization of cultures to a disturbing degree. Authentic dialogue threatens to be overwhelmed by mere imposition of a kind of uniform thinking where all people are expected to assume the same set of contemporary secular attitudes. Romano Guardini's insights into power and technology help explain the phenomenon witnessed all too frequently today, particularly in the way technology tends to create a one-dimensional model and way of thought wherever it goes. Latin America's tradition of *mestizaje*—whereby cultures engage and transform in ways other than superficial syncretism or simple absorption of one by another—is a hopeful alternative to the impositions of globalization, but it is nevertheless unclear that healthy processes of cultural interaction will prevail. One of the worst features of technological culture is its radical destruction of the important unity among past, present, and future. Human beings need wisdom over time to keep these three elements in appropriate balance. The past must be preserved in a healthy way to maintain identity over time. The wisdom it provides is important to face the challenges of present and future. Modern civilization, under the influence of technology, tends to undermine the past while casting a deterministic pall on the present as it heads to a future technology itself determines. There can be no question that the broader human and ethical dimensions of life face serious threats in this process. This is particularly so as modern people become more culturally uprooted, orphaned, at the mercy of cultural imagery that manipulates them to conform to the culture technology is creating, cut off from the transcendent. In the Pope's view, a culture of resistance, rooted in faith and the historically constituted identity of the people, is necessary.

NOTES

1. Father Mariano Fazio, theological expert at the Aparecida conference, explains,

> Even if it's a collective work, the document has a Bergoglio imprint. Many of the main ideas are typical of Bergoglio's spiritual and apostolic vision. In particular . . . it highlights the task of being missionary. . . . The document continually insists on the mission to those who are far away, to those who have left the Church . . . who have never been Christian or have forgotten that they have been. . . . This idea is typical of Bergoglio, and it's clear that it's what he did in Buenos Aires with the problem of the shantytowns.

In Piqué, *Pope Francis*, 136. I would add that the emphasis on Latin America's historical culture similarly echoes Bergoglio's own thought. References to the Aparecida document in this chapter are to be interpreted as Bergoglio's thinking.

2. Conference of the Bishops of Latin America and the Caribbean, *The Aparecida Document: Fifth General Conference of the Bishops of Latin America and the Caribbean* (Lexington, KY: Latin American Episcopal Conference

CELAM, 2014), 477. Hereafter referred to as *Aparecida*; all citations of this publication reference the numbered paragraphs.

3. Jorge Mario Bergoglio, *Educar: Exigencia y pasión; Desafíos para educadores cristianos* (Buenos Aires: Editorial Claretiana, 2013), 39.

4. Bergoglio, *Reflexiones espirituales*, 283.

5. Bergoglio, *Diálogos*, 54.

6. See the chapter "La dulce y confortadora alegría de predicar," found in Bergoglio, *El verdadero poder*, 302–15.

7. "Nican Mopohua: Here It Is Told," c. 1556, para. 119, available online at http://pages.ucsd.edu/~dkjordan/nahuatl/nican/nican5.html.

8. Bergoglio, *La nación por construir*, 58; Ivereigh, *Great Reformer*, 268–69.

9. Bergoglio's homilies for the feast of San Cayetano from 1999 to 2005 have been collected in Bergoglio, *Ponerse la patria al hombro*, 97–138.

10. Bonard, *Nuestra fe es revolucionaria*, 98–102.

11. See the chapter titled "El Señor del Milagro [Salta]," found in Bergoglio, *Reflexiones espirituales*, 291–95.

12. Bergoglio, *El verdadero poder*, 280.

13. Bergoglio, *Educar: Exigencia y pasión*, 34. Saint Toribio of Mogrovejo (1538–1606) was Archbishop of Lima.

14. Bergoglio, *El verdadero poder*, 34, 37–38.

15. Bergoglio, *La nación por construir*, 35–36; Bergoglio, *Educar: Exigencia y pasión*, 90.

16. Bonard, *Nuestra fe es revolucionaria*, 70.

17. Bergoglio, *El verdadero poder*, 111–21.

18. Bergoglio, *Reflexiones en esperanza*, 281.

19. John Paul II, quoted in Bergoglio, *Reflexiones en esperanza*, 281–82.

20. Bergoglio, *El verdadero poder*, 112.

21. Bergoglio, *Mente abierta*, 15–16.

22. Bonard, *Nuestra fe es revolucionaria*, 133–37.

23. Jorge Mario Bergoglio, *Education for Choosing Life: Proposals for Difficult Times*, trans. Deborah Cole (San Francisco: Ignatius Press, 2014), 110–11; emphasis original.

24. Francis, *Enviados a hacer el bien: Reflexiones y meditaciones* (Buenos Aires: Agape Libros, 2013), 103.

25. Ibid., 104.

26. Bergoglio, *La nación por construir*, 43–48, 68.

27. See his Easter 2004 discussion in Bergoglio, *Educar: Elegir la vida*, 98–106.

28. The following is from Francis, *Enviados a hacer el bien*, 105–10.

29. From the chapter "God Lives in the City," found in Francis, *Only Love Can Save Us*, 36.
30. Francis, *Only Love Can Save Us*, 39.
31. Ibid., 39–40.
32. Ibid., 42–43.
33. Bergoglio and Skorka, *Sobre el cielo*, 150.
34. Bergoglio, *El verdadero poder*, 103.
35. Bergoglio, *La nación por construir*, 23–24.
36. Ibid., 26–27.
37. Ibid., 25.
38. Bergoglio references the work of Ismael Quiles in *Reflexiones en esperanza*, n53, 28–30.
39. Bergoglio, *La nación por construir*, 25.
40. Bonard, *Nuestra fe es revolucionaria*, 54–55.
41. Bergoglio and Skorka, *Sobre el cielo*, 150–51.
42. See particularly Romano Guardini, *The End of the Modern World*, rev. ed. (Wilmington, DE: ISI Books, 2001). Guardini is arguably *the* greatest influence on Pope Francis among authors from this century. In 1986, at a difficult moment in Bergoglio's life, after Jesuit general Father Peter Hans Kolvenbach had imposed new Jesuit leadership in Argentina—clearly anti-Bergoglian in orientation—the future pope took a sabbatical to Germany to do a doctoral thesis on Guardini, although he never completed it and returned to Argentina by the end of the year. Ivereigh, *Great Reformer*, 197–99.
43. See the chapter "*Duc in altum*: El pensamiento social de Juan Pablo II," found in Bergoglio, *El verdadero poder*, 289.
44. Emphasis original.
45. Bergoglio, *Educar: Elegir la vida*, 46.
46. Bergoglio, *Education for Choosing Life*, 97; emphasis original.
47. Ibid., 99; emphasis original.
48. Ibid., 94.
49. Bergoglio and Skorka, *Sobre el cielo*, 105.
50. Bergoglio, *Educar: Elegir la vida*, 139.
51. Rubín and Ambrogetti, *El jesuita*, 28.
52. As Cardinal, Bergoglio discussed the issue of the various forms of orphanhood. See Bergoglio, *La nación por construir*, 19–22. A longer discussion can be found in Bergoglio, *Educar: Exigencia y pasión*, 105–18; my following discussion draws from this work.
53. Bergoglio, *Educar: Exigencia y pasión*, 110–11.
54. Ibid., 113–14.
55. Bergoglio, *El verdadero poder*, 66.

56. John Paul II, *Fides et ratio* (Boston: Pauline Books and Media, 1998), 91, 112–13. Also published by The Holy See (Vatican website), September 14, 1998, http://w2.vatican.va/content/john-paul-ii/en/encyclicals/documents/hf_jp-ii_enc_14091998_fides-et-ratio.html.

57. Bergoglio, *Ponerse la patria al hombro*, 85.

58. The internal quotations in this passage are from Guardini, *End of the Modern World*, 63–64.

6

BERGOGLIO AND THE POLITICAL ORDER

As Archbishop and Cardinal in Buenos Aires, Bergoglio had no hesitation to address political topics. He saw himself and was seen by others as a "true citizen." If he thought he could use his moral authority to promote the common good, he saw it as his duty to do so. In 2009, during his yearly August 7 address on the Feast of San Cayetano, he stated frankly, "For years this country has not cared for the people."[1] In his condemnations of human trafficking and contemporary slavery, against which he organized processions, Bergoglio issued criticisms of a historic nature. On September 11, 2013, he made a strident proclamation:

> At school they taught us that slavery was abolished, but do you know what that is? A fairy tale! . . . In this city workers are exploited in secret sweatshops, and if they are immigrants, they have no chance of escaping. In this city there are children who live in the street for years! . . . In this city there are men who make money and feed on the flesh of their brothers, the flesh of all these slaves—men and women—the flesh Jesus took on and for which he died is worth less than an animal's meat, that's what is happening in our city! We care more for a dog than for these slaves of ours![2]

In this chapter, we consider Bergoglio's reflections on politics. While his thinking on politics has depth, it must be noted at the outset that it is in no way systematic or comprehensive. He speaks as a pastor and citizen, not as a political philosopher. This presents some challenges in terms of presentation. There are important dimensions of political thinking that he does not address, and his discussion of politics in the conventional sense is quite limited. He is far more interested in the cultural roots of politics, what he terms *political anthropology*. In light of these considerations this chapter is divided into three parts: The first advances his thought with respect to the fundamental themes of Catholic social thought concerning politics: the common good, the role of the state, the principle of subsidiarity, freedom, and rights. These treatments evince Bergoglio's characteristic focus on the concrete and the particular, with reservations concerning abstraction. They additionally insist on the content of Revelation for their deepest understanding and realization. The second section of this chapter is more uniquely and thoroughly Bergoglio, as he discusses the cultural roots of a successful political order. These include a recognition of what transcends politics, a respect for truth and objectivity, the need for solidarity, and, finally, a deep sense of historical roots, particularly as these are manifest in personalities who best represent the moral rootedness of a nation's politics. It is characteristic of Bergoglio to use Scripture and literary narrative to underline his points. These are particularly evident in his frequent use of the parable of the Good Samaritan as a kind of metaphor for a healthy nation and his reference to Argentina's national poem, *Martín Fierro*. The third part of the chapter treats the political challenges of today, with emphasis on Bergoglio's concerns about the centralization of power, authoritarianism, and the difficulties of formulating an adequate political culture amid contemporary challenges.

I. POLITICS: THE FUNDAMENTAL VISION

The political order has long been a concern for Bergoglio. As with all aspects of the social order, it either reflects and encourages the moral good, and becomes a way of inculturating the Gospel, or it does not. Nevertheless, the political order is especially important because of its nature. It is worth noting at the outset that in Bergoglio's native Argentina, the Catholic Church has been involved in the political order since colonial times. At the time of the nation's independence, particularly in the key years from 1810 to 1816, the Church was very much present, as prominent clergymen participated in the Congress of Tucumán, which declared the nation's independence on July 9, 1816. The people were predominantly Catholic. We recall the developments in Catholic thought that had already been made by the early nineteenth century, particularly with respect to Francisco Suárez and his theory of popular sovereignty. The Bourbons had assumed a completely centralized and exclusionary view of the colonies, completely closed to local participation, which actually prompted the fundamentally Catholic motivations for independence.[3] Bergoglio reflects these same roots in his very classical view of politics, which go back to ancient Greece. On numerous occasions he has cited Aristotle's definition of man as a "political animal," by which he means to say that the human being is oriented by nature to life in political community. Families congregate in villages, but their striving for a better and for a more fully human life prompts them to create the political community for a shared pursuit of the good life in its highest and most comprehensive sense. It is this view of people as oriented to a common commitment to the good life that is the fundamental root of the classically republican and democratic traditions in Western political philosophy.[4] Bergoglio embraces this belief. For him, the political society can only perdure if it remains a vocation to satisfy needs in common. This goes to the very meaning of being a citizen, "to feel oneself called, convoked to a good, to a finality with meaning . . . and to keep the appointment."[5] In today's vocabulary, we can speak of a participatory democracy, which, so long as extrinsic and partial interests do not capture it, holds much hope to end the exclusion that has so often beset democracy in Latin America (*Aparecida*, 75).

Before we proceed with a discussion of politics, it is important to clarify some of the terminology Bergoglio frequently uses. For him, *country* is a geographical reference where geography and politics overlap. The *state* or *nation* refers to the national political organization, with its institutions embodied in its history and laws. The state as "an active subject . . . as promoter and the primary responsible [agent] of the common good, based on the principles of subsidiarity and solidarity, has a fundamental and nontransferable role in the search for integral development, as articulator of interests of distinctive sectors and social actors, establishing the rules of the game that promote social cohesion."[6] The state is, in other words, political authority in its widest and most fundamental sense, existing in the most intrinsic relation to the common good. Finally, there is *patria*, or "fatherland." This is the country or nation understood as a historical inheritance, which would include the state in its present form but carries the deeper sense of the entire national project with its associated values and culture considered historically. In this sense *patria* goes deeper and gives the people a genuine sense of identity. It is a legacy to be respected and improved upon.[7] One sees here the connection between *patria* and the sense of the necessary link among past, present, and future previously discussed in chapter 5.

The Pope reaffirms the classical and Catholic conception of the common good in his first apostolic exhortation, *Evangelii gaudium* (*EG*), and in his second encyclical letter, *Laudato si'* (*LS*).[8] It is a development of a conception that goes all the way back to Aristotle, who saw that the very existence of politics is tied to the existence of this highest of human goods. It was considered highest because it was the good of many as opposed to the good of one; it included in a comprehensive sense all other goods pursued in common, as a way of ordering and prioritizing them. The common good, then, is "the sum total of social conditions which allow people, either as groups or as individuals, to reach their fulfillment more fully and more easily" (*LS*, 156). The common good is no mere collection of individual goods. What makes it common is that it is brought about by properly common action characterized by common intention. The common good is a collection of goods, in which every citizen participates, in such a way that the participation in and the enjoyment by one does not imply a corresponding lack of participation in or lack of enjoyment by another. Consider such public goods as national defense, public health, and public education. If they are properly constituted, each citizen benefits, and the benefit conferred by one does not entail a loss to another. *The* common good is the total sum of all such goods, and its realization is the proper function of politics. The common good must be society's primary goal. Everyone is responsible to contribute to it in a way corresponding to one's position and capacity.

In order to understand Bergoglio, this last point needs special emphasis. Bergoglio's greatest achievements concerning the Catholic Church's teaching on the common good lie in no discourse or presentation of the doctrine but in his example and his call to active participation. José María Poirier, head of the journal *Criterio*, refers to Bergoglio as a "political animal" precisely for his depth of engagement with the promotion of civil society.⁹ For this reason, Bergoglio enjoys great prestige among the working class, business people, and a wide variety of social organizations. As mentioned previously, he initiated Diálogo Argentino at a time of national political and economic collapse. He constructed a wide tent of participation, bringing in a broad array of social sectors, different churches, and other faiths. Then-president Eduardo Duhalde testifies that the initiative "established clear grounds for indispensable agreements and tackled transitory or long-term solutions for varied problems concerning health, political reform, social and labor problems, and the functioning of the three powers of the state."¹⁰

Bergoglio is aware that the common good cannot be realized without a living sense of unity among the people. With his practical bent, he understands that the young are the future, and he particularly encourages their participation in civic life. He says, "I invite young people to enter politics and become responsible; politics is one of the most important forms of charity." Aware that the politics in many nations has become reduced to fights among entrenched interests, he hopes the young will be a "transversal generation"—that is, people who will transcend party and interests to work "for the common good, [as] it's necessary to deliver politics from the circumstances that have soiled it." Concerning the flight of the young from the nation, he referenced a poster, which read, "Ezeiza [the international airport] is not the only way out." The way out, Bergoglio says, "lies in work, in community organizations that guide the people, that give up some more personal things for the common good. Being a politician involves many sacrifices. And to young people I would say: Work in your country, as you can."¹¹

In his understanding of the state as the agent primarily responsible for the common good, Bergoglio, following the principles of Catholic social teaching, is careful to distinguish political authority properly exercised from any systematic tendency toward centralism and authoritarianism. As we have already seen, he has always opposed the centralizing tendencies of modernity in general. In his statement on the role of the state, he is careful to affirm the principle of subsidiarity, which is central to his thinking. Pope Pius XI, in his 1931 encyclical *Quadragesimo anno* (*QA*), gave the principle its classic formulation as follows: "Just as it is gravely wrong to take from individuals what they can accomplish by their own initiative and industry and give it to the community, so also it is an injustice and at the same time a grave evil and disturbance of right order to assign to a greater and higher association what lesser and subordinate organizations can do. For every social activity ought of its very nature to furnish help to the members of the body social and never destroy and absorb them" (QA, 79). To clarify, "greater and higher associations" refers to levels of public authority, culminating in the state proper. "Lesser and subordinate organizations" refers to social groups below the state, beginning with the family, branching out to include other voluntary organizations, such as local communities, states or provinces, and civic, cultural, and professional organizations. These are the communities people join freely, which generate most of social life, to which the people give themselves and from which they profit immensely. The latter organizations arise from the nature of the human person as social, which gives rise to the spontaneous tendency to form associations. In other words, the principle of subsidiarity opposes the tendency simply to transfer social responsibilities and powers to the state. This would be a violation of the fundamental rights of people to organize their own lives. In practice the principle of subsidiarity means that, for example, a family should normally be allowed to govern itself. This would also hold true of other forms of association and even to more local forms of government. The right of the lesser associations to regulate themselves should be respected by the state. However, the principle does not reduce simply to libertarianism or an antigovernment ideology. The state may intervene in a family matter when the family is incapable of resolving it, as in some cases of neglect or abuse. Moreover, if private associations are in conflict, the state may have a role in resolving social discord in the service of the common good. Finally, local government may simply be inadequate to solve a problem—say, the pollution of a river that runs through several states. In such cases, the common good may demand intervention by the state. Subsidiarity does place a burden of proof, however, on the state, when the latter would seek to regulate the affairs of a lesser association. The principle of subsidiarity is, therefore, a principle in need of practical wisdom to be used well. It is not an ideological sledgehammer designed to give ready-made answers to all questions about appropriate government activity.

Subsidiarity exists to promote the health and vitality of the civil society. Bergoglio writes, "our people, who know how to organize themselves spontaneously and naturally in the national community[—]protagonist of this new social linkage[—]asks for a place of consultation, control, and creative participation in all areas of social life that involve them. The leadership must accompany this vitality of the new linkage."[12] Therefore, subsidiarity, properly understood, is a hermeneutical principle for the interpretation of the common good, emphasizing that it is an abundance of life and a plethora of multiple goods and not a restriction on the pursuit of goods. The common good is far more abundant and real when a multitude of people and organizations pursue a wide variety of goods. There are multiple goods just as there are multiple virtues. People and communities are better, and acquire a greater depth of common good, the more that multiple goods and forms of excellence are pursued.[13] This is yet another manifestation of the broader social principle of unity in diversity, the old Ignatian principle.

Freedom and rights are such an important component in any discussion of politics today that they must be treated here. This is not an area of great development in Bergoglio's thought. Political theory generally treats these areas as a matter of reasoned principle, stressing their universality. Bergoglio's political thought, as we have seen, is almost always contextualized by history as related to specific forms of inculturation. His discussion of freedom is no exception. He does not treat freedom in the mode of classical or modern liberalism, which, in Hobbes and Locke, begins with a hypothetical individual in a state of nature, an individual without a past. The problem with this approach, in Bergoglio's view, is that freedom so conceived lacks any clear sense of what ends are to be pursued. In becoming an end in itself, this kind of liberty "locks one in oneself." The individual is in one sense enthroned, but only within himself; it is an empty, negative freedom. Liberty so conceived may indeed tell one that he should not commit an injustice against his neighbor, but to avoid injustice is only the very beginning of what it means to be just. Modern, indeterminate liberty tends to leave us without an adequate orientation to what ends we should pursue in the use of freedom. Although clearly seeing positive elements in the growing awareness of universal human rights, Bergoglio sees the promise of freedom likely to be unfulfilled with the inadequate underlying anthropology of modern liberalism. He writes, "Particularly important has been the advance in the consciousness of the rights of children, along with the rights of men and women, of the equality of rights of minorities. But it is necessary to take a further step: *it will not be through the exalting of individualism that the rights of the person will be given their proper place.* The ultimate right of a person is not only that no one impedes him from achieving his ends but that he effectively achieves them."[14]

The larger issue surrounding liberty is precisely its purpose or ends. Modern liberalism has never had an adequate answer to that, preferring to allow people to choose their ends for themselves. Bergoglio believes the ends are to be found in human nature understood in the light of Revelation. He sees liberty in a much broader context, embodied in a people and their history. Freedom, first of all, is not simply the freedom of isolated individuals but the freedom of entire peoples to be allowed to have their own history and culture in the first place. Nevertheless, much of modern history deprived so many peoples from having such a right. Like all human goods, liberty adequately taken must be linked to charity and the logic of the Incarnation, which propels us toward love of neighbor and orientation to the common good. As such, it must be exercised in the context of love and truth, as part of the struggle to live a mature human life. To understand it simply as indeterminate is one of the worst possible fruits of modern, abstract approaches that strip us of our humanity. Such false freedom is one of the major culprits in the dissolution of social bonds. It is the task of a real and revitalized freedom to reconstruct those ties.[15]

Rooted in the conviction that politics is fundamentally oriented to the common good, the highest human good in this world, Bergoglio holds it in high esteem, despite the fact that in recent decades it has been denigrated both in his native Argentina and around the world. Nonetheless, in its highest sense, politics flows from God's Commandments and the Gospel, which are inseparable from the common good from Bergoglio's Christian perspective.[16] He often refers to politics as "a lofty vocation and one of the highest forms of charity" (*EG*, 205). In his 2015 address to the Congress of the United States, he said, "Your own responsibility as members of Congress is to enable this country . . . to grow as a nation. You are the face of its peoples, their representatives. You are called to defend and preserve the dignity of your fellow citizens in the tireless and demanding pursuit of the common good, for this is the chief aim of politics." He compares the work of the representatives to that of Moses and his people, in that they are called "to keep alive their sense of unity by means of just legislation." In doing so, their work is "to protect, by means of the law, the image and likeness fashioned by God on every human face."[17] He wishes to correct the widespread but false notion that charity is limited to the personal, individual level. It must also become embodied institutionally. When love takes a social and structured form, it is charity in the widest sense, because here the loving desires of many people are made permanent.[18]

Bergoglio has frequently referred to Saint Augustine's work as a way of explicating the fundamental meaning and purposes of politics and its relationship with faith and history. Augustine faced the total collapse of civilization as he knew it. Politics was a reality with seemingly no good consequences. How was he to maintain hope in God without being completely unrealistic in the face of unimaginable destruction? In the midst of this, he worked out the great synthesis, *The City of God*. He saw that there were ultimately two cities—the worldly, characterized by self-love, and the heavenly, characterized by love of God and neighbor. Interestingly, Bergoglio identifies the love pertaining to the heavenly city with the will for the common good. Therefore, the love of God includes the social dimension. Members of the heavenly city seek the common good; members of the earthly city view the common only as an instrument for selfish pursuit. Neither of the two cities is historical. They are both eschatological. Throughout history, however, they are mixed; all historical cities contain both. So what does that mean for politics in history? Augustine clearly rejected the ancient idea of identifying the state with the divine. He also rejected the proposition that the heavenly city was attainable in history. However, history does open the space for God's action to transform mankind. The heavenly city cannot be realized now in the sense of being consummated. Yet the transforming work of grace in history does begin now with our cooperation. There is no false determinism in any direction. There is hope. With the promise of the eternal city, we have hope that things can be made better with the help of God's grace. Yet, we must get our hands dirty and work for it. We must reject the false purity of the Donatists, who took the doctrine of the new heaven and the new earth to be a mandate to remain uncontaminated by the world while waiting for the coming of the heavenly city. But there is no such purity to be found in history, wherein the two cities intermingle. We work not because our efforts bring down heaven on earth, but, filled with hope, we do work for something more human, more reflective of the new heaven and the new earth.[19]

II. POLITICAL ANTHROPOLOGY AND CIVIC CULTURE

While not discounting the necessary institutional components of politics, Bergoglio has always emphasized that a healthy politics can only be rooted in an adequate anthropology and culture. Ultimately government is ideally a reflection of the people governed and proceeds in a manner consonant with their values and culture. In his native Argentina, although always praising the nation's traditional culture, Bergoglio always bemoaned what he saw as a lack of adequate political anthropology and culture.[20] It would, furthermore, be fair to say that Argentina's political difficulties are an essential component of the backdrop for his political thought. With this in mind, we proceed to consider his thinking in these important areas.

Pope Francis's thinking on political culture focuses on four themes. The reader will note that his thinking in these areas is very much dependent on his historical-theological roots and cultural reflections already considered in chapters 2, 3, and 4. It would be fair to say that he believes that a successful politics leading to the realization of the common good can only occur if there is widespread recognition of politics as composed of the following four elements: (1) a strong sense that politics represents and points toward a reality that transcends it and to which it is beholden, (2) a common conviction that politics is about objective truths that harmonize a variety of interests—in other words, in politics there is indeed a whole greater than its parts, (3) a belief that politics is an exercise in social solidarity that accepts the existence of pluralism in unity, and (4) the common sense that politics in a given nation has historical roots that provide inspiration, models of behavior, and consonance with the nation's broader cultural values.

Transcendence—the first of the four elements we associate with Bergoglio's notion of a healthy politics—begins with the understanding of the person understood in relationship with God, the belief that human personhood is only fully understood with the ultimate source of personhood in God revealed in Christ. With this basis, politics can only be a service to people. The common good is never simply majority rule, for it must preserve the dignity of each and every person. This understanding of the transcendence of the person provides the basis for the necessary recognition of inalienable human rights. Transcendence is also supported by the Christian understandings of the earthly city as a reflection, however pale, of the heavenly city. As we have seen in Bergoglio's consideration of Saint Augustine, one of the true implications of Christian eschatology is to open the door of hope for genuine human improvement. We can even say there is room for a utopian vision so long as we understand this "as the form hope takes in a concrete historical situation."[21] In this light, political authority can again only be a form of service, wherein power is always employed in ways guided by a moral framework that includes transcendent understandings of the person and the ends of politics. Politics must be liberated from any practice of domination.[22]

One of Bergoglio's most longstanding and repeated themes is the priority of the whole over the part—what we'll identify as the second of the four elements Bergoglio includes in a healthy politics. In fact, nowhere is the theme of the greater good more important to Bergoglio than in his discussion of politics. Evidently this is a principle that can only be realized if there is a consensus that politics is about objective goals, which can only be realized if there is a shared understanding of the goods to be pursued. Obviously in the democratic politics of today there will always be a variety of interests, which can and do conflict with one another. However, it stands to reason that a political society has to have a sense of objective goals of sufficient depth and amplitude to accommodate the variety of interests. It is essential that the state not be captured by any particular interest or coalition of interests. Nevertheless, this cannot occur without a substantial sense of objective goods to be pursued. Pope Francis recognizes that, in the absence of such a sense, politics degenerates necessarily into a clash of interests without hope of peaceful resolution. In the absence of a clear objective sense of where politics needs to go, only confusion and conflict result.[23]

Since assuming the Chair of Saint Peter, Pope Francis has strongly reiterated the theme of solidarity as a disposition underlying political life[24]—which we term the third of the four elements necessary to Bergoglio's understanding of a healthy politics. *Solidarity*, as defined by the *Compendium of the Social Doctrine of the Church* (*CSD*), "highlights in a particular way the intrinsic social nature of the human person, the equality of all in dignity and rights, and the common path of individuals and peoples towards an ever more committed unity" (*CSD*, 192).²⁵ Solidarity goes far beyond the increasing recognition that people are politically, economically, and culturally interdependent. Nor is it a mere sentiment of distress experienced when one views the effects of social injustice. At the macro or state level, solidarity must inform the entire ordering of institutions, creating veritable "structures of solidarity" (*CSD*, 192–93). Yet it is equally a real personal virtue necessary to a healthy political culture. Solidarity is "a firm and persevering determination to commit oneself to the common good," by which is meant "the good of all and of each individual, because we are all really responsible for all." Social justice is a "fundamental social virtue" that exists "in the sphere of justice . . . directed par excellence to the common good" (*CSD*, 193). Therefore, solidarity bridges the individual and collective levels without reducing one to the other. It affirms the common good and the legitimate autonomy of the individual while avoiding the foibles of both individualism, in which social justice is reduced to whatever individuals might agree to, and collectivism, which swallows up the dignity of the person. At its highest level, solidarity is an extension of the true meaning of friendship and love. Pope Francis writes in *Laudato si'* that "love, overflowing with small gestures of mutual care, is also civic and political. . . . Love for society and commitment to the common good are outstanding expressions of a charity, which affects . . . 'macro-relationships, social, economic, and political ones.' That is why the Church set before the world the ideal of a 'civilization of love.' . . . 'In order to make society more human, more worthy of the human person, love in social life—political, economic, and cultural—must be given renewed value, becoming the constant and highest norm for all activity.'"²⁶

Prior to becoming Pope, Bergoglio was fond of using the biblical narrative of Zacchaeus (Luke 19:1–10) as an example of the conversion to solidarity. Zacchaeus has become a wealthy man by breaking the bonds of solidarity for self-interest. He is enclosed in his own selfish vision. Bergoglio asks if we have had enough of our own hardheaded and foolish ways, which lead us to the pain and social isolation of Zacchaeus. It is so easy to fall back on the same old habits, even when they do not lead to peace and joy. Zacchaeus did not choose the path of this kind of resignation, however. In the tax collector's decision to climb the sycamore tree to see the passing Jesus, Bergoglio sees the decision "to allow himself to be seen by God." This is a key move, which the Cardinal used to ask his listeners if they, too, were willing to put aside their "prejudices, ideologies, and modes of insensitivity" that prevent them from seeing both their own suffering and that of others.[27] When Jesus calls out to Zacchaeus, the tax collector responds with an open heart. In Zacchaeus's act of climbing down the tree, Bergoglio sees the tax collector symbolically lowering himself from his former sense of self-sufficiency. This coming down from his own self-centered pursuits, to embrace attitudes of patient work instead of getting rich quickly by cheating others, symbolizes Zacchaeus's conversion to solidarity. The reformed tax collector immediately announces he is giving half of his wealth to the poor and promises fourfold recompense to anyone he cheated. Jesus equates salvation with this conversion to solidarity.[28]

And, finally, the fourth element critical to achieving a healthy politics, Bergoglio would say, is that an adequate political anthropology must have a sense of historical rootedness. There is a historically accumulated wisdom from which lessons, both good and bad, from the past are derived. As we saw in the previous chapter, there must be a real unity among past, present, and future, for the human person is constituted a historical being. Nowhere is this statement more true than in the political world. As politics involves people in the fullness of their humanity, positively and negatively, it is subject to all of the foibles and temptations that beset humanity, making real progress difficult but not impossible. One must learn the lessons of the past, even when painful. The past is not to be understood here as something that codifies the present and determines the future. Rather the consideration of the genius or heroism of an archetypal figure can be a source of creativity and hope for the future. Many of the biggest temptations in politics are related to the misappropriation of the relationship among past, present, and future. The temptation to take refuge in the past and pretend it can be brought back must be avoided, as it often involves a kind of idealization that fails to consider the past in its concrete fullness. Equally to be avoided is the idea that politics can simply start from scratch tomorrow, bypassing history altogether. The political culture needs neither naive optimism nor pessimism but real projects rooted in the best of the nation's cultural richness that can withstand the test of time.[29]

III. NARRATIVES OF CIVIC VIRTUE: *EL GAUCHO MARTÍN FIERRO*, MANUEL BELGRANO, EL CURA BROCHERO, AND THE GOOD SAMARITAN

Probably related to his background in literature, which he taught earlier in his Jesuit career, Bergoglio enjoys using literary references in his teaching. Argentines could not help but rejoice when, speaking before the United Nations on September 25, 2015, Bergoglio referenced Argentina's greatest epic poem, *Martín Fierro*. Here we discuss his use of this great work and follow it with an examination of other examples of civic virtue he draws from the lives of Argentine founding father Manuel Belgrano and the recently beatified "Cura Brochero."[30] Finally we see how Bergoglio uses the parable of the Good Samaritan to illustrate a proper sense of civic responsibility.

Bergoglio has long been aware of the need for a political culture of resistance to domination, but he conceives of it in ways particular to his deeper anthropology, spirituality, and understanding of culture. Therefore, while always oriented to the poor and aware of the need for social justice, he has always distanced himself from the ideological trends of his time, seeing in their shortsightedness dimensions of the invasion of metropolitan hegemony broadly considered, as well as their lack of rootedness in what properly comes from the people themselves. A striking example of this came with Argentina's economic and political collapse starting at the end of 2001, after it defaulted on its external debt. Setting in motion the *Diálogo Argentino*, yet never using it as an avenue to expand power, Bergoglio delivered a series of discourses to educators in Buenos Aires that "reflect, with particular depth and genius, the Cardinal's vision concerning the national project."[31] It would not pass for a political discourse conventionally conceived, nor is it simply an affirmation of the importance of the Catholic Church; it is what he saw as appropriate for a religious leader to say to renew the nation's broken civic culture. Characteristically aware that past, present, and future are always inextricably intertwined, Bergoglio argued that authentic renewal must come from what is one's own and that real renewal comes only from *el pueblo fiel* (the faithful people). He explained what was needed via an extensive exegesis of Argentina's national epic poem, *Martín Fierro*. It was written by José Hernández in the 1870s, when much of Argentina's traditional life, particularly that of the gaucho, was already receding in the face of all that comes with modernization, industrialization, and centralization. What accompanied this change was considerable injustice and cultural upheaval, much of which was characteristically of foreign origin. Political and economic power were becoming separate from the people, particularly the gauchos, long a symbol of Argentine identity. The dominant model of power was exclusionary, centered on particular exclusionary economic and social class interests.

Martín Fierro is a work of protest, a classic story of a good man being done in by an exclusionary, unjust system, with all of the accompanying lies, rationalizations, and displacement. *Martín Fierro* represents, in one sense, a throwback to a life that was disappearing; yet Bergoglio sees in it much more, in that the gaucho's protest is a perennial one, on behalf of the true values of the people, without which there can be no viable national dignity. At the outset of his discourse, then-Cardinal Bergoglio noted that at first glance the work appears remote from the Argentina of today. The setting is rural Argentina in the 1800s, and for 86 percent of the Argentines who today live in cities, it can seem a world very distant. Bergoglio uses this incongruency, however, to introduce a second one, which is all too relevant: the globalized culture that comes from the outside and the traditional culture of the nation. In a sense, the conflicts depicted in the poem—particularly the gaucho Martín Fierro's struggle to keep alive his identity and cultural values in the face of changes coming from outside gaucho culture—are the same conflicts today: Argentines continue to struggle to maintain their way of life in the midst of an invading globalized culture. A second factor uniting contemporary Argentina with the epic poem is that the nation is a continuation of a common history.[32] What makes the poem a national poem is that its fictional characters reflect real people whose lives, thoughts, ideals, and decisions are in fact a part of today's reality. Bergoglio appeals to the nation's conscience, begging the people not to forget that they are a historical people and to acknowledge that for this reason the lessons of the poem are in fact perennial.[33]

The poem begins with the articulation of the social ideal. This is not a story simply of an idyllic past but the ideal—that which is being looked forward to. Here the gaucho lives according to the rhythms of nature, where his "glory is to live free like the bird in the heavens. . . . No one takes from me what God gave me / What the world gave me is what I leave with / . . . I make my bed in clover / And the stars cover me."[34] Martín Fierro and his wife have worked honestly and diligently. Bergoglio interprets this first part of the poem as a statement of a healthy and integrated life lived in community, respecting its origins. This is because the true ideal is something already in the people, not a mythology they have to be fed from the outside. They have common objectives, many links, and common experiences. There is a natural law and an inheritance that pertains to the people's history: "I have known this land where the man of the countryside lived with his children and mother . . . it was beautiful to see how he passed his days. . . . What a marvel! How the gaucho lived always joyful and well mounted and ready to work."[35]

The poem is fundamentally a work of protest, whose purpose is to stand in opposition to the dominant model, which was accompanied by the presence of gringos (foreigners). The system excludes the gaucho, strips him of his life, dignity, and identity, along with many others. The poem's call is not to go back in time but for inclusion of the gaucho: "He is poor in his orphanhood / From fortune to castaway / Because no one had the courage / To defend his race / The gaucho must have home, / School, church and rights."[36] Nonetheless, Bergoglio insists, the people *already have* within them the resources to resist. It comes from popular wisdom. If not, then why does a poem such as this ever become a national epic in the first place? It became so because people can recognize the injustice of the system and the reality of an alternative way of looking at things. It is to the existing popular culture that the work addresses itself. Martín Fierro speaks of the dignity of his homeland on behalf of popular wisdom. He speaks for the dignity of the people, in charge of their own destiny through work, love, fraternity, and festivity. The people need first their own heritage in the work of national reconstruction, which can only be the work of all. The nation must come to recognize again that participation is necessary in all walks of life. To use the language of today, the epic poem is an appeal for inclusion. Such can only truly come about "from below," in the sense that it emerges from the life of the people: "May God permit / That things get better / But it must always be remembered / To do the work well / That the fire that heats / Must always come from below."[37]

A good polity can only be rooted in the virtues of a people. Then-Cardinal Bergoglio proceeds, based on the text, to identify forms of virtue and ways of life necessary to revitalize the political and social order. He reiterates that the text is not about the past but the future we need to construct that is rooted in the nation's historical culture. First, there is the contrast between "prudence" and *picardía*. In Argentina, *picardía* is essentially being astute in a self-serving way, knowing how to get the best for oneself in a given situation. Bergoglio sees the nation as beset by those who acquire knowledge and use it to benefit themselves. The gaucho believes it is better to learn "good things" rather than adopt such egoistic attitudes. Second, the poem criticizes the success ethic of the modern world, which leaves many poor and excluded. The gaucho counsels against greed and against being servile toward the rich while ignoring the poor. The third virtue that must revive the people is, as Martín Fierro recommends, respect for the elderly, especially when they become weak, and service to the needy: "The stork when he is old / Loses his sight / And procures / To care for himself in his old age / All his little children / Learn from the storks / This example of tenderness." In an Argentina where countless elderly suffer with inadequate retirements, at times living in the streets, the poem's enjoinder hits home with considerable moral force. The poem's fourth civic virtue Bergoglio identifies as an ethic of honesty: "The man of reason, unlike the 'bird with bended beaks,' should never steal, because there is no shame in being poor / But there is in being a thief." Argentines generally believe that the political class uses their positions to help themselves to the public treasury. Fifth, the gaucho pleads for the virtue of an honest and sincere use of language, to sing with genuine feeling and meaning and not just for the joy of talking.[38]

Education is indeed central to the needs of the people, but not a mere technocratic education—rather, one that immerses the people in their own identity and cultural history. This will issue in new projects for our time but always understanding that the new must be rooted in the present and the past, not in a radical uprooting of the people from all that is theirs. Virtues are necessary, and Bergoglio discusses how the classic work underlines the importance of truth and the virtue of diligent work while criticizing the ethic of easy money and dishonorable living to achieve it. The ethic of individualism and noninvolvement must be overcome by an ethic of determined, fraternal justice to create a loving and indomitable nation. In one of the most famous lines of the poem, the character Martín Fierro warns that disunity among brothers leads to their being devoured by those from the outside: "Brothers, be united / Because this is the first law / Have union that is true / In whatever times you live / Because if you fight among yourselves / Those from outside will devour you."[39]

Bergoglio finds a spirit similar to Martín Fierro's in Argentine patriot, hero, and founding father Manuel Belgrano.[40] Bergoglio is fond of citing Belgrano as an exemplar of civic and Christian virtue, although—as Argentine president Domingo Sarmiento would say—Belgrano was one of the few who would never have to seek pardon from history, being neither rich nor successful as those terms would come to be defined. Belgrano died in penury, largely because he gave his possessions away. He was a man who truly "put the nation on his shoulders" in literal and striking ways. His entire life witnessed to his belief that one can only create a good nation by embodying the virtues one wants to see in it. Belgrano never sought self-interest, fame, or gain at anyone's expense. Belgrano knew that a leader had to be one with the people, calling them to realize the best of themselves and their culture. He foresaw and always fought against the notion of a leadership of elites distant from the people. Although he was in a sense a utopian, he was so only in the sense that he challenged the people to be the very best that they could be within the framework of their own Christian understandings. Bergoglio often cites him as a man of creativity but always in the sense of one who combined historical realism and a vision for the future that was within the reach of the people if only they would live out their historical destiny. Belgrano was a man of truth, who understood that the only true revolution had to be based on the truth, the truth of history, the truth of the people, and the truth of what is genuinely conducive to their betterment. Belgrano knew there were no historical shortcuts to being a great nation. Sometimes ridiculed for being weak and pious, Belgrano insisted on the highest standards for the army of independence. He knew the nation could not be morally superior to the people fighting for it, that in the conduct of the present was the future. For this reason he held the army to strict moral standards in everything concerning the treatment of the people. Like the character Martín Fierro, Belgrano knew that the people had to stay united in order to avoid being enslaved by outside forces.

Related to this end of creating and preserving a people with a clear sense of identity, Belgrano's greatest long-term commitment was not to military exploits but to the cause of education. In fact, he exhausted his personal resources for this cause, founding schools himself and donating money to start others. He believed in universal education as the best way to raise up the poor but did not just talk about it. "To found schools is to cultivate souls" was his belief. The school was the place of contact with the vibrancy of one's known history and culture. Belgrano's vision of education is what is today termed *integral human development*. Bergoglio cites Belgrano while underlining a central point taken from Paul VI's *Populorum progressio*: The ultimate criterion of development is universality in two senses—true development must be for "each man and the whole man," and it is also the formula for true education.[41]

Similar concerns for development properly conceived motivate the Pope to discuss another Argentine hero. In his first year in the Chair of Saint Peter, Pope Francis beatified José Gabriel del Rosario Brochero, Argentine priest from the Province of Córdoba, popularly known as "El Cura Brochero." In a way so particular to his thought, Bergoglio sees in "El Cura Brochero" a model for both religious and civic virtue. In his letter to the Argentine Episcopal Conference, Bergoglio emphasized how this priest embodied "a currently relevant approach to the Gospel. He was a pioneer in going out to the geographical and existential peripheries to take God's love and mercy to everyone."[42] José Gabriel del Rosario Brochero was born in 1840 and ordained in 1862. In 1869 he was given the pastorship of a very remote and arid region in the Córdoba mountains where there were ten thousand widely dispersed parishioners, lacking roads and schools and in a grave state of material and moral poverty. Brochero, as Pope Francis said in the Angelus Address the day after the beatification, "was untiring in the rescue of souls of a mountainous population very poor, isolated, and forgotten, left to the ravages of alcoholism and violence."[43] A unique feature of his ministry was his administration of the spiritual exercises of Saint Ignatius to the poor and uneducated laity. Yet Brochero also worked "for the common good that the great dignity of every person as a child of God deserves."[44] El Cura Brochero "left an inerasable print on the beautiful landscape of the Traslasierra [mountain region in Córdoba] with the help of his 'sheep,' building roads, schools, chapels, post offices, and a retreat house in the village of Tránsito."[45] He built a school for young women, repaired roads and canals, visited all the prisoners, and argued with civic officials in favor of freeing those he believed rehabilitated. Near the end of his life, Brochero asked the national authorities to build a railway to connect one town to another so that the insular people could have an outlet to the city.[46] Indefatigable, he never separated his evangelical work from building the civic community.

In a homily celebrated May 25, 2003, then-Cardinal Bergoglio gave an extended treatment of the parable of the Good Samaritan, using it to demonstrate the fundamental option for how to reconstruct a nation. In the nation, he contends, are a very large number of assaults against the common good of the people, and the victims of various kinds pile up higher and higher. The parable of the Good Samaritan contains within it all the dynamic elements of the nation's internal struggle in its attempt to construct a national identity. Although the victim in the story is presumably one who encountered bad fortune, the other figures in the story choose their course of action: the one who commits the assault, the various people who look away and construct excuses for not helping, and, finally, the Good Samaritan himself.

The account is a parable and metaphor—but a very real and concrete one—for the entire nation. Assaults that leave behind victims are part of the nation's daily story, and so are the actions of the passersby and the Samaritan man. The latter represents Christ Himself, who makes Himself neighbor to one He has never met before. This is one of the key points of the homily: The parable is neither about abstract ideas or theories about how to make a nation nor a fable with a moral attached. We either help the victims, or we do not. In our daily decisions to be like the Samaritan or leave people on the side of the road, we answer the question of our own identity, both individually and collectively as a nation. There is no escaping the imperative to choose: one either includes, excludes, or cooperates with the exclusion. Another central point of Bergoglio's homily is that the geographic, cultural, political, and religious differences among the people do not count. In the parable, the professionally religious and the respected man end up choosing the wrong side, while the hero is a member of a despised group, the Samaritans. Bergoglio claims that we know who the assailants are, for they are the same as always—those who seek power and wealth and lack any scruples. He notes, furthermore, that the parable interestingly does not actually focus on them; rather, it takes them and their deeds as a given. The Samaritan does not bemoan the state of society nor theorize as to why things are the way they are. That, however, is what many do; they use the reality of the wounded to construct an explanation about who is responsible, an account they place in opposition to other people who have alternative or conflicting explanations. Hence the reality of the wounded becomes a pretext for endless contention, a struggle for power. Nonetheless, we can only classify these people who emphasize their theories to explain the tragedy with the passersby; they seek to explain, but they do not come to the aid of the victim.

Bergoglio has praise for the culture of the people, because he notes that, despite the mounting tragedies, many still follow the example of the Samaritan and help their neighbor in need. One hears the echo of "el pueblo fiel," discussed in chapter 3. Bergoglio elaborates that there are many ways to be one of the passersby. He underlines most those who look away—which he sees as a metaphor for those who look to a reality that seems more pleasant, excluding from view the victims and their pressing needs. They want simply to replace the nation's identity with another that comes from outside, which is largely illusion. Bergoglio notes that there is a kind of unity between the assailants and the passersby; they benefit mutually while the nation sinks into hopelessness. He concludes that every Argentine faces the reality the Good Samaritan faces: Daily life presents everyone the option to choose which character they will be—assailant, passerby, or one who gives succor to his neighbor. The Good Samaritan seeks neither recognition nor reward.

IV. THE POLITICS OF FRAGMENTATION AND THE TECHNOLOGICAL IMPERATIVE

When we consider Bergoglio's vision of political anthropology and his rather classical understanding of the function of politics for the common good, we might get the impression that he has a somewhat unrealistic view of the political world. But that impression would be mistaken. Bergoglio is fully aware of how far the actual world of politics is from the ideals he proposes. Politics can only approximate a pursuit of the common good under two circumstances: (1) there must be a common will, and (2) there must be common ends. What would supply these under any circumstances? Clearly such commonality would have to be established within the existing political culture. In a world where the Gospel was inculturated, commonality of will and ends would come naturally, already embodied in social forms and practices. Yet, as we have seen, Bergoglio is aware that faith has ceased to be at the forefront of cultural production; today the work of believers can only be characterized as a new attempt to evangelize societies no longer Christian in their social mores and structures.

As politics lost its base in epistemological and moral unity provided by the culture in which it was embedded, politics as the pursuit of the common good has ceded its space to other forces. Since the middle of the 1700s, politics in the grand sense has lost out to "economic space, social space, and juridical forms." Economic theory, sociology, and law have replaced politics. Bergoglio's views here go back to his essentially critical view of liberalism as a political ideology. Under liberalism, a struggle among various interests replaces the common good; in this struggle, whatever is left of the common culture of the people is relativized if not excluded. Striking examples would be laws that mandated legal abortion in the United States in 1973 and gay marriage in Argentina in 2010; in both cases, the changes in law excluded the thinking of nonelites, vast majorities of whom were not supportive of the measures. Therefore, politics in democratic societies today simply reflects a fracturing of visions. Worth noting is that politics comes no longer to be understood as the noble search and realization of the common good but, rather, becomes identified precisely by conflict among interests.[47]

Obviously each nation has its own peculiarities, but it seems fair to say that in Bergoglio's thinking there are two overarching and interrelated trends that persistently promote a fractured and fragmented politics: The first are the impacts of globalization, whose negative aspect is characterized by liberalism and imperialism. As it tends to homogenize cultures and impose a common vision, it is obvious that the politics of individual nations must cede economic, political, and cultural space to the imperatives of globalization. Therefore, in the largest sense politics has to become weaker—that is, it can deal in authoritative fashion over an ever-diminishing field. For example, in *Laudato si'* Pope Francis mentions that in the face of so many threats to the common good of the environment "it is remarkable how weak international political responses have been. . . . There are too many special interests, and economic interests easily end up trumping the common good" (*LS*, 54). The same could be said of any number of other issues—such as global poverty, refugees, and problems related to immigration. A second passage from the same paragraph of *Laudato si'* underlines the second persistent trend that fractures our politics: "The alliance between the economy and technology ends up sidelining anything unrelated to its immediate interests" (*LS*, 54). As we have already seen, globalization for Bergoglio is, in its cultural dimension, a kind of one-dimensional thinking, a tendency only intensified by the technocratic mentality that drives it.

At this point it is appropriate to note that Romano Guardini—who has so influenced Bergoglio's thinking, as we recall—was concerned about technology and culture generally but particularly with respect to their influence on politics, because the technocratic paradigm is the predominant factor that transforms politics into a struggle for power in an environment where the sense of limits on power inevitably deteriorates. We recall the discussion from chapter 5, where Guardini's concerns were developed, particularly the tendency for the way of thinking intrinsic to technological development tends to prevail in society generally. As technology itself has no properly human, ethical ends, its use and expansion tend to be justified in terms of utility or security, which, without an objective moral framework, are indistinguishable from power itself. In this climate technology's indubitable successes lead to a kind of glorification of the specific type of reasoning behind them—that is, experimental, scientific reasoning. One need only consider how people today generally consider politicians as opposed to technological icons such as Bill Gates or Steve Jobs. The former suffer from the perception of politics as an unresolvable conflict among self-centered interests; few question that the latter have brought about enormous contributions, and still fewer question whether the impacts of technology might be something other than good. The accompanying myth of inevitable progress through science only solidifies the tendency. Guardini writes that "there is a fateful inclination to utilize power ever more completely, both scientifically and technically, yet not to acknowledge it, preferring to hide it behind aspects of 'utility,' 'welfare,' 'progress,' and so forth. This is one reason why man governs without a corresponding sense of government. Thus power has come to be exercised in a manner that is not ethically determined; the most telling example of this is the modern business corporation."[48]

Guardini notes that "power acquires characteristics only Revelation can interpret." One of the distinguishing characteristics of our postmodern politics accompanied by the technological imperative is the loss of the sense that people have that they are in control of what occurs around them. This is perhaps particularly true in politics. Contemporary man "no longer feels that *he*, personally, is acting." He feels, rather, "like one element in a chain of events." As others are in the same predicament, "there is a growing sense of there being no one at all who acts, only [an] intangible, invisible, indefinable something which derides questioning." The result is a declining sense of personal responsibility for social outcomes across the board but perhaps especially in the political. The empty space created, however, does not remain. It "is succeeded by a faithlessness which hardens into an attitude, and into this no-man's-land stalks another initiative, the demonic."[49] In the final analysis, the growing and accumulating power associated with technology, unchecked by ethics, is simply evil.

In borrowing from Guardini's views, Bergoglio does not mean to suggest any type of hopelessness here, as though negative outcomes in the future are guaranteed. He does offer a lengthy disquisition on the book of Revelation. Following Guardini, Bergoglio does not see in John's Apocalypse a definitive account of endlessly worse times. Rather he sees "a book of consolation" that God wanted to put in the hands of His Church at the end of the apostolic period.[50] However, the consolation is needed, because the trials and tribulations are indeed real and historically accumulating. He references the work of Hans Urs von Balthasar as well, who, we should note, shares Bergoglio's concerns about a technologically driven culture. "Wherever modern technological civilization penetrates," Balthasar writes, ". . . it also infuses a post-Christian, secular, atheistic consciousness as well." This trend seems intrinsic, not accidental, as "these fetishes cast a previously unknown spell precisely because they are manipulable." Technology began as a means by which peoples could make progress but eventually took center stage, and ultimately the truly personal has been sacrificed to it. The most striking example of this is perhaps the way that contemporary political leaders simply accept massive job losses, knowing they are permanent, knowing the incalculable harm they cause societies and families, as though there were no alternative to it; the mandates of technology become embodied in definitions of efficiency unquestioned by people. Balthasar, along the same lines as Guardini, characterizes power of this kind as simply evil.

> This technocracy, this manipulation of things and of man (who has himself become a thing) can no longer be recognized as a phenomenon originating in power. For it is characteristic of the resultant manipulation that it does not actually apply force, nor does it confront man openly in the form of coercion; he is subject to it without violence and without external conflict. In contrast to all relationships based on power, modern manipulation simply ignores the aspect of free will in man; *thus it pursues a quasi-anonymous annihilation of personal existence that is even more radical than that undertaken by force. This is what makes the modern technocracies . . . much more menacing.*[51]

Surrendering to technological imperative, without a vision of the common good proper to it, politics increasingly operates over the heads of people. Laws and policies are increasingly separate from them. The political system increasingly feels obligated to attend to the technological imperative, expressed by the desires of those who own and control the technology. Those in public office seem to surrender more and more to the reality that money and power drive everything. Pope Francis writes, "One cause of this situation is found in our relationship with money, since we calmly accept its dominion over ourselves and our societies. . . . We have created new idols. The worship of the ancient calf has returned in a new and ruthless guise in the . . . dictatorship of an impersonal [technologically driven] economy, lacking a truly human purpose. . . . The thirst for power and possessions knows no limits."[52]

Politics suffers in this context again in a special way from the sense of uprootedness characteristic of modern culture. As impersonal processes replace the role of people at multiple levels, politics loses what for Bergoglio is its necessary historical continuity. A healthy politics must unify the personal, the objective, and the collective, and it is only in a living and historically rooted sense of politics that such convergence takes place.[53] When it is absent, the field is replaced by ideologies that always lead to irreconcilable differences. This is because the modern ideologies all took parts of the Christian understandings and ran with them but left other constitutive dimensions behind. The best example of this is seen in the modern struggle between individualism and collectivism. If we look at the thinking that informed the Jesuit missions, the dignity of each person coexisted with a strong sense of solidarity. When the Christian influences ceased to be dominant in the public square, this union dissipated. Lacking historical perspective, the modern ideologies of collectivism and individualism emphasized abstract concepts, losing the real lessons of history. Much of modern political thinking came to be a series of divisions between various expressions of individualism versus collectivism, accompanied by competing theories of what government should do and should not do. With contradictory starting points, and a one-sidedness that tended to make each side blind to its own faults, politics could only be the place of conflict and ongoing power struggle, with the sense of the common good ever in decline.

It is for these reasons that modern politics is often characterized by "sterile confrontations," the results of which characteristically leave out many people. One conflict is between an "adolescent progressivism" versus those who seek to bring back an idealized version of the past. Neither truly grasps real history. The first thinks that the past can simply be left behind. This is usually accompanied by a false assumption that there is little to learn from the past. A striking example of this was in celebrations of national independence in contemporary Argentina during the presidency of Cristina Fernández de Kirchner. It is customary for the president to speak on July 9, recalling the heroism and the virtues of Argentina's great founders—such as José de San Martín and Manuel Belgrano. But in recent years the Independence Day speech has made little to no reference to the founding at all. Instead, it has emphasized the president's divisive political agenda, followed by a political event attended only by supporters of the president's party. This is adolescent progressivism at its worst. The focus is only on how one political party has the answers for the future. It inevitably slips into increasing authoritarianism, as all who oppose the vision of progress presented are rightly to be suppressed.[54] In this worldview the past is something to be used only to the extent that examples to highlight today's political agenda can be extracted from it. Moreover, believing oneself and one's party to be the only true voice of progress inevitably demonizes the opposition. The only sense of the common good that remains is the agenda of the self-proclaimed progressivism—or, worse, "profane messianism."[55]

One form of opposition is the political expression of what in chapter 5 was called the search for a cultural refuge. This attitude rightly resists adolescent progressivism but by seeking to use the political system to bring back an idealized past. It is not the past in its fullness but the parts of it one appreciated. This leads to an agenda of resistance but has two major flaws: First, it fails to appreciate the extent to which the past contained many injustices not thought important enough to address. Second, there is often an element of unreality in the thought that the past could truly be brought back anyway. It becomes a politics of resentment and division of a different kind. To give a contemporary example, in the United States, some pine for the days of *Leave It to Beaver* or *The Andy Griffith Show*, easily forgetting that those were also times of institutionalized segregation. This is also a vision that accepts considerable exclusion.

The historical uprootedness of contemporary politics is perhaps best illustrated by the degree to which it leads to terrible results around the world for the extremes of the age spectrum. When people do not care to learn from the past they depreciate the lives of the aged. When they fail to take responsibility for the future all the hard work of begetting and raising children is similarly depreciated. The very old and the very young are an inconvenience to those with no long-term vision of the common good. So it is not surprising that the political system often does little to better the plight of either the very old or the very young. The culture of contraception and abortion around the world in recent decades is one good example: "I am astonished," Bergoglio remarked in an interview, "by the low birth rates here in Italy; this is how we lose our link to the future."[56] So is the consideration of poor children around the globe. Some of Cardinal Bergoglio's most moving and harshest language was reserved to condemn how children were treated. One striking example was his mention that there was a law in Buenos Aires forbidding the use of horses to carry carts, while one frequently sees children pushing carts, looking through dumpsters. Is this not worse, allowing children to push the carts? Moreover, there existed rings of pedophiles in the neighborhoods of Chacarita and Floresta in Buenos Aires, where young people between five and fifteen years of age are the targets of sex tourism. Half of the children of Argentina live in poverty. Clearly they face a future of indigence, malnutrition, and problematic personal relations. Bergoglio speaks of tours operating for the express purpose of ogling human disgrace.[57] On the other side of the spectrum the aged are neglected by a society that believes they have no wisdom to offer. Pope Francis has long spoken of the "hidden euthanasia of the elderly, who are abandoned instead of being considered a memory, a link to our own past and a source of wisdom for our present."[58]

Nominalism, secularism, and relativism round out the severe political challenges of our time. Nominalism in politics is part and parcel of the loss of epistemological unity and coherence discussed in the previous chapter. In politics today words have a great deal of mobility, related to the autonomy of signs, creating a world of illusions. Ideas and words come to predominate over reality, contradicting one of Bergoglio's longstanding convictions—namely, that reality is more important than ideas. Consider, for example, what has become of the language of rights since the 1500s. Initially conceived as an area of rightful autonomy linked to an increase in both personal and common good, language today increasingly becomes inseparable from the pursuit of particular interests lacking any real connection with the common good or even morality. Consider the full meaning of what the following terms mean in the concrete for their most devoted advocates: *Reproductive rights* means over fifty million abortions in the United States and the right to have a late-term abortion when there is no threat to health in the sense in which the term has been traditionally conceived. Abortion and contraception access are regularly called *health care*, despite the fact that very few claim even today that they take contraceptives or have abortions to improve their health. To others *gun rights* means the right to have access to any weapon whatsoever without government scrutiny, a right held to be absolute and depending in no way on any kind of result in terms of violent crime or accidental killings. Then there is the famous *collateral damage*, whereby the death of the innocent is equated with the destruction of a building. Bergoglio says that politics is reduced to an exercise in rhetoric in these cases. Politicians use words and language to promote themselves rather than to capture the real "signs of the times."[59]

Secularism is another contemporary political problem, particularly in the developed world. Recall from chapter 2 where we discussed how Bergoglio saw imperial invasion as the desire to destroy the inculturated faith. The faith is a vision of a genuinely common good, in opposition to domination by foreign interests. Just as the Jesuits mission had to be destroyed so the imperial projects from Europe could live, so does contemporary globalization need to privatize religion and increasingly reduce its influence over political life. Secularism can also be seen as a systematic failure to see the past as a source of creativity and values for today. In both *Evangelii gaudium* and *Laudato si'* Pope Francis references the problem in contemporary politics. Secularism, he says, "entail[s] privatizing religions in an attempt to reduce them to the quiet obscurity of the individual's conscience or to relegate them to the enclosed precincts of churches, synagogues, or mosques. This would represent, in effect, a new form of authoritarianism" (*EG*, 255). And he contends that the political world can benefit from "the wisdom of the biblical accounts" when considering the environment (*LS*, 65–75), that political solutions can be found by "religions in dialogue with science" (*LS*, 199–201), and even that the Trinity provides a model for relationships among all creatures (*LS*, 238–40). Above and beyond specific references to the *Laudato si'*, much of the document is an expression of how the Christian tradition provides wisdom for a true politics oriented to the global common good.

Finally, we come to the problem of moral relativism and politics. Pope Francis's predecessor made this theme characteristic of his papacy, popularly remembered in an expression used in a homily just prior to the papal conclave that elected Benedict XVI, where he spoke of the "dictatorship of relativism." Although not always identified as such, it is a very significant theme for Bergoglio. As we have seen, relativism in contemporary politics is not, in his account, complete. Relativism is the attitude to be taken toward the traditional Christian morality as a justification for ridding the public square of it. One often hears that, for example, in the context of Christian complaints about the influence of secularism with respect to sexuality and family life that Christians must not "impose their views." Rather they should limit themselves to the solutions provided by secularists, highlighted by a sex education that emphasizes biology and technique, careful to exclude moral judgments. On the other hand, as we have seen, Bergoglio sees in the hegemony of globalization the enshrining of a technocratic paradigm that is anything but relative. It leads to the imposition of very definite policies from which there can be no opposition. This adds a kind of multiplied force to the concerns raised by Pope John Paul II who feared modern democracy's unknowing slip into a new kind of totalitarianism. It is not seen because secular relativism is only sensitive to one kind of political imposition: that which emanates from traditional religious influences. Bergoglio understands that the relativistic mentality, in the context of globalization and technocracy, actually tends to totalitarianism. Again we have a hegemony conceived from the metropolitan centers threatening the integrity, autonomy, and even existence of what is rightful to people: a dignity derived from their own history and culture. Hence his views allow us to see the truth of what John Paul II said concerning ethical relativism today with a multiplied force: "Today, when many countries have seen the fall of ideologies [that] bound politics to a totalitarian conception of the world . . . there is no less grave a danger that the fundamental rights of the human person will be denied. . . . This is the risk between an alliance between democracy and ethical relativism, which would remove any sure moral reference point from political and social life. . . . Indeed . . . then ideas and convictions can easily be manipulated for reasons of power . . . [which] easily turns into open or thinly disguised totalitarianism."[60]

In conclusion, we have seen in this chapter that Bergoglio emphasizes particular themes from the body of Catholic social teaching concerning politics—yet always in a way reflecting his characteristic preoccupation for reality over ideas. He joins the established body of Catholic Church teaching in its insistence on the common good as an independent moral norm by which politics must be evaluated. His thinking concerning modern freedom witnesses to concerns shared by his predecessors, particularly how a descent into relativism threatens to transform the discourse on rights into a justification for an advancing authoritarian state while genuine rights are compromised. His most frequently addressed concerns are for the development of an adequate political culture, which he sees as lacking in his native Argentina. Nevertheless, he believes that the nation can still find a renewed stability in its historical roots and learn from the cultural witnesses of men like Manuel Belgrano, "El Cura Brochero," and fictional gaucho Martín Fierro. Nevertheless, the project of creating an adequate political culture faces fundamental challenges in light of the centralizing political trends associated with globalization and the nominalism, secularism, and relativism characteristic of the unidimensional monoculture that comes from the politics of globalism.

NOTES

1. Piqué, *Pope Francis*, 141.
2. Ibid., 152.
3. The best work explaining the Catholic, scholastic roots of the independence movement in Latin America is O. Carlos Stoetzer, *The Scholastic Roots of the Spanish American Revolution* (New York: Fordham University Press, 1979).
4. Bergoglio, *Educar: Exigencia y pasión*, 160.
5. Bergoglio, *La nación por construir*, 41.
6. Jorge Mario Bergoglio, *Nosotros como ciudadanos, nosotros como pueblo: Hacia un bicentenario en justicia y solidaridad, 2010–2016* (Buenos Aires: Editorial Claretiana, 2011), 77.
7. Rubín and Ambrogetti, *El jesuita*, 112, 164–65.
8. Francis, *Evangelii gaudium*, 123, 182–83, 203, 217–37; Francis, *Laudato si'*, 156–58.
9. Piqué, *Pope Francis*, 112.
10. Ibid., 114.
11. Ibid., 156.
12. Bergoglio, *Ponerse la patria*, 19–20.
13. The best philosophical discussion of the meaning of the common good in relationship to the pursuit of individual goods is found in Simon, *Philosophy of Democratic Government*, 36–71. The genius of this presentation is in the way it shows that diversity in unity can be preserved without in any way compromising either a robust understanding the common good or the pursuit of a multiplicity of diverse goods.
14. Bergoglio, *Education for Choosing Life*, 108; emphasis original.
15. Bergoglio, *El verdadero poder*, 284; Bergoglio, *La nación por construir*, 49–50; Bergoglio, *Education for Choosing Life*, 104–8.
16. Rubín and Ambrogetti, *El jesuita*, 83.
17. Francis, *Apostolic Journey of His Holiness Pope Francis to Cuba, to the United States of America and Visit to the United Nations Headquarters (19–28 September 2015): Visit to the Joint Session of the United States Congress; Address of the Holy Father; United States Capitol, Washington, D.C., Thursday, 24 September 2015*, The Holy See (Vatican website), September 24, 2015, https://w2.vatican.va/content/francesco/en/speeches/2015/september/documents/papa-francesco_20150924_usa-us-congress.html.
18. Bergoglio, *El verdadero*, 99.
19. Bergoglio, *Educar: Exigencia y pasión*, 147–51.
20. Bergoglio, *Reflexiones en esperanza*, 271.
21. Bergoglio, *Educar, elegir la vida*, 13.

22. Ibid., 147–51. Bergoglio, *Reflexiones en esperanza*, 282.

23. Ibid., 258, 272.

24. Francis, *Evangelii gaudium*, 189. The affirmations of solidarity are often done using other terminology, as in *Laudato si'*, where he speaks of "Civic and Political Love" (part 5, 228–32). Francis, *Laudato si'*, The Holy See (Vatican website), May 24, 2015, http://w2.vatican.va/content/francesco/en/encyclicals/documents/papa-francesco_20150524_enciclica-laudato-si.html.

25. Pontifical Council for Justice and Peace, *Compendium of the Social Doctrine of the Church* (Washington, DC: United States Conference of Catholic Bishops, 2004) (also published by The Holy See [Vatican website], May 26, 2006, http://www.vatican.va/roman_curia/pontifical_councils/justpeace/documents/rc_pc_justpeace_doc_20060526_compendio-dott-soc_en.html).

26. Francis, *Laudato si'*, 231. The internal quotations are from the following: Benedict XVI, *Caritas in veritate*, The Holy See (Vatican website), June 29, 2009, http://w2.vatican.va/content/benedict-xvi/en/encyclicals/documents/hf_ben-xvi_enc_20090629_caritas-in-veritate.html, 2; Paul VI, *Message . . . for the Celebration of the Day of Peace*, The Holy See (Vatican website), January 1, 1977, https://w2.vatican.va/content/paul-vi/en/messages/peace/documents/hf_p-vi_mes_19761208_x-world-day-for-peace.html, 68; and CDS, 582. Bergoglio discusses solidarity in his *Reflexiones en esperanza*, 285–88.

27. Bergoglio, *Ponerse la patria*, 52.

28. Ibid., 50–52.

29. Bergoglio, *Nosotros como ciudadanos*, 31–34; Bergoglio, *La nación por construir*, 19–21.

30. Brochero is scheduled to be canonized in October 2016 by Pope Francis.

31. Rubín and Ambrogetti, *El jesuita*, 167.

32. Bergoglio, *Educar: Exigencia y pasión*, 155–56.

33. Ibid., 153.

34. From José Hernández, *El gaucho Martín Fierro* (Alicante, Sp.: Biblioteca Virtual Miguel de Cervantes, 2000), nos. 16–17. The numbers refer to the poem's standard stanzas. In what follows, unless otherwise indicated, quotations from *El gaucho Martín Fierro* are translated from the text in Bergoglio, *Educar: Exigencia y pasión*. The reader should be aware that *El gaucho Martín Fierro* is part 1 of 2 of the larger work *Martín Fierro*.

35. Hernández, *El gaucho Martín Fierro*, nos. 23, 35.

36. Ibid., quoted in Bergoglio, *Educar: Exigencia y pasión*, 167.

37. Bergoglio, *Educar: Exigencia y pasión*, 171–72.

38. The discussion of the virtues here is from ibid., 175–83.

39. Hernández, *El gaucho Martín Fierro*, quoted in Bergoglio, *Educar: Exigencia y pasión*, 183. Pope Francis used the same quotation in his discourse to

the United Nations on September 24, 2015. See Francis, *Apostolic Journey . . . Address of the Holy Father*.

40. Bergoglio discusses Belgrano in Bergoglio, *Educar: Elegir la vida*, 20–31.

41. Ibid., 31. The quotation is from *PP*, 14.

42. Francis, *Letter of Holy Father Francis to the President of the Bishops' Conference of Argentina on the Occasion of the Beatification of Father José Gabriel Brochero*, The Holy See (Vatican website), September 14, 2013, https://w2.vatican.va/content/francesco/en/letters/2013/documents/papa-francesco_20130914_beatificazione-brochero.html.

43. Infobae, "Francisco: 'Que se multipliquen los sacerdotes que imiten al cura Brochero,'" September 15, 2013, http://www.infobae.com/2013/09/15/1508962-francisco-que-se-multipliquen-los-sacerdotes-que-imiten-al-cura-Brochero.

44. Francis, *Letter . . . to the President of the Bishops' Conference of Argentina*.

45. Infobae, "Francisco: 'Que se multipliquen los sacerdotes.'"

46. Oscar Caiero, "Las palabras de Brochero," *La Gaceta (Sección Literaria)*, January 30, 2000, 1. *La Gaceta* is the largest newspaper in northwest Argentina, with headquarters in Tucumán.

47. Bergoglio, *Reflexiones en esperanza*, 258.

48. Guardini, *Power and Responsibility* (New York: Sheed and Ward, 1957), 14–15.

49. Ibid., 7–8.

50. Discourse on Revelation is found in Bergoglio, *Mente abierta, corazón creyente*, 137–68.

51. Hans Urs Von Balthasar, *Theo-Drama: Theological Dramatic Theory*, vol. 4: *The Action* (San Francisco: Ignatius Press, 1994), 65, 159; emphasis mine.

52. Francis, *Evangelii gaudium*, 55–56.

53. Bergoglio, *Reflexiones en esperanza*, 283–85.

54. The account here is based on my own twenty trips to Argentina, almost all of which have fallen during the annual celebration of Argentina's Independence Day, July 9. In 2014, the president, Cristina Fernández de Kirchner, gave a very brief speech at the formal celebration in Argentina's version of Independence Hall, the Casa Historica in San Miguel de Tucumán. Afterward, there was a separate event, completely partisan, at the enclosed horseracing track (*hipódromo*), where the president gave a highly partisan speech. A good portion of the talk was devoted to attacking political rivals. The Kirchner presidency has in recent years increasingly sought legal restrictions on the press and has tried to corral the nation's judiciary.

55. Bergoglio, *Reflexiones en esperanza*, 267–68.

56. Andrea Tornielli and Giacomo Galeazzi, *This Economy Kills: Pope Francis on Capitalism and Social Justice*, trans. Demetrio S. Yocum (Collegeville, MN: Liturgical Press, 2015), 148.

57. Bonard, *Nuestra fe es revolucionaria*, 145–47.

58. Tornielli and Galeazzi, *This Economy Kills*, 148.

59. Bergoglio, *Reflexiones en esperanza*, 273–74. The examples are mine, given that the discourse on nominalism provided no examples.

60. John Paul II, *Veritatis splendor*, The Holy See (Vatican website), August 6, 1993, http://w2.vatican.va/content/john-paul-ii/en/encyclicals/documents/hf_jp-ii_enc_06081993_veritatis-splendor.html, 101. Bergoglio cites this same passage in *La nación por construir*, 23.

7

ECONOMICS
Globalization, Poverty, and Work

Pope Francis's teachings related to economics have attracted more public attention than the issues discussed in previous chapters. Complaints have come from pundits and some scholars in the United States. The critics make the broad claim that the Pope either does not understand or does not appreciate the free-market system, which his critics tout as having raised millions out of poverty. This ties into a second set of criticisms—accusations that the Pope is a Marxist, communist, socialist, or at least centralizing statist. In the minds of some, the conclusion is foregone because of his history as an Argentine, even more specifically a Peronist. This fact supposedly supports the charge that the Pope only understands a capitalism corrupted by a centralizing state.[1] Some of the criticism can only be readily dismissed by anyone actually familiar with the Pope's thought. Bergoglio emerged from the same historical-cultural background that Peronism did, but this is a very long way from meaning that the Pope sees the political economy of former Argentine president Juan Domingo Perón as a model for today. In fact the record does not even support Bergoglio's having offered unequivocal support for Peronism even during that president's lifetime. The claims that Bergoglio is a Marxist or communist are too absurd to merit serious treatment. Even the claim that he is essentially a centralized statist concerning economic matters should be held in strong suspicion by anyone familiar with his writings on political matters. The evils of a centralized state under rationalist assumptions is in fact the Pope's longest-standing fear. It is safe to say that the Pope's critics have broader problems with the Catholic Church's social teaching; they resist the Church's perennial demand that economics answer to moral criteria independent of the market. Indeed the Pope himself seems to see these criticisms as repetition of old canards coming from those who do not wish to consider the moral dimension of economic life. Far from advocating Marxism, the Pope says he is simply trying to reiterate the desire that "any father or mother would want to have for their children: an aspiration that should be within the reach of all but which we sadly see is increasingly unavailable to the majority: land, housing, work. It is strange, but if I talk about this, there are those who think the Pope is a communist."[2]

What is of interest is to clarify the Pope's actual thinking on these matters. He has spoken about economic matters as he has deemed necessary as a pastor. Economics is an important component of the life of the people, and pastors cannot be indifferent to it. Bergoglio does not write as an economist. On economic matters the Pope has made it very clear that his teaching in this area is intended to be seen as part and parcel of the Catholic Church's established teachings. Among the less-discussed passages from *Evangelii gaudium* is Francis's clarification that "this Exhortation is not a social document, and for reflection on those different themes . . . [that is,] . . . the many grave social questions affecting today's world . . . we have a most suitable tool in the *Compendium of the Social Doctrine of the Church*, whose study and use I heartily recommend" (*EG*, 184). I do not cite this passage to indicate an unwillingness to use *Evangelii gaudium* as a source for the Pope's social thinking. I do cite it to justify citing the Church's actual social teaching on economic matters as part of the exposition of the Pope's thinking. The summary of that teaching here is not intended to be systematic but, rather, to place in context what the Pope has had to say about economic matters, centering on the themes of property, inequality, the fundamental role of the state, and the impacts of globalization. In the following we first summarize the relevant features of this teaching for the consideration of the Pope's views. Having done so, we then consider his thinking in the important areas he has addressed: (1) globalization, including international finance, (2) poverty and social debt, and (3) work.

I. BACKGROUND: CHURCH SOCIAL TEACHING ON ECONOMICS

The Catholic Church's teaching on economic matters in the modern period goes back to Pope Leo XIII's landmark encyclical, *Rerum novarum* (1891). Written in the context of the Industrial Revolution, prior to most of what would become an extensive set of regulatory legislation in most of the developed world, the Catholic Church formulated a view of economic life rooted in its belief that economic activity should reflect and serve both the transcendent dignity of the human person and the common good considered comprehensively—that is, including the economic order. Moreover, the state had the obligation to preserve and promote the common good. This was to be done in a way to distance the Church from two extremes: (1) socialism, understood to mean the absence of fundamental property rights, and (2) laissez-faire liberalism, which would simply turn economic activity over to the free market, accepting the results of economic competition in the name of preserving individual liberty.

Key to the Catholic Church's position and the heart of its arguments against both extremes has always been its understanding of property rights. First, the Church would essentially affirm the right to own property against Marxism, contending that property ownership is good for people, that natural law affirms the right of a family to own property and engage in economic activity as a way of procuring its needs. The state absolutely has no right to take away these rights. Moreover, the Church contended that it is precisely the poor who suffer the most if the little they have is taken from them. This commitment undergirds the Church's confirmation of the principle of subsidiarity in economic matters. The state has no right to interfere in the capacity of the family to earn a living and reasonably provide for its future. It would be appropriate to say that the Catholic Church strongly reaffirmed the right to private property, focusing on the needs and rights of the family and the communities in which they live. This is accompanied by the argument that socialized property is less attended to and cared for than is private property because people take less responsibility for things that are not theirs; on the other hand, people work harder and care more for goods that are or will become their own property.[3]

Surrounding the right to private property is a moral obligation and social principle that distinguishes Catholic teaching from classical liberal thought. These interrelated norms are (1) the social nature of property and (2) the universal destination of goods. The latter is based on the theological notion that God created the world and all of its natural goods for the good of all, and, therefore, the earth and all its fruits by the strictest demand of justice must be for all people.[4] This provides the moral basis for the second principle—that is, the social function of property, which begins by recalling that Christianity never supported an unlimited right to private property. Private-property rights are subject to the higher principle of common use, derived from the universal destination of goods. This principle does not oppose private property, but it does regulate it. As Pope Paul VI pointed out in *Populorum progressio*, private property is essentially an instrument to realize the principle of the universal destination of goods; it is a means to something higher, not an end in itself. Beyond this, the Catholic Church's social teaching mandates recognition of the social function of property ownership. The universal destination of goods imposes serious obligations on owners and the state. Owners are not free to use their resources without considering the social repercussions of any particular kind of use. They must consider the common good. Therefore, in extreme cases, the state may properly intervene to address inappropriate exercises of property rights. In extreme cases this may include expropriation of private property (*PP*, 22–24).

In the attempt to implement the universal destination of goods, the role of the state is critical. Again, Church teaching does not come down in a way that would satisfy the laissez-faire liberal or the statist. We have already covered the principle of subsidiarity in our discussion of politics. It has considerable force when it comes to economic issues. The Catholic Church clearly prefers—from its belief in the dignity of the person and in love as the greatest of the virtues—that the just distribution of goods be realized through the will of the actual decision makers and not primarily through the interventions of the state. Nonetheless, as we have noted, subsidiarity is not simply an ideological argument against state intervention. If the private sphere cannot arrive at a just solution, state intervention may be necessary. It will always be in the realm of prudent judgment to determine whether or not or to what the degree the state should be involved. For example, is it desirable to have the state involved in the provision of health care? One can see immediately that it is not a simple question. Some emphasize the fact that the purely private system has left many out, while others claim that state intervention lowers the quality of care and drives up the costs of government. Even Catholics in good faith become divided once the discussion comes to the details of state involvement.

The Catholic doctrine of the state concerning economic matters goes back to its fundamental view of the state as the principal agent for attaining the common good. As Paul VI clearly indicated in *Populorum progressio*, state interventions may well be necessary (*PP*, 24). In doing so the state must avoid, as John Paul II warned in *Centesimus annus*, "an inordinate increase in public agencies, which are dominated more by bureaucratic ways of thinking than by concern for serving their clients, and which are accompanied by an enormous increase in spending" (*CA*, 48). People have a right to use their talents as they wish to earn a living, provide for their families, and contribute to the common good through their efforts. Although much of the discussion of these matters focuses on questions of intervention, this is not the state's primary task in economic matters. Rather, the state's primary function is to "determine an appropriate juridical framework for regulating economic affairs . . . which presumes a certain equality between the parties, such that one party would not be so powerful as to practically reduce the other to subservience" (*CA*, 15). It is often forgotten that if the state could achieve this primary juridical function the number of issues related to intervention might significantly be reduced. The state should work in conjunction with the market, seeking always a prudent balance between allowance for economic initiative on the part of citizens and state regulation. In order for the free market to achieve its purpose of attaining the universal destination of goods, the state has a necessary role to play in determining the meaning and direction of a nation's economic development (*CA*, 48). There is fodder here for both liberals and conservatives in the United States, but an honest reading of the Catholic Church's social doctrine demonstrates its ideological independence.

The Church's social teaching has a particular concern about inequality, particularly when millions of people are living in poverty. This concern goes to the very core of the Gospel. Jesus's preaching from the beginning was an announcement of "good tidings for the poor" and was meant "to set at liberty those who are oppressed" (Luke 4:18–19). The Church's love for the poor is rooted in the Gospels and beatitudes and includes material as well as cultural poverty. The principle of the universal destination of goods directly implies concern for those who lack the goods they need to live. Hence the Catholic Church teaches that public policies must give primacy to these people, a principle it has long called the preferential option for the poor. Poverty is no expression of God's will but an injustice to be remedied. The fight against poverty can never simply be an impersonal act of legal justice. Its end is that the poor should be recognized in all their dignity and take their places as full and contributing members of society. The principle of solidarity, central to the Church's social doctrine, demands this goal of full social inclusion.

All of this discussion concerning the universal destination of goods, the social role of property, and the role of the state bears directly on the problem of poverty, placing it front and center in the consideration of public policies as well as in the consciences of those who are in a position to help. Considering contemporary obstacles to overcoming poverty—which is becoming ever more significant—the *Compendium of the Social Doctrine of the Church* observes that the "use of new technologies and knowledge . . . have a *universal destination*; they too must be placed in a context of legal norms and social rules according to the criteria of justice, equity, and respect for human rights. . . . The new discoveries and technologies . . . risk becoming sources of unemployment and increasing the gap between the developed and underdeveloped areas . . . if they remain in the wealthier countries or in the hands of a small number of powerful groups" (*CSD*, 283; emphasis mine). In other words, when we consider the ongoing technological transformation of society, we are bound to consider in each case the economic and social impacts on people. Technological change, as with all economic activity, must answer to the common good and the ethical principles upon which the Catholic Church's social teaching has always insisted.

Catholic social teaching has some relevant observations concerning globalization and international finance relevant to understanding the Pope's discussion of these themes. The Church acknowledges that globalization opens the door to new sources of solidarity and cooperation. Yet, economic globalization needs to be guided by the broader principles of social teaching, particularly the universal destination of goods, the preferential option for the poor, and the recognition of a global common good. Near the top of the list of concerns is recognition of the right of development or "the fundamental right of peoples to subsistence and progress." This is especially relevant in the light of the massive debt of many developing nations. Church teaching speaks of "the urgency of rethinking the economy" in a context where "present economic, social, and cultural structures are ill-equipped to meet the demands of genuine development." A fundamental problem is the "loss of effectiveness of nation-states in directing the dynamics of national economic financial systems. . . . Because of the new bonds of interdependence among global operators, the traditional defensive measures of States appear to be destined to failure and . . . the very notion of a national market recedes into the background." This calls for "a greater commitment on the part of the international community to exercise a strong guiding role." While the list of rights expands in the developed world, in the poor nations the "right to food and drinkable water, to housing and security, to self-determination and independence . . . are still far from being guaranteed and realized." The Church does not see evidence that these problems are on the way to being solved by the commercial and financial relations associated with economic globalization. Rather there are "indications aplenty that point to a trend of increasing inequalities, both between advanced countries and developing countries and within industrialized countries" (*CSD*, 450, 564, 370, 365, 362).

The Church expresses some particular concerns with reference to the financial sector. In an era where the international transfer of money is extremely rapid, "financial transactions far surpass that of real transactions" involving the transfer of actual goods and services. Hence there is a risk that these markets develop "according to a mentality that has only itself as a point of reference, without being connected to the real foundations of the economy" (*CSD*, 368). Speculative economic activity, whereby financial instruments are bought and sold with a view to gain without the production of any real goods or services in between, abounds in the world economy. The Church's social teaching calls for regulation and stability of financial markets. Catholic social doctrine has proven prophetic in this area with the global financial meltdown of 2008, which was fueled by speculative economic activity related to real estate. Looking at the financial world of today recalls Pius XI's 1913 discussion in *Quadragesimo anno*. "The virtual degradation of the majesty of the state" is evident to all, he wrote almost a hundred years ago, "which, although it ought to sit on high like a . . . supreme arbitress, free from all partiality, and intent upon the one common good and justice, is become a slave, surrendered and delivered to the passions and greed of men. . . . The dictatorship is being most forcibly exercised by those who, since they hold the money and completely control it, control credit also and rule the lending of money." And in international relations there is "a no less deadly and accursed international imperialism of money whose country is where profit is."[5]

II. POPE FRANCIS ON GLOBALIZATION

In considering Pope Francis's particular insights, we begin by recalling Romano Guardini, discussed in chapters 4 and 5. Modern man, for Guardini, becomes technological man, and this will increasingly have a determining force on humanity's self-understanding and social order, particularly in the economic order. Technological man sees nature as a given but not in the sense of the classical, medieval, or early modern periods, wherein nature imposed limitations and constraints. There is no teleology in nature for technological man. Nature is rather the prime matter out of which anything can be made.[6] The motive of technology is power pure and simple. One of Guardini's deepest concerns is what happens to personal freedom in the context of the technocratic mentality. Even as far back as the 1950s he noted that people felt compelled to have the latest commodities produced by modern technology.[7] Additionally, technological power becomes inherently more centralized and concentrated, fueling the economic competitiveness that inevitably generates more losers than winners over time. Moreover, the imperatives of technological development and the market determine the kinds and amount of work available. It is common today to consider job loss in the private and even public sectors as inevitable or the only reasonable alternative. Thus opponents are quickly written off as left- or right-wing extremists who lack the requisite rationality to understand the world they live in. At the same time what is functionally considered to be "good" policy must make a profit or balance the books. Even in democratic societies impersonal economic factors come to prevail over any meaningful human sense of what the common good is.

Related to Guardini's insights, in the political world of today "experts" have come to replace statesmen. In the developing world, despite the enormity of unmet human needs, economic policy decisions have in recent decades come to be more and more determined by a few hundred bankers and economists living in the developed world, via the mechanisms imposed by institutions such as the International Monetary Fund and the World Bank. It is worth noting here that policy advice is no longer limited to obviously economic issues such as trade and budget policies; witness the United Nations's stunning critique of the Catholic Church's sexual ethics. The UN saw in traditional morality opposition to its preferred model of development, wherein, as has been said, the birth of a calf is viewed as a potential source of profit and the birth of a human being as surplus stock or a debit.

It is precisely through modern developments in the economic order that the developments discussed by Guardini have been most palpable. In the premodern era economic activity was bound by independent, moral criteria that often restricted individual decision making. The moral condemnation of usury is perhaps the most well known of these, but moral guidance was far more extensive than this alone. There were very serious discussions concerning justice in exchanges, most notably in the theories concerning the just wage and the just price. Additionally, in a theme that went back to Aristotle, moneymaking in itself was morally suspect. Moral restrictions concerning the accumulation of wealth were ultimately of two kinds: First and foremost were moral restraints on the very idea of moneymaking as an end in itself. Second were moral restrictions concerning the methods of making money through various kinds of exchanges. In a real sense the development of modern capitalism can be seen as an ongoing process of removing moral constraints on the economic behavior of individuals.[8] Contemporary economic civilization increasingly permits market considerations alone, in the absence of any moral criteria, to determine economic outcomes. Market rationality has proceeded to penetrate the entire society, considerably redefining the role of the state and, increasingly, all social institutions. Whereas the state formerly regulated the economy precisely to ensure that economic results conformed to moral criteria—most notably the common good—today increasingly the state refrains from interventions so motivated. The move toward deregulation of economic activity in the West witnesses to the phenomenon. The unregulated market is precisely the mechanism by which power becomes more concentrated, unleashing the disturbing trends Guardini so perspicaciously discussed.

Pope Francis's teaching concerning the global economy must be understood in light of this. There is no inherent problem with a system that respects private property, the right of economic initiative, and free markets per se. Nor is he opposed to industrialization. It would be fair to say that he makes two interrelated criticisms: first, there is the problem of reducing the broad conception of value humanly and ethically speaking to mere economic value, which inevitably places the pursuit of profit above all other values; second, and as a result of the first, market values come to prevail over other values in all dimensions of social life.[9] Here Pope Francis trains his characteristic focus on what is real and historical. He is not interested in discussions of "capitalism" or how, hypothetically, "the market economy"—not dominated by multinational enterprises and financial monopolies in a context of a healthy democracy and the flowering of all the classical virtues—potentially solves the world's economic problems. His issue is that the actual functioning of the global economic system is unlike this ideal construct, and his concern is the real lives of the people, particularly in the developing world.[10] Concerning the distortion of values, Francis says with characteristic bluntness,

> It is no longer the person who commands but money, money, cash commands. . . . Men and women are sacrificed to the idols of profit and consumption: it is the "culture of waste." If a computer breaks, it is a tragedy; but poverty end[s] up being considered normal. If there are children . . . who have nothing to eat, that is not news. . . . And yet these things enter into normality: that some homeless people should freeze to death on the street. . . . On the contrary, when the stock market drops ten points in some cities, it constitutes a tragedy.[11]

At the macroeconomic level, the same problem is the source of the neoliberalism that Bergoglio has long condemned. This doctrine holds that economics is a science of cause and effect, patterned to the extent possible after the sciences of nature. Hence the economy must be organized purely by economic criteria, wherein the profit motive is constitutive and determining, elevating efficiency—conceived in material and profit-oriented terms—to the position of controlling criterion. In this perspective, there is no place for any attempt to modify the economy based on values extrinsic to the economy so conceived. Bergoglio, with Catholic social teaching, rejects this approach. As the economy concerns what is good for people, it must be held accountable to independent and properly human ethical norms, the determining value being the universal common good. Seen in this light, the neoliberal economic projects fail on human grounds; the dominating values of efficiency and profit making promote considerable exclusion and intolerable inequality. In the blunt language of *Evangelii gaudium*, "Such an economy kills" (*EG*, 53). The mere fact that Marxist solutions failed should not mean that we should now accept the capitalist system as is. Rather, Francis reminds us that developed Western democracies, most identified with capitalism, are characterized by their own persistent failures to preserve social justice and morality rooted in a sound anthropology.[12] In conclusion, neoliberalism is un-Christian, an antipode to the Gospel; and the Gospel, in conjunction with the Catholic Church's social teaching that flows from it, insists instead on the primacy of self-giving, solidarity, and creating opportunities for all as necessary and dominant criteria.[13]

Concerning economic globalization more specifically, most of Francis's criticism is part and parcel of two larger themes in his social thought we have already explored: (1) it is a manifestation of a one-dimensional technocratic paradigm that relativizes and diminishes the role of important human values in social organization, and (2) it is the predominant contemporary example of a scheme of "metropolitan hegemony," rooted in Enlightenment thinking, which imposes itself on weaker peoples and weaker nations. Let us now look at his writings with respect to these themes in order. First, the technocratic paradigm generates its own sense of imperatives, which ultimately reduce to expanding the power of technology in ways no longer restrained by a broader set of human and moral norms.[14] We must recall that much of the economic and political force behind the technocratic paradigm is tied to economic motivations such as efficiency, itself dependent on imperatives to cut costs and to expand output. As a result the economy becomes increasingly independent, viewed as having its own internal norms driven by market imperatives, themselves inseparable from the drives to accumulate money and hence power. In *Evangelii gaudium*, Francis writes that "the thirst for power and possessions knows no limits. . . . In this [economic] system, which tends to devour everything [that] stands in the way of increased profits, whatever is fragile . . . is defenseless before the interests of a deified market, which becomes the only rule" (*EG*, 56). Recall that in the previous chapter we considered Francis's concern that politics, as the quest for the common good, has ceded space in recent decades to the economy. In other words, the economy comes to be seen as an autonomous system with its own rules that the political system must respect. So if economic theory says that we need to reduce inflation via punishing increases in interest rates that throw an economy into recession, discarding workers and augmenting poverty, then the political system must cooperate. The state's role in defending the common good in economic life increasingly declines. Pope Francis strongly resists the ideas of an economic system that answers to no moral criteria external to it. He writes that "the dignity of each human person and the pursuit of the common good are concerns [that] ought to shape all economic policies" (*EG*, 203). Yet, reflecting how deeply embedded are the interrelated market and technocratic paradigms he mentions that words like *ethics*, *solidarity*, a *God of justice*, and *distribution* are often considered "irksome" by the proponents of the dominant model (*EG*, 203). That is because this vocabulary questions the logic of the system. Pope Francis discourages the tendency simply to place our trust in impersonal mandates, writing that "we can no longer trust in the unseen forces and the invisible hand of the market. Growth in justice requires . . . decisions, programs, mechanisms, and processes specifically geared to a better distribution of income, the creation of sources of employment, and an integral promotion of the poor that goes beyond a simple welfare mentality" (*EG*, 204).

Economic globalization, in its uniform aspects, "is essentially imperialist and instrumentally liberal."[15] As such it can be categorized as a project of "metropolitan hegemony," an "enlightenment project" to undermine and eliminate whatever stands in its way. Hence the criticism of economic globalization is of a piece with the cultural critique already advanced. Globalization is not necessarily the same as liberalism; globalization could conceivably open societies to stimulating contact with other cultures and economies. However, in point of fact, the uniform liberalizing tendencies are there, and it is probably in the economic realm, so close to the driving force of technology, where these tendencies are the strongest. In the Aparecida document, we read that "financial institutions and transnational companies are becoming stronger to the point that local economies are becoming subordinated, especially weakening the local States, which seem ever more powerless to carry out development projects at the service of their populations, especially when it involves long-term investments with no immediate dividends. International extractive industries and agribusiness often do not respect the economic, social cultural, and environmental rights of the local populations and do not assume their responsibilities" (*Aparecida*, 66).

In both *Evangelii gaudium* and *Laudato si'* Pope Francis laments the undermining of local economies and smaller businesses, resulting from competition with the multinational conglomerates. In *Laudato si'* he speaks of the need to preserve sources of employment often lost through global competition while praising the work of "laborers and craftsmen" tied to the local economy (*LS*, 124). There is a need, he contends, to preserve "productive diversity," particularly "small-scale food-production systems" (*LS*, 129). Furthermore he supports "cooperatives" that "are being developed to exploit renewable sources of energy which ensure local self-sufficiency and even the sale of surplus energy." The state should assume the role of preserving local economies, but the neoliberalism accompanying globalization mandates a reduced role for the state. Nonetheless, the Pope has always defended the role of the state on economic matters "to develop more rigorous regulations, procedures, and controls" (*LS*, 179). Moreover, "civil authorities have the right and duty to adopt clear and firm measures in support of small producers and differentiated production. To ensure economic freedom from which all can effectively benefit, restraints occasionally have to be imposed on those possessing greater resources and financial power. To claim economic freedom while real conditions bar many people from actual access to it, and while possibilities for employment continue to shrink, is to practice a doublespeak which brings politics into disrepute" (*LS*, 129).

Within the limits of subsidiarity, the Pope defends a robust role for the state with respect to the material components of the common good, considering the privatization of social promotion and social assistance "antihuman." The key point seems to be that privatization is ultimately incompatible with the state's responsibility to ensure results compatible with the common good in that it leaves the results to some considerable degree to chance.[16]

The Pope considers the financial sector of particular concern in today's global economy. He sees a "new idolatry of money." As is characteristic of his thinking, he sees this as a profoundly human crisis rooted in the loss of the sense of the dignity of the person. In some sense, new idolatry is an old sin. Yet, it has taken on some distinctive forms in our time. He writes, "We have created new idols. The worship of the ancient golden calf (Exodus 32:1–35) has returned in a new and ruthless guise in the idolatry of money and the dictatorship of an impersonal economy lacking a truly human purpose" (*EG*, 48). One of the causes he underlines is the autonomy of the financial sector. Grafted onto the ideology of the autonomy of the market, finance becomes a source of domination and control. Consider the crushing role that places on developing nations (*EG*, 56). And this is no new theme for Francis. When Argentina's economy collapsed in 2001, he spoke about it in the strongest terms:

> Throughout this time, there has been economic financial terrorism proper. And it has had its consequences which are not hard to see: more rich people, more poor people, and a drastically reduced middle class. There have been other less-circumstantial consequences, such as the disaster in the field of education. At this moment in the city of Buenos Aires and in its residential suburbs, there are two million young people who neither study nor work. Given the barbarous form assumed by the financial globalization in Argentina, the church in this country has always taken the indications contained in the magisterium as its points of reference . . . [as in] John Paul II's allocution *Ecclesia in America*.[17]

Francis specifically references *Quadragesimo anno*, reminding us that Pope Pius XI wrote during a similar crisis, the onset of the Great Depression, characterizing "the speculative economic model with the power to impoverish millions of families from one minute to the next as 'the international imperialism of money,'" which, he says, is "a definition that never loses its pertinence" and "has a biblical root."[18] He continues:

When Moses went up to the mountain to receive God's law, the people became guilty of idolatry in fabricating the golden calf. Today's imperialism of money also has an unequivocally idolatrous face. It is curious how idolatry always goes hand in glove with gold..... So the new imperialism of money even takes work away, which is the one expression of the dignity of man, of his creativity, the image of God's own creativity. The speculative economy does not even have any further need of labor. It bows down to the idol of cash, which is self-generating. This is why there is no remorse in turning millions of workers out of their jobs.[19]

With respect to Argentina's economic collapse, Francis also has negative words for the global community and financial organizations like the International Monetary Fund, of which he says, "I don't think man is central to their thinking, despite all the fine things they say. They always recommend governments to adopt their rigid directives, always talk about ethics and transparency, but they seem to be . . . devoid of goodness."[20]

As many people outside the financial sector may not have a very good understanding of "the speculative economy," I would like here to spend some time explaining what the Pope means when he shares his concerns about it. I recall the work of great Thomist philosopher Yves R. Simon, who wrote with perspicacity on the subject. He used the unfamiliar term *one-way exchanges*, noting with concern that they were common in the market economy.[21] One can only imagine what he would have thought of the degree to which his observations in 1950 apply today! One-way exchanges occur whenever someone buys something at one price and then sells it a higher price though no value has been added in the meantime. When such exchanges proliferate, they create a moral problem in the economic realm. The link among investment, production, and profit is disturbed when speculators "invest" in ways that merely siphon off society's wealth to enrich themselves while providing no service. Moreover, speculation can contribute to a breakdown of the economic order. Some people make money producing nothing and provide no genuine human service, while others labor for very little. As Nobel laureate Paul Krugman puts it, "Certainly these days many vast fortunes come not from building something but from consistently guessing what other investors are going to do in a few days, or sometimes a second or two, ahead of the pack."[22]

Speculative economic activity has grown exponentially in our time, and "speculative finance has in our time become a kind of secondary economy of its own," as I have previously explained. "The sheer magnitude is staggering. As Foster and Magdoff put it, 'stock markets and currency trading have become little more than giant casinos where the number and value of transactions have increased far out of proportion to the underlying economy.'"[23] In fact, world currency markets trade up to $4 trillion a day, which "means that more money circulates in the financial markets in five days than in an entire year in the real economy."[24] As I have previously observed:

> This means that ninety percent or more of this market has nothing to do with the underlying economy of buying and selling goods. It approximates pure speculation. Money drifts away from expansion in production to financial speculation, with the generation of more and more types of financial products and speculative gains that only a specialist can keep up with. One can bet on the future value of almost anything. Although many people are familiar with futures markets, wherein one speculates on the future value of a commodity, few are aware that today ninety percent of this activity is in the financial sector of the economy, betting on the prices of currencies, municipal bonds, treasury bonds, stocks, interest rates, and various indices. In 2003 the [US] Department of Defense created one in conjunction with a private company betting on the likelihood of assassinations and terrorist attacks. In 2007 a hedge fund, Amaranth Advisors, lost six billion dollars in one week betting incorrectly on natural gas prices. It is precisely the search for the "one-way exchange," the motivation to earn profit merely by a hoped-for change in the price, that was behind the speculative mania that took hold of the US housing market.[25]

"Speculative mania," write Foster and Magdoff:

> is characterized by a rapid increase in the quantity of debt and equally rapid decrease in its quality. Heavy borrowing is used to buy up financial assets, not based on the income streams they will generate, but merely on the assumption of increasing prices for these assets. This is what economist Hyman Minsky famously called "Ponzi finance" or hyperspeculation. CDOs, with their exposure to subprime mortgages or financial "toxic waste," increasingly took this classic

form. Not just mortgage lenders and subprime borrowers were caught up in the frenzy. A growing crowd of real estate speculators got into the business of buying houses in order to sell them at higher prices.[26]

Of course the entire house of cards collapsed because so many of the financial instruments being bought and sold all over the world were backed up by failed mortgages. We ended up with a situation frightening and farcical. The chairman of the US Federal Reserve had to go to Congress in 2008 to inform them that the banking system was on the verge of collapse due to the fact that billions of dollars of "assets" held by these banks, as they were ultimately backed by failed mortgages, were worthless. The proposed solution reminds us of how Third World debt was and is resolved: The people will have to pay billions of dollars for debts they did not accrue. Literally, the people of the United States were "asked" to take their hard-earned money and purchase useless pieces of paper so that the financial system would not collapse completely. All of this is what lies behind the Pope's concerns about the impacts of financial markets in the world today.

III. POVERTY AND SOCIAL DEBT

Pope Francis has placed the need to include the poor in society front and center in his pastoral outreach. His approach is very Christocentric and consistent with the Catholic Church's social doctrine. He writes, "Our faith in Christ, who became poor, and was always close to the poor, is the basis of our concern for the integral development of society's most neglected members" (*EG*, 186). He wishes to underline that the commitment here is fundamentally theological. Christ Himself "became poor" (2 Corinthians 8:9). Poverty is an integral part of the entire biblical account of redemption. Jesus's mother, central to the entire drama of salvation, was poor, his father a laboring man. Gospel accounts reveal how Jesus chose to live in the midst of worldly poverty, having been born in a manger, where the first to greet Him were poor men of the fields. At His presentation in the temple, His mother and father offered two turtledoves, the traditional sacrificial gift to God made by those who could not afford a lamb. From the outset of His public life, Jesus claimed that His mission was "to preach good news to the poor"

(Luke 2:24). Perhaps the most powerful of all Christological references on this point is in Matthew 25, the account of the Final Judgment, wherein Jesus clearly states that He Himself is the recipient when we choose to feed the hungry, clothe the naked, and visit the prisoner (*EG*, 197). This is the basis for the principle of the Catholic Church's social doctrine that Pope Francis strongly reaffirms, the preferential option for the poor, which is "a special form of primacy of Christian charity, to which the whole tradition of the Church bears witness" (*EG*, 198). It is fair to say that Francis's commitment to and belief in "el pueblo fiel," formed decades ago in Buenos Aires, is echoed when he says, "This is why I want a Church that is poor and for the poor" (*EG*, 198). He insists that the demands to love the poor through acts of justice and mercy are so clear "that no ecclesial interpretation has the right to relativize it." Concern to implement this divine, biblical mandate in this area is a mandate to action as binding as any commitment to doctrine (*EG*, 194). In Buenos Aires he was fond of repeating the story of the deacon Saint Lawrence who lived in Rome in the third century: the Roman emperor Valerian demanded that within a short period of time Lawrence bring him all the treasures of the Church. In a few days, Lawrence returned with a group of poor people, saying, "These are the treasures of the Church." There is much more here than a demand for charity. The full Christocentric interpretation of the poor and poverty demands nothing less than the full incorporation of the poor into society.[27]

The last theme to be discussed here is social debt. In his opening talk at the Social Debts of Our Time, a seminar held in Buenos Aires in 2009, then-Cardinal Bergoglio addressed the theme.[28] The concept for his talk derived from a statement made by the Argentine bishops in 2008, who said that the social debt is the nation's greatest debt, not the *external debt* owed foreign lenders. In the process of international lending, however, many injustices occurred. First of all, much of that debt had been privately accumulated, and there is nothing just in asking all Argentines or citizens of any nation to assume debts they did not choose to accumulate and from which they derived little to no benefit. In the midst of paying off the foreign debt, a broader debt to the poor accumulated, and this is the root of this notion of *social* debt. It is not simply a financial concept but a broader moral one, an "existential debt crisis" that goes to the very meaning of life, which includes a sense of belonging in society. Serious damage has been done to so many in this regard.

The poor grow in number, and the middle class collapses. The immorality comes from the fact that the economic exclusion from society's benefits is ultimately the result of human choices that were made when other choices could have been made. The poor remain victims of social policy. It is an anthropological issue because social debt ultimately has to do with what is due to the human person precisely as a human. The Catholic Church has long recognized the rights of the poor to life, work, and inclusion in society's benefits. There needs to be a major reorientation of social policy toward the common good, which necessitates inclusion. Francis makes specific reference here to the issue of the massive export of capital, which besets many developing nations. He recalls that Paul VI addresses the issue in *Populorum progressio*, where he invites consideration of the enormous damage done when capital is exported purely for personal financial gain. He also recalls the treatment of the theme in *Caritas in veritate*, where Benedict XVI appeals to the broader context in which wealth is produced: the "requirements of justice" include "due consideration for the way in which the capital was generated and the harm to individuals that will result if it is not used where it is produced."[29] In other words, since wealth is a social creation, there is something wrong if the profit is simply exported with no consideration for the people who helped produce it and the broader contributions of the home nation that assisted the production of the wealth in the first place, such as infrastructure, legal protections, and benefits produced for business by taxpayers. Francis made reference to the fact that in the midst of so much poverty Argentines held 150 billion dollars abroad, with an additional two billion leaving the country monthly.[30]

IV. POPE FRANCIS ON WORK

Pope Francis frames his discussion of work in the broader context of Catholic social teaching in a way that unites it with his own fundamental perspective.[31] The Church's social teaching is tethered to the Gospel itself. It is a necessary implication of the very logic of the Incarnation; it is part of what it means to inculturate the Gospel. That is so because Catholic social teaching puts flesh on the fundamental Christian commitments of solidarity and seeking communion with others in accord with our nature as human beings. To fail to proclaim and, more importantly, live out what is contained in this teaching is to alter the Christian message into a spiritualty that either is hidden from the world or fatally succumbs to the individualism of the culture surrounding us.

His treatment links work to three fundamental spiritual principles: First, it is related to communion; work is an expression of the social dimension of the person, who lives in solidarity with others. Second, when people work, they do so in a context of a mutual recognition of one another and their work as gifts. Third, the world of work must be a place where, to use one of Bergoglio's fundamental themes, we renounce the tendency to want to occupy space; we must give space to others to be themselves and exercise their gifts, again in a spirit of mutual support as the Gospel mandates. Attitudes of competitiveness and distrust destroy the nature of work.

Work is the key to the entire social question for a number of reasons, particularly today. Work goes back to divine mandates that themselves go back to the very origins of the human person discussed in Genesis. Humans are called to subdue the earth, but not merely in the sense of exercising power for its own sake. Rather, work is an expression of our fundamental freedom and existence as creatures of reason. We exercise self-determination, but in a manner that cooperates with God's work of creation, not against it. In our free decision to collaborate, we participate in creation to make life better and more fully human. It is essential to preserve the biblical vision of work as a free decision to cooperate, in solidarity with other free people, with God's work of creation, for the betterment of one's self, family, and the society in which one lives. We must remember that Jesus Himself "comes into our history . . . with the presence of Saint Joseph, the legal father who cares for him and also teaches him his work. Jesus . . . [learned] the craft of carpenter from Saint Joseph in his workshop in Nazareth, sharing with him the commitment, effort, satisfaction, and also the difficulties of every day."[32] This is the basis for a veritable "Gospel of Work," opening up the doors to the richest understandings of the dignity of work and worker.[33]

This vision is seriously threatened today by the technocratic paradigm previously described in the discussions of culture and Romano Guardini's writings. One of the most pernicious impacts of this technocratic mode of thinking is what it does to the world of work. First, human beings are reduced to a "factor of production," similar to other factors. In the second phase of this line of reasoning, human beings are treated like objects—used and discarded. When either the profit motive or the technological imperative or both together dictate that human beings are to be deprived of their work, this is billed as an "inevitability," part of the price for "progress" so conceived. The fundamental truth that human beings are discarded against their will by some other human beings' act of will is obscured and vociferously denied by proponents of the system. The exercise of power hides behind a veneer of impersonality, the following of a line of rationality that sees workers as objects and instruments. Lost is the understanding so well laid out by John Paul II in *Laborem exercens*, which underlines that neither the worker nor the work itself can ever be reduced in this way. Rather, "the basis for determining the value of human work is not primarily the kind of work being done but the fact that the one doing it is a person. The sources of the dignity of work are to be sought primarily in the subjective dimension, not in the objective one" (*LE*, 6). "In the modern period," moreover:

> the Christian truth about work [has] to oppose the various trends of materialistic and economistic thought. . . . For certain supporters of such ideas, work was understood and treated as a sort of "merchandise" that the worker . . . sells to the employer. . . . [In the context of] the quickening process of the development of a one-sidedly materialistic civilization . . . there is a confusion or even a reversal of the order laid down from the beginning by the words of the book of Genesis: man is treated as an instrument of production, whereas he . . . ought to be treated as the effective subject of work and its true maker and creator. (*LE*, 7)

This framework of understanding is strongly reasserted by Pope Francis in *Laudato si'*, where the vision of *Laborem exercens* is incorporated into a wider framework emphasizing all of creation. Pope Francis develops the significance of the creation narratives to affirm the centrality of the creator, the dignity of the person created by God, and the relationship of the human person with God, others, and creation (*LS*, 65–75). In this context, where "man is the source, the focus, and the aim of all economic and social life . . . work should be the setting for this rich personal growth, where many aspects of life come into play: creativity, planning for the future, developing our talents, living out our values, relating to others, giving glory to God" (*LS*, 127). Echoing the thoughts of John Paul II and Benedict XVI, Francis writes:

> We were created with a vocation to work. The goal should not be that technological progress increasingly replaces human work, for this would be detrimental to humanity. Work is a necessity, part of the meaning of life on this earth, a path to growth, human development and personal fulfillment. . . . Yet the orientation of the economy has favored a kind of technological progress in which laying off workers and replacing them with machines . . . reduce the costs of production. The loss of jobs "also [erodes] the network of relationship of trust, dependability, and respect for rules [that] are indispensable for any form of human coexistence."[34]

The contemporary human person must struggle to remain the true protagonist in the economic ordering of society to maintain freedom.

There are three interrelated concepts that flow from these theological and philosophical underpinnings: (1) work as related to property ownership, (2) the priority of labor over capital, and (3) the dignified wage. In the creation narratives, we see that the created world, though abundant, can only serve the human person through human toil. This is the true origin of the right to property. A human being cannot adequately work to provide for self and family without taking possession of some elements of creation. As John Paul II put it, the human person "takes them over through work and for work" (*LE*, 12). This remains the paradigm no matter how complicated production becomes. At the root of any process by which wealth is created remains the human person in relationship with the resources of nature. Labor is always the primary cause of production, and even the most complicated form of modern technology remains an instrument. Hence there is no basis for a conflict between capital and labor. To isolate instruments of production as a legitimate interest separate and in opposition to labor is the result of fundamental misunderstanding. No technological instrument or any other form of capital can "be possessed against labor[;] they cannot even be possessed for possession's sake, because the only legitimate title to their possession . . . is that they should serve labor and thus by serving labor that they should make possible the achievement of the first principle of this order—namely, the universal destination of goods and the right to common use of them" (*LE*, 14). Finally, people cannot realistically ever use work to acquire property and dignity unless they receive a dignified wage for their labor. This includes every worker, by which Francis means to include those who are currently forced to work informally. These, too, have a right to "fair remuneration, social security, and a pension." He wishes to join his voice with the Catholic Church's traditional demand for a just and dignified wage for all workers, even the "*cartoneros* [who collect and sell cardboard], those who live by recycling waste, street vendors, garment makers, craftspeople, fishermen, farmers . . . workers in companies in receivership, cooperatives, and common trades that are excluded from employment rights, who are denied the possibility of forming trade unions, who do not have an adequate or stable income."[35]

To conclude on Pope Francis's reflections on economics, it is abundantly clear that in his discussion of the universal destination of goods, subsidiarity, the role of the state, globalization, poverty, the common good, and economic liberalism generally he follows the lines of Catholic social teaching. In a time when considerable efforts have been made by some Catholic thinkers in the United States to reconcile Catholic social teaching with modern capitalism, it is important to go back and remind ourselves that Church teaching has always explicitly condemned economic liberalism not only in its absolute form but also at any point where the pursuit of wealth and profit is at odds with the common good.[36] Nor does Church teaching allow for the subtle way some thinkers attempt to reduce the robust Catholic notion of the common good to the results of the market system. I have gone over this ground elsewhere.[37] Nor does the fact that capitalism in one form or other contributed to lifting millions out of poverty in different times or places in any way allow for the Church's teaching to be restated along the lines of liberal capitalism. The Church's social teaching does not and must not cherry-pick examples to buttress ideologies. Pope Francis has in no way attempted to engage in discussions of economic theories. He is simply saying, as the Catholic Church has always said, that free-market principles are not enough—and for a simple reason. When we attempt to argue—as is argued so often today—that the free market should be acceded to because it is the best system, we cannot distinguish our argument from a claim, never explicitly stated, that the poor should be left to chance. Yves R. Simon made this point decades ago, and the argument has lost none of its force. We either take responsibility for the poor, or we do not. The free market as a point of historical fact does not guarantee that the prospects of the poor improve. But free-market principles *have* contributed to both the Great Depression and the recent financial meltdown of 2008. This is not to engage in any kind of propaganda against the free market but merely to say that it must be evaluated always by moral criteria external to it and that it needs to be regulated by public authority in ways that respect both solidarity and subsidiarity.

Pope Francis himself has said as much. In one interview he reiterates that he wrote nothing in *Evangelii gaudium* not already found in Church social doctrine. He remarks that he made only one statement directly evaluating economic theory: that trickle-down economic theory is not valid. This theory itself is not distinguishable from the economic liberalism the Catholic Church has always rejected, which we can take to mean that Francis rejects the notion that economic growth resulting from the free market always benefits the poor. He never denies that economic freedom has in many cases lifted up the poor; he merely denies that this is always the case to the point where the Catholic Church should simply endorse such theories and find in them all that needs to be said about the universal destination of goods, solidarity, and the role of the state. Concerning those who called him a Marxist because he referred to an economy that "kills," Pope Francis suggests that "perhaps whoever has made this comment does not know the social doctrine of the Church and, apparently, does not even know Marxism very well either."[38] Anyone who thinks the Pope's language is too strong might wish to reread Pius XI's discussion of the economic liberalism of his day, which he characterized as a "despotic economic dictatorship . . . in the hands of a few," where "no one can breathe against their will."[39]

NOTES

1. Summaries of the points raised by the Pope's critics can be found in the following: Amanda Erickson, "Some American Catholics Really Don't Like Pope Francis. Here's Why (For Conservatives, Sowing Confusion)," *Washington Post*, September 18, 2015, http://www.washingtonpost.com/sf/local/2015/09/18/francis-is-a-global-sensation-but-to-certain-traditional-catholics-his-message-rings-hollow/; Samuel Gregg, "*Laudato si'*: Well Intentioned, Economically Flawed," *The American Spectator*, June 19, 2015, http://spectator.

org/articles/63160/laudato-si'-well-intentioned-economically-flawed; Samuel Gregg, "Pope Francis and Poverty," The Corner, *National Review*, November 26, 2013, http://www.nationalreview.com/corner/365004/Pope-francis-and-poverty-samuel-gregg.; James V. Schall, "Concerning the 'Ecological' Path to Salvation," *Catholic World Reporter*, June 21, 2015, http://www.catholicworldreport.com/Item/3970/concerning_the_ecological_path_to_salvation.aspx.

2. Zenit staff, "Pope: Every Worker Has Right to Fair Pay," *Zenit*, October 28, 2014, http://www.zenit.org/en/articles/pope-every-worker-has-right-to-fair-pay.

3. The social encyclicals have continually reaffirmed these principles since *Rerum novarum*. There are various compilations of the social encyclicals; a volume with all the documents through John Paul II's pontificate is Michael Walsh and Brian Davies, eds., *Proclaiming Justice and Peace: Papal Documents from Rerum novarum to Centesimus annus* (Mystic, CT: Twenty-Third Publications, 1994). Private property rights are discussed in Pontifical Council for Justice and Peace, *Compendium of the Social Doctrine of the Church*, 176. The classic statement against socialism is in Leo XIII, *Rerum novarum*, 3–13, as found in the Walsh and Davies volume; this qualification is necessary, as *Rerum novarum* did not employ the later practice of numbering paragraphs in its original edition.

4. This principle, too, has been repeated continually in Catholic social teaching since *Rerum novarum*.

5. Pius XI, *Quadragesimo anno*, The Holy See (Vatican website), May 15, 1931, http://w2.vatican.va/content/pius-xi/en/encyclicals/documents/hf_p-xi_enc_19310515_quadragesimo-anno.html, 109, 106.

6. Guardini, *End of the Modern World*, 51–57.

7. Guardini discusses power and the person in *Power and Responsibility* (New York: Sheed and Ward, 1957).

8. The best one-volume discussion of the scholastic roots of economics, which came to inform Catholic social teaching, discussing usury, fair price, just wage, and speculative economic activity, is Odd Langholm, *Economics in the Medieval Schools: Wealth, Exchange, Value, Money, and Usery According to the Paris Theological Tradition* (New York: E. J. Brill, 1992).

9. See on this topic, for example, Bergoglio, *Diálogos*, 46.

10. This is one of the issues distinguishing Francis from Catholic neoconservatives in the United States, particularly Michael Novak, whose treatments of capitalism reference history mostly in highly selective ways, particularly when he minimizes the historically Catholic positions. For Novak, the moral problems central to capitalism are predominantly to be corrected by the flowering of individual virtues. This misses the central dynamic of capitalism's history.

Capitalist development has been a history of deliberately eliminating independent moral criteria from the evaluation of economic behavior, in the process stripping older moral criticisms of all their force. It demonstrates a profound misunderstanding to contend in such a context that the moral problems of capitalism are going to be solved by appeals to individual virtue when historical capitalism in practice emasculated the older moral criticisms with their associated virtues. This is what gives the Catholic neoconservative corpus its disturbing characteristic as largely a defense of the status quo, the one exception being their proclivity to adopt libertarian criticisms of government intervention. Moreover, these criticisms of government are frequently not in fact informed by moral criteria either but rather the kind of exaltation of individual liberty at odds with Catholic social teaching in the first place. I develop this criticism at length in Thomas R. Rourke, *A Conscience as Large as the World: Yves R. Simon versus the Catholic Neoconservatives* (Lanham, MD, and London: Rowman & Littlefield, 1997), 139–99. Andrea Tornielli and Giacomo Galeazzi critique Novak and George Weigel's treatments of Benedict XVI's social encyclical *Caritas in veritate* in *This Economy Kills*, 81–87.

11. See the chapter "The Cult of the God of Money," found in Francis, *Church of Mercy*, 113–14.

12. Bergoglio, *Diálogos*, 48. He cites Henri Tincq in this regard.

13. Ibid., 49.

14. The technocratic paradigm is developed in Francis, *Laudato si'*, 106–14.

15. Rubín and Ambrogetti, *El jesuita*, 150.

16. Bergoglio, *El verdadero poder*, 272.

17. Andrea Tornielli, *Jorge Bergoglio, Francisco* (New York: Vintage Español, 2013), 136.

18. Ibid., 137.

19. Ibid.

20. Tornielli and Galeazzi, *This Economy Kills*, 11.

21. Find his discussion of one-way exchanges in Yves R. Simon, *Work, Society and Culture*, ed. Vukan Kuic (New York: Fordham University Press, 1971), 34–39; and also in Simon, *Philosophy of Democratic Government*, 237–41.

22. Paul Krugman, "Unproductive Finance," *New York Times*, June 12, 2013, http://krugman.blogs.nytimes.com/2013/06/12/unproductive-finance/.

23. Thomas R. Rourke, "Moral Problems in Economic Organization in the Work of Yves R. Simon: Unequal Exchange and Man as the Principle of Integration," *Redeeming Philosophy: From Metaphysics to Aesthetics*, ed. John J. Conley, 323–24 (Washington, DC: Catholic University of America Press, 2014). The internal quotation is from Fred Magdoff, John Bellamy Foster, and Frederick H. Buttel, "An Overview," in Magdoff, Buttel, and Foster, eds.,

Hungry for Profit: The Agribusiness Threat to Farmers, Food and the Environment (New York: Monthly Review Press, 2001), 18.

24. Tornielli and Galeazzi, *This Economy Kills*, 75.

25. Rourke, "Moral Problems," 323–24.

26. A *CDO* is a collateralized debt obligation, a financial instrument developed in the 1990s that mixed together a variety of mortgages at different levels of risk. Quotation from John Bellamy Foster and Fred Magdoff, *The Great Financial Crisis: Causes and Consequences* (New York: Monthly Review Press, 2009), 96–97.

27. Rubín and Ambrogetti, *El jesuita*, 163, 159.

28. This discussion of social debt is from the chapter "Social Debt," found in Francis, *Only Love Can Save Us*, 105–14.

29. Benedict XVI, *Caritas in veritate*, 40.

30. Francis, *Only Love Can Save Us*, 113.

31. A summary of his arguments is found in the chapter "*Duc in altum*: El pensamiento social de Juan Pablo II," found in Bergoglio, *El verdadero poder*, 282–98. His immense debt to John Paul II on this topic is manifest throughout, although he integrates the discussion with his own fundamental commitment to inculturating evangelization.

32. Catherine Harmon, "Full Text: Pope Francis' Wednesday Audience Address on the Feast of St. Joseph the Worker," *Catholic World Report*, May 1, 2013, http://www.catholicworldreport.com/Blog/2224/full_text_Pope_francis_wednesday_audience_address_on_the_feast_of_st_joseph_the_worker.aspx.

33. The point concerning the "Gospel of Work" is from John Paul II, *Laborem exercens* (hereafter *LE*), The Holy See (Vatican website), September 14, 1981, http://w2.vatican.va/content/john-paul-ii/en/encyclicals/documents/hf_jp-ii_enc_14091981_laborem-exercens.html, 6.

34. Francis, *Laudato si'*, 128. The internal quotation is from Benedict XVI, *Caritas in veritate*, 101.

35. Zenit staff, "Pope: Every Worker."

36. Explicit rejections of capitalism understood as economic liberalism are found in, for example, Pius XI, *Quadragesimo anno*, 105–9; and John Paul II, *Laborem exercens*, 11–15. The criticisms are broad, ranging from a materialist anthropology to the tendencies toward a concentration of wealth that in fact does not systematically incorporate the poor.

37. I critiqued Catholic "neoconservatives" Michael Novak, Richard John Neuhaus, and George Weigel, who tend systematically to support free-market solutions to poverty and think the Catholic Church should also, in Rourke, *Conscience as Large as the World*. The book critiques in depth the theory that modern capitalism can accommodate the Catholic conception of the common good. My critiques fall as well on Father Robert Sirico, who claims that "we

must always work for moral objectives in the context of market realities." A more thorough rejection of Catholic social teaching would be hard to imagine. I discuss Sirico's economic personalism in Thomas R. Rourke and Rosita A. Chazarreta Rourke, *A Theory of Personalism* (Lanham, MD, and London: Lexington Books, 2005), 16–18; I contend that Sirico's personalism, when it comes to economic matters, does not meet the Catholic Church's moral standards.

38. The Pope's comments are found in Tornielli and Galeazzi, *This Economy Kills*, 151.

39. Pius XI, *Quadragesimo anno*, 105–6.

EPILOGUE

Perennial Challenges to Inculturation and *Laudato si'*

Pope Francis's social vision is a sustained reflection on what it means to inculturate the Gospel of Jesus Christ in the world today. It is a reflection that never ceases to penetrate more deeply the ultimate sources of the crises of our time and point in the direction of change. Although he is not the only Catholic or Christian thinker, even the only Pope, who has explored these themes, he brings to the table the uniqueness of his historical background. Pope Francis is a man of the South. This does not grant him any particular epistemological privileges unavailable to others, but it certainly does provide him an important and necessary perspective on globalization, international political economy, politics, and the cultural challenges of our time. The Holy Spirit has determined that a man of his particular background occupies the Chair of Saint Peter in our time, and people of wisdom will listen to what he has to say. The South is where most Catholics and Christians live. As Europe dies out, the product of its own suicide, the torch has been passed to the South, where the faith has over five hundred years of history. Alberto Methol Ferré was right: This is the time for Latin America to become a source church.

As we have seen in these chapters, inculturation of the Gospel has been central to Jorge Mario Bergoglio's social thinking. His Jesuit roots formed his reflections first and foremost. Certainly, from the outset, one of the first things we notice when studying him is that his mind and spirit have been formed by over fifty years of contemplating Jesus in the Gospels, in the manner spelled out by Saint Ignatius. He sees in the original Jesuit missions in Argentina the true embodiment of the Jesuit ideal in its time. The missions represent, moreover, the Christian ideal. The logic of the Incarnation propels the faithful to do what these Jesuits did—that is, go to the peripheries and bring Jesus Christ. The missionaries understood, unlike so many Christians today, that the Gospel was intended to penetrate every dimension of life. Salvation is no individualistic project to be attained in isolated individualism while leaving the world to operate on its own terms. The Jesuits, using the best theology and pastoral practice, sought to create nothing less than a Christian civilization. This left an indelible imprint on Jorge Mario Bergoglio. With this example in mind, he will forever refuse to be fooled into thinking that a world full of exclusion, poverty, unemployment, and inhuman inequalities is something to be accepted as inevitable. It is not. It is the result of intentional choices made by specific human beings who act under the judgment of God. The light of the Gospel taught Bergoglio that faith truly illuminates the social order.

One of the most important lessons Bergoglio has learned derives from the Christian understanding of time and its relationship to social possibilities. Christians must work in a sustained way over time to produce results that will never be perfect. Nevertheless, this is not an excuse for withdrawal or impatience. It is better to embark on a good, imperfect, but sustained project with solid evangelical bases than to try to "occupy space" or seize power. Christian humility and realism teach us that, in the wise provision of God, time is the playing out of real possibilities and must be respected. History, wisely appropriated, instructs us that time both imposes limits and opens doors of opportunities. From this wisdom flows one of Bergoglio's firmest foundations: social reality in all its forms must embody an understanding of continuity among past, present, and future.

In the forced dissolution of this great work of inculturated evangelization, Bergoglio saw the paradigm of how such noble work is always destroyed. The specific forms, times, personages, and ideologies may change, but the essential model has stayed the same since the time of the Enlightenment. There is a project of domination, rooted in one or other form of reason disincarnate from both history and the Incarnate Word's role in it. It is invariably a reductionism that severs the connection between people—both individually and collectively—and the transcendent God. Departing from the logic of the Incarnation, such projects always violate a second of Bergoglio's fundamental assumptions: reality—understood in its depth as grounded in Creation and the Incarnation—is more important than ideas. The projects of domination always speak in universal but abstract terms. Therefore, the universality attained is at the expense of some considerable elements of reality. The Jesuit missions were destroyed because they stood in the way of the centralizing political project of European monarchs. This was no historical accident. Imperialist logic mandated that the work of the Jesuits be destroyed. The Jesuits and the native peoples in their missions had their own priorities—moral and political values that flowed from their sense of evangelization under Saint Ignatius and ultimately Jesus Christ. This kind of diversity could not be tolerated because it conflicted at its roots with the imperial project. A Christian people, informed by the Gospel understandings of both the person and community, particularly when they live in a historically embodied Christian culture, will resist the ideological trappings of false universalism. They will understand that good and noble works are being destroyed for a chimera. For Europeans intent on dominating Latin America, the Jesuit missions represented a real alternative way of life that obviously appealed to people. The threat of such a countermodel to their projected political and economic imposition could not be tolerated. Bergoglio understood that in these tragic events was a paradigm of what continued to play out in the modern world. Whether the project of the centralizing state, the project of the international bourgeoisie, the universality of the free market, the universality of class struggle, the dictatorship of the proletariat, the spread of fascist hypernationalism, or today's dictatorship of relativism, Jorge Bergoglio would see, via the Ignatian discernment of spirits, that all are projects that destroy the work of the Gospel and seek to enslave people.

Through the prism of Vatican II and its aftermath in Latin America, Father Bergoglio would discern an authentic Christian response. This was no easy achievement. It placed him at odds with liberal, radical, and restorationist elements in his own order, the nation, and the world at large. Eschewing ideology, his leadership would never lose its focus on service to the people in a real Christian sense. Steering away from the currents that claimed to be *for* the people but were not *with* the people,

Bergoglio acted in many ways in unison with the strain of thought and practice in Argentina deemed *la teología del pueblo*—theology of the people. This school sympathized with the call for justice in the more well-known theology of liberation. Nevertheless, Bergoglio's theology resisted the elements that would work Enlightenment and Marxist premises into it. It also saw in the ideological elements in Marxism a dangerous tendency to reductionism and immanentism, negating the essential component of transcendence. In addition, Bergoglio would stay on the straight and narrow path by remaining centered in Paul VI's *Populorum progressio* and *Evangelii nuntiandi*. In this way Bergoglio would be a true reformer, adopting with regenerated force the missionary thrust he had first learned from Saint Ignatius. It would be difficult to overestimate how difficult this would be in his home country, which has been torn by conflicts between vanguardists and restorationists within the Catholic Church, paralleled by conflicts between radicals and the "national-security state" in the larger society. In the midst of this, Bergoglio focused on loving the poor, creatively serving their needs, forming new institutions, all while preaching the Gospel and resisting the ideologues on both sides. He was responsible for saving many lives, although he has always left it to others to tell these stories.[1]

Bergoglio always relied on this set of fundamental insights in forming his thinking about society. All of his reflections on culture are derived from the theory and practice of inculturating evangelization. So are his conclusions concerning what has gone wrong. Culture must maintain the pole of transcendence, respecting the true absolute norms given by the Gospel. These alone provide for true development and social peace. The actual culture of the people must be respected. They have the right to their own culture as it has developed over the centuries, particularly when the Gospel informs it. For this reason—again along the lines indicated by Paul VI in *Evangelii nuntiandi*—Bergoglio will be able to see the depth of faith in popular religious practices, assisting them and deepening them in the manner of a pastor, tying them to the larger and universal themes of the faith. His preaching on the August 7 Feast of San Cayetano provided rich syntheses of Church social teaching, tied to the popular devotion. Of course he has always preached that in Mary, Mother of Christ, Latin America is a family that has a mother. The now ever-present themes of "the culture of encounter" and the need for dialogue are based on his Gospel reflections.

EPILOGUE

What do the Gospels suggest Jesus would do if He were on the scene today? Would He stay in the rectory? Would He refuse to speak to public sinners? Pope Francis thinks not, and he has never thought so. Rooted in the Gospel understanding that all men and women are brothers and sisters, public sinners or not, Pope Francis believes Jesus would encounter them and dialogue with them in a way that always reflects the truth of who He is but also reflects the love who is God.

Contemporary culture presents many negative and challenging features, inevitable results of the absence of a unifying and transcendent center. The unifying tendencies of globalization create at best a pseudo-solidarity. In the modern person's center so often lie the pains of uprootedness and fragmentation. In Latin America, for example, where Christian culture is no longer the driving force of contemporary developments, the sense of inner dispersion comes from a declining sense of identity once provided by that culture. Globally the decline of the "profane messianism" of Marxism has left us with a new form of atheism often unrecognized as such. From Alberto Methol Ferré, Bergoglio adopted the view that the underlying assumption of today's "permissive cornucopia" and relativism is exactly atheism. The leading developments in culture, brought on by globalization, tend in the direction of a "globalization of indifference," not solidarity. Nevertheless, the obligation of hope remains at the center of personal and common life.

In the political order, belief in time over space and the priority of the whole over the part are the driving forces. Bergoglio's political thought is in strict continuity with the Catholic Church's social teaching concerning the central themes: the common good, the role of the state, subsidiarity, solidarity, and liberty. He does not address politics in terms of specific policies so much as he tries to speak to the need for a renewed political anthropology and culture. This may appear curious to those who follow politics. In the middle of a profound political, economic, and social breakdown, why did the Cardinal talk about the nineteenth-century epic poem *Martín Fierro*? Why would he talk about the virtues of a saint-priest, El Cura Brochero, when discussing politics? With inflation running rampant and the nation unable to maintain a president in office, why would a long sermon on the Good Samaritan or the narrative of Zacchaeus be appropriate? The answer lies in Bergoglio's long-term vision, of how a nation cannot really solve its problems without one, and his belief in the need to begin today to create a viable culture to support a healthy and democratic polity. The Cardinal knew how sterile it is simply to talk about policies when there is no state capable of solving the people's problems. So he did two things: he initiated the Diálogo Argentino, focused on the people's needs, and he began addressing the need for long-term change in political culture. He did so in the full knowledge that his preaching would not change the world tomorrow. He also managed to avoid the temptation to use his position to occupy public space in the manner of a political leader. His discussions of *Martín Fierro*, El Cura Brochero, Manuel Belgrano, and the Good Samaritan were all about the virtues the polity needed to heal its pathologies.

The theme of power and its contemporary manifestation looms large in Bergoglio's political thinking. It derives considerably from Romano Guardini, particularly in Guardini's assertion that power today has unique features, including an insidious, even demonic, element. This is the way power today does not speak in its own name but hides behind other words—such as *progress, utility, welfare*—and behind the language of inevitability. For example, how often one sees the enormous strength of tendencies fueled by the forces of technology and money in the context of the global market. In the last fifty years, countless millions of people have lost their access to land, livelihood, and the benefits of government and culture; yet those who make these decisions themselves often do not feel that they have exercised power over others. In their minds they were just following an imperative delivered from some pool of money, technology, the direction of the market, or someone over them. Bergoglio does not believe it is really this way. It is true that the depersonalizing sense of the mechanisms of power today may allow decision makers to *feel* they are not responsible for the terrible results. Revelation reminds us that we are ultimately responsible for the world we have built. So when, for example, international financial institutions or judicial institutions impose criteria on developing nations that cause untold suffering and these measures are taken to satisfy wealthy creditors in the developed world—even the predatory holders of vulture funds who can afford to wait[2]—distinctly moral decisions are being made.

Concerning the economy, the Pope's assertion that "this economy kills" caused a great deal of commotion and spawned a veritable resistance movement on the part of those deeply committed to expanding the role of the free market in the world. Nonetheless, it could ironically be said that it is in this area where Pope Francis is the most driven by established Church teaching. Some of the problem is misinterpretation. The Pope is not opposed to the free market in principle, understanding that there is a legitimate and worthy vocation of business, an expression of the fundamental liberty of the person. The actual problem is twofold: First, when the profit motive overrides more fundamental human values and society permits the failure to realize the universal destination of goods, then the social responsibilities of property remain unmet and, consequently, there is a moral problem. Second, there is the tendency to reduce all values to monetary values and increasingly not to recognize the terrible human losses when such a trend becomes pervasive. Today we see the integrity of a broad array of social institutions, from education to health care, being reduced to their business dimensions while many leaders fail to see anything wrong with this. Pope Francis, following Catholic social teaching, reaffirms the ethical dimensions of economic activity, particularly the universal destination of goods, the right to work, the priority of labor over capital, and the right of the state to intervene when necessary. Most of all, Francis seeks to preserve the most fundamental belief that economics must always answer to moral criteria independent of the market and that the state has a legitimate role in making such determinations, always subject to the principle of subsidiarity.

Much of the hostility toward Pope Francis has come from Catholics in the United States who have not faced up to the fact that Catholic social teaching simply does not support capitalism as it actually operates in the world today. The Catholic Church maintains an independent set of moral criteria according to which economic injustices abound. The Church does not echo conservative or libertarian ideology, which insists that the only injustices are those caused by state intervention. Yet the market left to itself contributed to the Great Depression, the Third World debt crisis, and the financial meltdown of 2008. The Pope criticizes only morally unacceptable results. It is the Pope who actually well understands how the system works, as he has never abandoned the Gospel or the Church's social teaching as his critics often do.

Recently Pope Francis issued the encyclical, *Laudato si'*. The larger Catholic framework of the encyclical, and its continuity with the Pope's longstanding thinking, has largely been missed in the subsequent discussion. The Pope systematically links the problems with the environment to the broader issues long discussed by Catholic social teaching, such as the unbridled search for profit, materialism, and consumerism. In a sense, he is adding a layer onto the established critiques of modern politics and economics already embodied in the social magisterium. Unfortunately in the political and cultural discourse *Laudato si'* has been reduced to "the Pope's encyclical on the environment." In a sense the claim is true. Nevertheless, it is fatally narrow to view it in this way, as it is a beautiful Catholic document that will hopefully be seen as a wonderful work of integration among the moral, social, economic, and political orders with the order of Creation. In truth one could take out all the specific discussion of environmental policies and still have a full, intelligible, and very Catholic document. Nonetheless, although the Pope had not really addressed the environment in any depth in his previous writings, and since *Laudato si'* is a contribution to the social magisterium of the Church, it is necessary to summarize briefly the new developments and then link the document to the broader themes of his thought already discussed.

The new features of the document begin with the kind of striking observation that has always attracted attention. The Pope states that we are making of the earth, our common home, "an immense pile of filth" (*LS*, 21), linked to the broader practices of what he has long lamented as our "throwaway culture" (*LS*, 22). He refers to the climate as "a common good," which signals a responsibility for government to oversee it to the extent possible and in accord with the dictates of prudence. He asserts, in what has become conventional wisdom, that climate change is being brought about by the accumulation of greenhouse gases in the atmosphere from the use of fossil fuels. Exacerbating the tendency to global warming is the loss of tropical forests (*LS*, 23–24). Echoing his characteristic concerns, he notes that the poor experience the worst impacts of climate change (*LS*, 25). He calls for substitutions to be found for fossil fuels (*LS*, 26). He proceeds to underline the problems with water, noting the loss of balance in recent decades such that supplies are often inadequate to demand. He emphasizes that access to clean water is a basic human right, as it is linked to the right to live (*LS*, 30). He considerably laments the loss of biodiversity, in opposition to those who believe that human beings have the right to send species into extinction, and affirms that every creature is a reflection of the creator

(*LS*, 33–35). The decline of "those richly biodiverse lungs," the Congo and Amazon basins, are of concern for both their biodiversity and their capacity to offset global-warming trends (*LS*, 32–42). He links all of these problems to the human environment in the belief that the same forces that cause environmental decline also contribute to social breakdown. As examples he specifically references the "current models of development"—globalization, technology, and the market—and the "throwaway culture," followed by "global inequity" (*LS*, 43–52). Reflecting his concerns that the modern state is so often inadequate to the task of addressing its responsibilities, he characterizes the response of governments to date as lamentably "weak" (*LS*, 53–59).

Chapter 2 of *Laudato si'* delivers a beautiful account of "The Gospel of Creation," where the Pope demonstrates the contribution of the biblical accounts of creation for the development of a suitable environmental ethic. In chapter 3, "The Human Roots of the Ecological Crisis," he summarizes, under the influence of Guardini, the related problem of power, technology, and globalization (*LS*, 102–14) and the negative impacts of "modern anthropocentrism" (*LS*, 115–36). In chapter 4, "Integral Ecology," he discusses how cultural trends negatively impact both the human and physical environments, particularly the loss of solidarity, globalizing trends that disrespect the local, and consumerism (*LS*, 141–46). He recommends public transportation (*LS*, 153) and behaviors on the individual level that contribute to the "ecology of daily life" (*LS*, 147–55). Nevertheless, at all levels there is "much to be done" (*LS*, 180). He believes far more international action is needed, particularly in the area of reducing carbon emissions (*LS*, 164, 170) and conserving energy (*LS*, 180).

Beyond the specific discussion of what are commonly recognized as environmental concerns, the document is influenced by the historical trajectory of Bergoglio's thinking—as we have examined throughout this book—at times in very direct ways and at other times from a distance. As we have seen, Bergoglio has longstanding convictions about inculturation, which result in a deep respect for the integrity of the local rooted in the sovereignty of the people. Such concerns run throughout *Laudato si'* and are reflected across the board in the treatment of economic, political, and cultural factors. The Pope sees the need to preserve the original identity, historically and culturally, of both people and places, even of archeological sites (*LS*, 143). He emphasizes the dignity of peoples (*LS*, 205), noting the valuable contributions of indigenous communities to a proper environmental ethic (*LS*, 146). In all aspects of planning, he insists that the local population be given a special place (*LS*, 183.) On the cultural front, he characteristically notes the centrality of religion in the culture of a people, not only for intrinsic reasons but also as a source of values and ideals that can help in creating a better environment in a better world (*LS*, 199). He specifically underlines the relevance of the biblical accounts of creation and of Catholic social thought (*LS*, 64–75).

In "The Ecology of Daily Life" (*LS*, 147–55) the Pope shares specifically his deep knowledge of the life of the poor. He commends poor people for the ways they support a healthy ecology despite tremendous challenges and limitations by creating a decent life through acts of love and solidarity (*LS*, 148). Moreover, concerning economic matters, he quotes Sirach 38:34 to restate a truth that technology is making us forget that "craftsmen . . . maintain the fabric of the world" (*LS*, 124). This is in the context of wanting to preserve patterns of local community subsistence, autonomy, and productive diversity, particularly through small-scale food-production systems, cooperatives, and preserving employment sources generally (*LS*, 124, 129, 179). Neither does he forget to mention the value of medicinal plants and the importance of maintaining the local flora and fauna (*LS*, 124, 168), echoing the concerns of the indigenous peoples and the Jesuit missionaries of old who served them.

Equally evident in the encyclical are Bergoglio's longstanding perceptions of the sources of today's problems in a globalizing hegemony characterized by "uniform thinking" and a culture oriented to the preservation of an imposed system that benefits entrenched interests and excludes millions. The global political economy is in many ways an example of the imperial and uniform thinking that destroyed the Jesuit missions (*LS*, 106). The global market has become the only rule (*LS*, 56). Associated with it is an increasingly powerful financial sector that operates according to its own criteria bereft of broader human values (*LS*, 189). Particularly distressing was when the financial system failed so egregiously and sent the world into a dangerous recession. Nonetheless, major reforms are still not forthcoming. Major flaws are often overlooked because the ideological system promotes an ideology of progress that is not questioned (*LS*, 60). As always the system of domination that comes from the developed world excludes a distressingly large number of people from the benefits of this progress in longstanding patterns of "social exclusion" (*LS*, 46). Poor people are as always unrepresented, having surrendered their sovereignty to decision makers who make decisions over their heads (*LS*, 48–49). The dominant culture is a "throwaway culture" characterized by "instant gratification" (*LS*, 22, 162).

The solution to the domination inherent in globalization can only be found in the building up everywhere of a true culture of encounter among peoples (*LS*, 47), creating bonds of solidarity and friendship, bonds that will hopefully become worldwide (*LS*, 14, 89–92, 142). In the world of today, such a culture must inevitably be a culture of resistance. Always rooted in history and the actual state of affairs, political change is critical, the Pope realizes. He has long bemoaned the "weak politics" resulting from the hegemonizing powers of market ideology and relativism, and he makes frequent reference to the insufficiency of political responses today (*LS*, 54, 57). There is a lamentable absence of political will (*LS*, 166) across the board to bring about needed reforms. Existing accords are either weak or unenforced (*LS*, 167, 169). The source of the incapacity lies in the focus on the short-term and the overall weakening of the nation-state in the face of the globalization process (*LS*, 175, 178, 197).

Of all the strains of thought discussed here, the most obvious and direct influence on the encyclical is clearly Romano Guardini with his insights into the person and power in our times. Francis cites him to the effect that the modern approach to nature does not see in it teleology or limits; it is rather a pure object (*LS*, 6, 11). Respect for nature and its limits has been replaced by "a tyrannical anthropocentrism" in which there are no limits (*LS*, 68–69). Guardini's treatment of the interplay between the related anthropocentrism and the "technocratic paradigm" really grounds the entire discussion in chapter 3, "The Human Roots of the Ecological Crisis" (*LS*, 101–37). The Pope reminds us that nothing guarantees that increased power will be used for good (*LS*, 104–5). There is a real danger that the reign of technology will be a genuine global domination (*LS*, 108). The technocratic paradigm already "tends to dominate economic and political life" (*LS*, 109). Indeed, there is a "loss of appreciation for the whole, for the relationships between things, and for the broader horizon, which then becomes irrelevant" (*LS*, 110).

The entire domain of ethics is inevitably reduced to relativism in such a context, as technology itself has no way of determining good from bad. Relativism thereby becomes part of the dominant hegemonic culture and the deepest root of its evils:

> The culture of relativism is the same disorder [that] drives one person to the advantage of another . . . imposing forced labor on them or enslaving them to pay their debts. The same kind of thinking leads to the sexual exploitation of children and abandonment of the elderly. . . . It is also the mindset of those who say, Let us allow the invisible forces of the market to regulate the economy and consider their impact on society and nature as collateral damage. . . . We should not think that political efforts or the force of law will be sufficient to prevent actions . . . [for] when the culture itself is corrupt and objective truth and universally valid principles are no longer upheld, then law can only be seen as arbitrary impositions or obstacles to be avoided. (*LS*, 123)

In conclusion, the Pope's thinking is rooted in a longstanding set of concerns grounded in his entire understanding of evangelization itself. The work of the Gospel is to incarnate the Word of God in all dimensions of life, in the process of creating a people. The social implications are many, all oriented toward respecting the deepest identity of the people as subjects before the Creator. It is the great challenge of our time to preserve the good ways of life—and particularly where the seeds of the Word of God have often long been present and growing—from the destructive and absolutizing forces of our time.

NOTES

1. Scavo, *Bergoglio's List*. This book tells of how the then-young Jesuit Provincial hid people and made arrangements for them to leave the country, all at considerable personal risk.

2. *Vulture funds* deliberately buy up what is seen as bad debt from developing nations—that is, debt that the indebted nation is unlikely to be able to pay. These funds take the risk that they can recoup this debt by pressing the matter in courts. This has particularly been a problem for Argentina. Under Néstor Kirchner's presidency, Argentina agreed to pay a certain percentage of its unpayable debt. Most of the holders of the debt agreed to it, but the so-

called vulture funds did not. They pressed the matter successfully in courts in the state of New York. Many find it reprehensible that funds held by wealthy speculators seek profits from nations in dire financial straits with millions of extremely poor people. At the time of this writing, new President Mauricio Macri is trying to conclude a deal that would give these funds most of what they demand as a way of trying to recoup Argentina's credit in international financial markets.

BIBLIOGRAPHY

Ackermann, Stephan. "The Church as Person in the Theology of Hans Urs von Balthasar." *Communio* 29 (Summer 2002): 238–49. http://www.communio-icr.com/files/AckermanFinal.pdf.

Albado, Omar César. "La pastoral popular en el pensamiento del padre Rafael Tello: Una contribución desde la Argentina a la teologia latinoamericana." In *Franciscanum* 55, no. 160 (December 2013): 219–45, http://revistas.usbbog.edu.co/index.php/Franciscanum/article/view/443/344.

Benedict XVI. *Caritas in veritate*. The Holy See (Vatican website). June 29, 2009. http://w2.vatican.va/content/benedict-xvi/en/encyclicals/documents/hf_ben-xvi_enc_20090629_caritas-in-veritate.html.

Bergoglio, Jorge Mario [Francis]. *Corrupción y pecado; Algunas reflexiones en torno al tema de la corrupción*. Buenos Aires: Editorial Claretiana, 2013.

———. *Diálogos entre Juan Pablo II y Fidel Castro*. Buenos Aires: Editorial de Ciencia y Cultura, 1998.

———. *Educar: Elegir la vida: Propuestas para tiempos difíciles*. 2nd ed., corrected and updated. Buenos Aires: Editorial Claretiana, 2013.

———. *Educar: Exigencia y pasión; Desafíos para educadores cristianos*. Buenos Aires: Editorial Claretiana, 2013.

———. *Education for Choosing Life: Proposals for Difficult Times*. Translated by Deborah Cole. San Francisco: Ignatius Press, 2014.

———. *El verdadero poder es el servicio*. 2nd ed. Buenos Aires: Editorial Claretiana, 2013.

———. "The Eucharist, Gift of God for the Life of the World: Catechesis Delivered by Jorge Mario Cardinal Bergoglio, International Eucharistic Congress, Quebec City, Canada, June 18, 2008." The Holy See (Vatican website). http://www.vatican.va/roman_curia/pont_committees/cucharist-congr/documents/rc_committ_euchar_doc_20080618_mistero-alleanza_en.html.

———. "For Man." In *A Generative Thought: An Introduction to the Works of Luigi Giussani*, edited by Elisa Buzzi, 79–83. Montreal and Kingston; London; Ithaca: McGill Queen's University Press, 2003. Chapter text available online at http://communio.stblogs.org/Pope Francis on the Religious Sense.pdf.

———. *In Him Alone Is Our Hope: Spiritual Exercises Given to His Brother Bishops in the Manner of Saint Ignatius of Loyola*. Translated by Vincent Capuano and Andrew Matt. New York: Magnificat, 2013.

———. *Meditaciones para religiosos*. Bilbao: Editorial Mensajero, 2014.

———. *Mente abierta, corazón creyente*. Buenos Aires: Editorial Claretiana, 2012.

———. *La nación por construir: Utopía, pensamiento y compromiso*. Buenos Aires: Editorial Claretiana, 2005.
———. *Nosotros como ciudadanos, nosotros como pueblo: Hacia un bicentenario en justicia y solidaridad, 2010–2016*. Buenos Aires: Claretiana, 2011.
———. *Ponerse la patria al hombro: Memoria y camino de esperanza*. Corrected and updated. Buenos Aires: Editorial Claretiana, 2013.
———. *Reflexiones en esperanza*. 1st ed. Madrid: Romana Editorial, 2013.
———. *Reflexiones espirituales sobre la vida apostólica*. Bilbao: Ediciones Mensajero, 2013.
———. *Sobre la acusación de sí mismo*. Buenos Aires: Editorial Claretiana, 2013.
———. *The Way of Humility: Corruption and Sin; On Self-Accusation*. San Francisco: Ignatius Press, 2013. English edition 2014, translated from the original Spanish by Helena Scott.
———. *See* Francis.
Bergoglio, Jorge Mario [Francis], and Abraham Skorka. *Sobre el cielo y la tierra*. New York: Vintage Español, 2013.
Bermúdez, Alejandro, ed. *Pope Francis: Our Brother, Our Friend*. San Francisco: Ignatius Press, 2013.
Boff, Leonardo, and Clodovis Boff. *Introducing Liberation Theology*. Maryknoll, NY: Orbis Books, 1987.
Bonard, Virginia. *Nuestra fe es revolucionaria*. Buenos Aires: Grupo Editorial Prensa, 2013.
Carriquiry, Guzmán. *El bicentenario de la independencia de los países latinoamericanos*. Madrid: Ediciones Encuentro, 2011.
Conference of the Bishops of Latin America and the Caribbean. *The Aparecida Document*. Lexington, KY: Latin American Episcopal Conference CELAM, 2014.
Congar, Yves. *True and False Reform in the Church*. Translated by Paul Philibert (Collegeville, MD: Liturgical Press, 2011.
Congregation for the Doctrine of the Faith. *Libertatis conscientia*. The Holy See (Vatican website). March 22, 1986. http://www.vatican.va/roman_curia/congregations/cfaith/documents/rc_con_cfaith_doc_19860322_freedom-liberation_en.html.
———. *Libertatis nuntius*. The Holy See (Vatican website). August 6, 1984. http://www.vatican.va/roman_curia/congregations/cfaith/documents/rc_con_cfaith_doc_19840806_theology-liberation_en.html.
Diócesis de Cruz del Eje. "Vida y obra de José del Rosario Brochero." José del Rosario Brochero (website). http://www.padrebrochero.com.ar/vida.html.
Eagleson, John, and Philip Scharper, eds. *Puebla and Beyond: Documentation and Commentary*. Translated by John Drury. Maryknoll, NY: Orbis Books, 1979.
Ellacuría, Ignacio, and Jon Sobrino, eds. *Mysterium Liberationis: Fundamental Concepts of Liberation Theology*. Maryknoll, NY: Orbis Books, 1993.
Foster, John Bellamy, and Fred Magdoff. *The Great Financial Crisis: Causes and Consequences*. New York: Monthly Review Press, 2009.
Francis [Jorge Mario Bergoglio]. *Apostolic Journey of His Holiness Pope Francis to Cuba, to the United States of America and Visit to the United Nations Headquarters (19–28 September 2015): Visit to the Joint Session of the United States Congress; Address of the Holy Father; United States Capitol, Washington, D.C., Thursday, 24 September 2015*. The Holy See (Vatican website). September 24, 2015. https://w2.vatican.va/content/francesco/en/speeches/2015/september/documents/papa-francesco_20150924_usa-us-congress.html.
———. *Church of Mercy: A Vision for the Church*. Chicago: Loyola Press, 2014.
———. *Enviados a hacer el bien: Reflexiones y meditaciones*. Buenos Aires: Agape Libros, 2013.
———. *Evangelii gaudium*. The Holy See (Vatican website). November 24, 2013. http://w2.vatican.va/content/francesco/en/apost_exhortations/documents/papa-francesco_esortazione-ap_20131124_evangelii-gaudium.html.
———. *Laudato si'*. The Holy See (Vatican website). May 24, 2015. http://w2.vatican.va/content/francesco/en/encyclicals/documents/papa-francesco_20150524_enciclica-laudato-si.html.

BIBLIOGRAPHY

———. *Letter of Holy Father Francis to the President of the Bishops' Conference of Argentina on the Occasion of the Beatification of Father José Gabriel Brochero.* The Holy See (Vatican website). September 14, 2013. https://w2.vatican.va/content/francesco/en/letters/2013/documents/papa-francesco_20130914_beatificazione-brochero.html.

———. *Only Love Can Save Us: Letters, Homilies, and Talks of Cardinal Jorge Bergoglio.* Translated by Gerard Seramik. Huntington, IN: Our Sunday Visitor, Inc., 2013.

———. *Por la senda de la paz.* Buenos Aires: Agape Libros, 2014.

———. *Que no les roben la esperanza: Catequésis durante las audiencias de los miércoles.* Buenos Aires: Agape Libros, 2013.

———. See Bergoglio, Jorge Mario.

Fúrlong Cárdiff, Guillermo. *Los jesuitas y la cultura rioplatense.* Buenos Aires: Editorial Biblos, 1994.

Gregg, Samuel. "*Laudato si'*: Well Intentioned, Economically Flawed." *The American Spectator.* June 19, 2015. http://spectator.org/articles/63160/laudato-si'-well-intentioned-economically-flawed.

———. "Pope Francis and Poverty." The Corner. *National Review.* November 26, 2013. http://www.nationalreview.com/corner/365004/pope-francis-and-poverty-samuel-gregg.

Gremillion, Joseph. *The Gospel of Peace and Justice.* Maryknoll, NY: Orbis Books, 1976.

Guardini, Romano. *The End of the Modern World.* Rev. ed. Wilmington, DE: ISI Books, 2001.

———. *Power and Responsibility.* New York: Sheed and Ward, 1957.

Gutiérrez, Gustavo. *The Density of the Present: Selected Writings.* Maryknoll, NY: Orbis Books, 1999.

———. *On Job: God-Talk and the Suffering of the Innocent.* Translated by Matthew J. O'Connell. Maryknoll, NY: Orbis Books, 1987.

———. *Theology of Liberation: History, Politics, and Salvation.* Rev. ed. Translated and edited by Sister Caridad Inda and John Eagleson. Maryknoll, NY: Orbis Books, 1988.

———. *We Drink from Our Own Wells: The Spiritual Journey of a People.* Translated by Matthew J. O'Connell. Maryknoll, NY: Orbis Books, 1984.

Gutiérrez, Gustavo, and Gerhard Müller. *Del lado de los pobres: Teología de la liberación.* Madrid: San Pablo, 2013.

Harmon, Catherine. "Full Text: Pope Francis' Wednesday Audience Address on the Feast of St. Joseph the Worker." *Catholic World Report.* May 1, 2013. http://www.catholicworldreport.com/Blog/2224/full_text_pope_francis_wednesday_audience_address_on_the_feast_of_st_joseph_the_worker.aspx.

Hernández, José. *El gaucho Martín Fierro.* Alicante, Sp.: Biblioteca Virtual Miguel de Cervantes, 2000.

Ivereigh, Austen A. *Catholicism and Politics in Argentina: 1810–1960.* New York: Saint Martin's Press, 1996.

———. *The Great Reformer: Francis and the Making of a Radical Pope.* New York: Henry Holt, 2014.

Jamut, Gustavo E. *365 días con el Papa Francisco.* Buenos Aires: San Pablo, 2014.

Jederías y Loyot, Julián. *La leyenda negra y la verdad histórica.* Clásicos de Historia 65. Available online at https://www.dropbox.com/s/4cc6qljbyxg3giq/Juderias.pdf?dl=0.

John Paul II. *Centesimus annus.* The Holy See (Vatican website). May 1, 1991. http://w2.vatican.va/content/john-paul-ii/en/encyclicals/documents/hf_jp-ii_enc_01051991_centesimus-annus.html.

———. *Ecclesia in America.* The Holy See (Vatican website). January 22, 1999. http://w2.vatican.va/content/john-paul-ii/en/apost_exhortations/documents/hf_jp-ii_exh_22011999_ecclesia-in-america.html.

———. *Fides et ratio.* Boston: Pauline Books and Media, 1998. Also published by The Holy See (Vatican website). September 14, 1998. http://w2.vatican.va/content/john-paul-ii/en/encyclicals/documents/hf_jp-ii_enc_14091998_fides-et-ratio.html.

———. *Laborem exercens.* The Holy See (Vatican website). September 14, 1981. http://w2.vatican.va/content/john-paul-ii/en/encyclicals/documents/hf_jp-ii_enc_14091981_laborem-exercens.html.

———. *Sollicitudo rei socialis*, The Holy See (Vatican website), December 30, 1987. http://w2.vatican.va/content/john-paul-ii/en/encyclicals/documents/hf_jp-ii_enc_30121987_sollicitudo-rei-socialis.html.
———.*Veritatis splendor*. The Holy See (Vatican website). August 6, 1993. http://w2.vatican.va/content/john-paul-ii/en/encyclicals/documents/hf_jp-ii_enc_06081993_veritatis-splendor.html.
John XXIII. *Mater et magistra*. The Holy See (Vatican website), May 15, 1961, http://w2.vatican.va/content/john-xxiii/en/encyclicals/documents/hf_j-xxiii_enc_15051961_mater.html.
———. *Pacem in terris*. The Holy See (Vatican website). April 11, 1963. http://w2.vatican.va/content/john-xxiii/en/encyclicals/documents/hf_j-xxiii_enc_11041963_pacem.html.
Langholm, Odd. *Economics in the Medieval Schools: Wealth, Exchange, Value, Money, and Usery According to the Paris Theological Tradition*. New York: E. J. Brill, 1992.
Latin American Bishops. *Justice*. From the Medellín Documents. Second General Conference of Latin American Bishops, Medellín, Colombia, September 6, 1968. Text found online at http://www.shc.edu/theolibrary/resources/medjust.htm
———. *Peace*. From the Medellín Documents. Second General Conference of Latin American Bishops, Medellín, Colombia, September 6, 1968. Text found online at http://www.shc.edu/theolibrary/resources/medpeace.htm.
———. *Poverty of the Church*. From the Medellín Documents. Second General Conference of Latin American Bishops, Medellín, Colombia. September 6, 1968. Text found online at http://www.shc.edu/theolibrary/resources/medpov.htm.
Leo XIII. *Rerum novarum*. The Holy See (Vatican website). May 15, 1891. http://w2.vatican.va/content/leo-xiii/en/encyclicals/documents/hf_l-xiii_enc_15051891_rerum-novarum.html.
Loprete, Carlos A. *Iberoamerica: Historia de su civilización y cultura*. Upper Saddle River, NJ: Prentice Hall, 1995.
Magdoff, Fred, John Bellamy Foster, and Frederick H. Buttel, eds. *Hungry for Profit: The Agribusiness Threat to Farmers, Food, and the Environment*. New York: Monthly Review Press, 2001.
Methol Ferré, Alberto, and Alver Metalli. *El papa y el filósofo*. Buenos Aires: Editorial Biblos, 2013.
Paul VI. *Evangelii nuntiandi*. The Holy See (Vatican website). December 8, 1975. http://w2.vatican.va/content/paul-vi/en/apost_exhortations/documents/hf_p-vi_exh_19751208_evangelii-nuntiandi.html.
———. *Gaudium et spes*. The Holy See (Vatican website). December 7, 1965. http://www.vatican.va/archive/hist_councils/ii_vatican_council/documents/vat-ii_const_19651207_gaudium-et-spes_en.html.
———. *Lumen gentium*. The Holy See (Vatican website). November 21, 1964, http://www.vatican.va/archive/hist_councils/ii_vatican_council/documents/vat-ii_const_19641121_lumen-gentium_en.html.
———. *Message . . . for the Celebration of the Day of Peace*. The Holy See (Vatican website). January 1, 1977. https://w2.vatican.va/content/paul-vi/en/messages/peace/documents/hf_p-vi_mes_19761208_x-world-day-for-peace.html.
———. *Populorum progressio*. The Holy See (Vatican website). March 26, 1967. http://w2.vatican.va/content/paul-vi/en/encyclicals/documents/hf_p-vi_enc_26031967_populorum.html
Piqué, Elisabetta. *Pope Francis: Life and Revolution*. London: Darton, Longman and Todd, Ltd., 2014.
Pius XI. *Quadragesimo anno*. The Holy See (Vatican website). May 15, 1931. http://w2.vatican.va/content/pius-xi/en/encyclicals/documents/hf_p-xi_enc_19310515_quadragesimo-anno.html.
Pontifical Council for Justice and Peace. *Compendium of the Social Doctrine of the Church*. Washington, DC: United States Conference of Catholic Bishops, 2004. Also published by The Holy See (Vatican website). May 26, 2006. http://www.vatican.va/roman_curia/

pontifical_councils/justpeace/documents/rc_pc_justpeace_doc_20060526_compendio-dott-soc_en.html.
Presas, Juan Antonio. *Luján: La ciudad mariana del país*. Buenos Aires: Editorial Claretiana, 1982.
Ratzinger, Joseph. *Principles of Catholic Theology*. San Francisco: Ignatius Press, 1987.
———. *Theological Highlights of Vatican II*. New York: Paulist Press, 1966.
Rourke, Thomas R. *A Conscience as Large as the World: Yves R. Simon versus the Catholic Neoconservatives*. Lanham, MD, and London: Rowman & Littlefield, 1997.
———. "Liberation Theology." In *Encyclopedia of Catholic Social Thought, Social Sciences and Social Policy*, vol. 2, ed. Michael L. Coulter, Stephen M. Krason, Richard S. Myers, and Joseph A. Varacalli, 629–37. Lanham, MD: Scarecrow Press, 2007.
———. "Moral Problems in Economic Organization in the Work of Yves R. Simon: Unequal Exchange and Man as the Principle of Integration." In *Redeeming Philosophy: From Metaphysics to Aesthetics*, ed. John J. Conley, 313–32. Washington, DC: Catholic University of America Press, 2014.
Rourke, Thomas R., and Rosita A. Chazarreta Rourke. *A Theory of Personalism*. Lanham, MD, and London: Lexington Books, 2005.
Rubín, Sergio, and Francesca Ambrogetti, eds. *El jesuita: Conversaciones con Cardenal Jorge Bergoglio, S.J.* Buenos Aires: Vergara Editor, 2010 [reprinted in 2013 as *El jesuita: La historia de Francisco, el papa argentino*].
Scannone, Juan Carlos. "La filosofía de la liberación: Características, vigencia actual." *Teología y Vida* 50 (2009): 59–73.
———. "La filosofía de la liberación en la Argentina." *Tábano*, no. 9 (2013): 11–25.
———. "La irrupción del pobre y la pregunta filosófica en América Latina." In *La irrupción del pobre y quehacer filosófico; Hacia una nueva racionalidad*, ed. Juan C. Scannone and Marcelo Perine, 123–40. Buenos Aires: Editorial Bonum, 1993.
———. *Teología de la liberación y praxis popular*. Salamanca: Sígueme: 1976.
———. "Theology, Popular Culture, and Discernment." In *Frontiers of Theology in Latin America*, ed. Rosino Gibellini, trans. John Drury, 213–39. Maryknoll: NY: Orbis Books, 1979.
Scavo, Nello. *Bergoglio's List: How a Young Francis Defied a Dictatorship and Saved Dozens of Lives*. Translated by Bret Thoman. Charlotte, NC: Saint Benedict's Press, 2014.
Schall, James V. "Concerning the 'Ecological' Path to Salvation." *Catholic World Reporter*. June 21, 2015. http://www.catholicworldreport.com/Item/3970/concerning_the_ecological_path_to_salvation.aspx.
Sigmund, Paul E. *Liberation Theology at the Crossroads: Democracy or Revolution?* New York and Oxford: Oxford University Press, 1990.
Simon, Yves R. *Philosophy of Democratic Government*. Notre Dame, IN: University of Notre Dame Press, 1993.
———. *Work, Society and Culture*. Edited by Vukan Kuic. New York: Fordham University Press, 1971.
Sobrino, Jon. *Christology at the Crossroads*. Maryknoll, NY: Orbis Books, 1978.
Spadaro, Antonio. "A Big Heart Open to God." *America: The National Catholic Review*. September 30, 2013. http://www.americamagazine.org/pope-interview.
Stoetzer, O. Carlos. *The Scholastic Roots of the Spanish American Revolution*. New York: Fordham University Press, 1979.
Suárez, Francisco. *"De legibus, ac deo legislatore."* In *Classics of International Law*, ed. James Scott Brown. London: Clarendon Press, 1949.
Synod of Bishops. *Justice in the World*. The Holy See (Vatican website). November 30, 1971, http://www.vatican.va/roman_curia/synod/documents/rc_synod_doc_19711130_giustizia_po.html (available here only in Portuguese) (available in English at http://www.shc.edu/theolibrary/resources/synodjw.htm).
Tello, Rafael. *Puebla y cultura I*. Buenos Aires: Editorial Patria Grande, 2011.
Tornielli, Andrea. *Francis: Pope of a New World*. San Francisco: Ignatius Press, 2013.
———. *Jorge Bergoglio, Francisco*. New York: Vintage Español, 2013.

Tornielli, Andrea, and Giacomo Galeazzi. *This Economy Kills: Pope Francis on Capitalism and Social Justice*. Translated by Demetrio S. Yocum. Collegeville, MN: Liturgical Press, 2015.
Valeriano, Antonio. "Nican Mopohua: Here It Is Told," c. 1556. Available online at http://pages.ucsd.edu/~dkjordan/nahuatl/nican/nican5.html.
Vallely, Paul. *Struggle for the Soul of Catholicism*. London: Bloomsbury, 2015.
———. *Untying the Knots*. London: Bloomsbury, 2013.
Walsh, Michael, and Brian Davies, eds. *Proclaiming Justice and Peace: Papal Documents from Rerum novarum through Centesimus annus*. Mystic, CT: Twenty-Third Publications, 1994.

INDEX

abortion, 154, 159–160
absolutism, 16, 26, 32, 37, 101
Angelelli, Bishop Enrique (Argentina), 72
anthropology, 93, 95, 110–111, 113, 134, 142–153, 184, 199
antinomies. *See* Bergoglio, Jorge Mario, on antinomies
Aparecida (Fifth General Conference of Latin American Bishops), 1, 3, 71, 81, 86–87, 101, 104–105, 110, 112, 113, 115, 116–117, 120, 135, 178
Aquinas, Thomas St., 27
Aramburu, Cardinal Juan Carlos (Argentina), 78
Argentina, 2–3, 5, 9, 15–16, 29, 36–37, 39, 64, 66, 67, 71, 72–73, 84, 93, 94, 113, 134, 140, 142, 147, 153, 160, 162, 167, 181, 184–185
Aristotle, 154, 176
Arrupe, Father Pedro, 64
asistencialismo (assitancism), 19
Augustine, Saint, 109, 141–142, 143
authority, civil (in Francisco Suárez), 28–29, 114

baptism, 20, 74
Bárzana, Alonso de, Fr., 17
base communities (comunidades eclesiales de base), 59–61
Belgrano, Manuel (General), 3, 11, 146, 150–151, 158, 200

Benedict XVI (Pope), 49, 112, 184, 187
Bergoglio, Jorge Mario,: and abstract thought, 31–34, 118–119; and adolescent progressivism, 34, 123, 158–159; and antinomies, 25, 116; on Belgrano, Manuel (Argentine founding father), *see* Belgrano, Manuel; on Brochero, *see* Brochero, El Cura; on Calvinism, 34–36, 101; on child abuse, 133; on civic culture, *see* Bergoglio, Jorge Mario, on politics; on common good, *see* common good; on country (definition), 135; on "culture of encounter," *see* culture of encounter; on disregard for young and old, 159–160; on economics, 11–12, 21, 167–190, 200, 204; on education, 149; on "elitism of the spirit", 89; on Enlightenment, *see* Enlightenment; on environment, 201–204; on finance, 95, 169, 173, 180, 183; on freedom and rights, 139–140, 173, 180; on globalization, *see* globalization; on The Good Samaritan (parable), *see* The Good Samaritan; and Guardini, Romano, *see* Guardini, Romano; and historical continuity (past, present and future), 30, 39, 101, 107, 109, 124, 136, 145, 146, 149, 150, 157, 196; on ideologies, *see* ideology; and inculturation, *see* inculturation (of

215

Gospel); and Jesuit Missions, *see* Jesuit Missions; and *kerygma*, *see* kerygma ; on labor over capital, 188–189, 200; on Locke, John, *see* Locke, John; and liberation theology, *see* liberation theology; on liberty, 140, 199; on *Martín Fierro* (Argentine epic), *see* Martin Fierro; on market (free), 168, 176, 200; on money, 176, 179, 180, 182, 200; and Mary, *see* Mary; on nominalism, 162; on *patria* (fatherland), 136; on politics, 10, 133–162, 205; and popular religiosity, *see* popular religion; on poverty, 169; on private property, 168, 170, 200; on relativism, *see* relativism; and Saint Augustine, *see* Saint Augustine; and Saint Ignatius, *see* Saint Ignatius of Loyola; on secularism, 160; on social debt, 11, 169, 184; on social justice, 143, 146; on solidarity, *see* solidarity; on speculation, 95, 174, 181–182; on state, 134, 137, 168–169, 179, 199, 200, 202, 204; and Suárez, Francisco, *see* Suárez, Francisco; on subsidiarity, 11, 137, 169, 179, 189, 199; on technology, 121–124, 127, 128, 149, 155, 156–157, 157, 161, 172, 175, 177, 186, 200, 204, 205–206; and theology of the people, *see* teología del pueblo; and transcendence, *see* transcendence; on virtue, 143–153; on wages, 188; on weak thinking, 126–127, 205; on work, 169, 185–190. *See also* Pope Francis.
Black Legend, 38–39
Bolívar, Simon, 85
Bourbon(s) (Reforms), 30–31, 134
Brazil, 2, 3
Brochero, El Cura, (Fr. José Gabriel), 11, 144, 150, 151–152, 162, 199–200
Buenos Aires, 5, 78, 113, 115, 117, 146, 159–160, 183, 186

Caacupé, Virgen of (Paraguay), 18
capitalism, 74, 80, 176–177, 189
Caritas in veritate (Benedict XVI encyclical, 2007), 51, 183
cartoneros (cardboard collectors), 189
Carriquiry, Guzmán, 38–39

catechumens, 21
Catholic Church, 8–9, 19, 21–23, 26, 30, 37–38, 50, 62, 72, 85–87, 89–91, 93, 95, 101, 103, 104, 109–110, 112, 114, 116, 136, 169–170, 175, 184, 190; in Argentina, 7, 19, 32; in Latin America,. *See also* Latin America 5, 9, 33, 49; social teaching of, 11, 64, 83, 92, 157, 168–169, 171, 172–174, 176, 181, 198, 199, 200–201, 203
Centesimus annus (John Paul II), 171
Christology, 59, 94
citizens, 134, 136
Comisíon Episcopal para la Pastoral (COEPAL – Argentina), 72
comunidades eclesiales de base. See comunidades eclesiales de base
common good, 26–27, 32, 93–94, 114, 120, 133, 134, 136, 137, 138, 140, 142, 143, 151, 153–154, 157, 157–158, 162, 171, 173, 176, 177, 189–190, 199, 203
common use, 170, 189
Conference of Latin America Bishops. *See* Aparecida, Medellín, Puebla
Congregation for the Doctrine of the Faith, 63, 71, 83
conquistadores, 38
contraception, 159–160
Córdoba (Argentina), 151–152
counterpositions, 23
criollos, 30, 39
Cross, 104, 106
culture, 3, 10, 21, 74, 95, 101–102, 107, 108, 115, 118–119, 122, 125, 127, 128, 142, 153, 155, 199; of encounter, 10, 95, 101, 109, 112, 114–115, 118, 120, 198, 205; of images, 126; Latin American, 74–75, 79, 103, 104; modern and postmodern, 76, 113–114, 123, 126, 157; of orphanhood, 125–126; political, *see* Bergoglio, Jorge Mario, on politics; popular, 74–75, 103–104, 153, 203; of shipwreck, 125; throwaway, 124, 203, 205; urban, 95, 117, 118

Del Valle, Padre, 20
dependency theory, 62, 76

Diálogo Argentino, 105, 136, 145, 146, 199
dictatorship of relativism, 160, 198
Donatists, 141
Dostoyevsky, Fyodor, 78
Duhalde, Eduardo, 136

earth, 202
Ecclesia in America (John Paul II), 180
encomenderos, 17
economics, 77, 95, 119. *See also* Bergoglio, Jorge Mario, on economics
Ejército Revolucionario Popular ("Montoneros"), 64
elitism (spiritual), 89
Enlightenment, 16, 19, 32, 36–37, 39, 66–67, 76, 81, 86, 177, 196–198
eschatology, 109, 143, 184
Eucharist, 112–113
Europe, 29–30, 36, 38, 62, 195, 196
Evangelii Gaudium, *(The Joy of the Gospel*, Francis), 88, 93, 115–116, 136, 160, 168, 177, 178, 179, 190
Evangelii Nuntiandi (Paul VI), 8, 47, 53–57, 61, 64, 66–67, 78–80, 81, 88, 104, 198, 199
evangelization, 53–57, 79, 80, 88, 91–92, 93, 101, 104–105, 198

Fides et ratio (John Paul II), 126–127
finance. *See* Bergoglio, Jorge Mario, on finance
Fiorito, Father Miguel Angel, 65
Foster, Joseph Bellamy, 182
fragmentation, 33, 122, 126, 153, 199; epistemological, 126–127
freedom. *See* Bergoglio, Jorge Mario, on freedom and rights

gaucho, 145, 146, 147–149
Gaudium et Spes (Vatican II Document), 8, 47, 49, 50, 54, 66, 83
Gera, Father Lucio, 9, 71, 72–73, 78
globalization, 7, 10, 11, 85–86, 95, 101, 118–119, 120, 122, 128, 154–155, 161–162, 168–169, 172–174, 177, 178–179, 180, 189, 195, 199, 203–205; of indifference, 120

The Good Samaritan (parable), 105, 152–153, 199–200
Gospel, 15–16, 18, 20–21, 32, 33, 36, 39, 59, 74, 83, 89, 95, 102, 106, 112, 115, 128, 153, 171, 177, 185, 199, 206
Great Depression, 180, 190, 201
Guadalupe, Our Lady of, 104
Guaraní, 17, 30, 36
Guardini, Romano, 7, 121, 127–128, 155–156, 174, 175, 176, 186, 200, 203, 205
Gutiérrez, Gustavo, 59, 71, 75, 81–82, 83

Hernández, José, 146
Hispanic culture, 32, 37
historical thinking (importance of). *See* Bergoglio, Jorge Mario, and historical continuity
Hobbes, Thomas, 139
Holy Spirit, 23, 101, 195
hope, 108–109, 141, 199

identity, 125, 128, 149, 153, 199, 203
ideology, 76–77, 80, 87, 146, 157, 198, 204
Iglesias, Enrique V., 83
Ignatian (Rule, spirituality), 23, 34, 39, 91, 92, 94, 101, 111, 138, 197
Ignatius, Saint, of Loyola, 17, 20–21, 23, 25, 36, 65, 151, 195, 196, 197, 198
immanetism, 89, 126, 198
imperialism, 8, 30, 111, 117, 152, 157, 176, 179, 197
Incarnate Word, 16, 17, 20, 21, 32, 39, 78, 112
Incarnation, 17, 92, 95, 102, 111, 128, 140, 185, 196, 197
inculturation (of the Gospel), 7, 15, 21–23, 25–26, 32, 33, 34–36, 39, 78, 80, 85, 88, 92, 95, 101, 107, 110, 113, 115, 116, 128, 139, 160, 195, 196, 197, 198, 203, 204
independence (of Argentina), 30, 158
indigenous communities, 203
individualism, 74, 114, 143, 149, 157, 185
industrialization, 176
International Monetary Fund, 175, 181
integral liberation (development), 59, 83, 151

Jesuits, 23, 25–26, 28, 30, 34–35, 39, 65, 196, 204
Jesuit missions, 7–8, 17–21, 23, 25, 29–30, 31, 33, 39, 64, 85, 93, 157, 195, 196, 204
Jesuit reductions. *See* Jesuit missions
Jesus Christ, 21–23, 34, 35, 53, 78, 79, 89–92, 104, 111–113, 144, 152, 196, 197
Jews (Judaism), 61, 95, 116
John, Saint Paul II, Pope (Karol Wojtyla), 51, 64, 84, 111, 113, 126, 160–161, 171, 186–187
Joseph, Saint, 186
Juan Diego, Saint, 104

kenosis, 17
kerygma , 54, 91
Kirchner (Néstor and Cristina, Argentine Presidents), 6–7, 158
Krugman, Paul, 182

Laborem exercens (John Paul II), 11, 186–189
Las Casas, Bartolomé de (Dom.), 38, 79
latifundia, 51
Latin America, 1–4, 21, 26, 32, 36, 39, 47–48, 56, 62, 64, 66, 75–76, 78–80, 82, 84–86, 101, 103, 104, 115, 128, 195, 196, 197, 198, 199; spirituality, 82–83
Laudato Si', 12, 121–122, 136, 143, 154, 160, 179, 187, 190, 195, 200, 203–206
Lawrence, Saint, 184
Leo XIII, Pope, 169
liberalism, 29, 36–37, 76, 80, 84, 110, 118–119, 139–140, 154, 169, 178, 189–190
liberation theology, 2–4, 8–9, 47, 59–65, 66, 71, 72, 75, 77, 78, 81, 82–84, 197–198
libertarianism, 137, 201
Libertatis conscientia, 4, 63
Libertatis nuntius, 4, 63
Lima Vaz, Henrique de, 86
Locke, John,, 139
Luján, Virgen of (shrine), 21, 105
Lumen gentium, 47, 48, 49, 66, 83

Magdoff, Fred, 182
magisterium, 77–78
Mane Nobiscum Domine (John Paul II), 113
market economy, 171, 176, 204
Martín de Porres, Saint, 79
Martín Fierro (Argentine epic), 2, 134, 146–147, 162, 199
Marxism, 2, 29, 61, 63, 72, 74, 75–76, 78, 80, 81, 83, 87, 167–169, 177, 190, 198, 199
Mary (Mother of Jesus), 56, 78, 80, 104, 106, 126, 198
materialism, 202, 204
Medellín (Second General Conference of Latin American Bishops), 47, 58–59, 66, 72, 80
memory, 108–109, 125, 160
Methol Ferré, Alberto, 1, 4, 9, 38, 72, 85–87, 195, 199
Minsky, Hyman, 182
missions. *See* Jesuit missions
Moses, 140
Movimiento de sacerdotes del tercer mundo (Third World Priests Movement), 65, 74
Müller, Father Gerard, 71, 83–84

natural law, 169
neoliberalism, 84, 176–177, 178
New Testament, 94
nominalism, 10, 160

Old Testament, 116
one-way exchanges, 181
On Job: God-Talk and the Suffering of the Innocent (Gutiérrez), 81–82

Paraguay, 3, 16, 18
la patria grande, 85
patronato, 36
Paul, Saint, 53–54, 89
Paul VI, Pope, 1–2, 47, 51–57, 61, 66–67, 78, 101, 170, 184, 186, 198, 199
People of God, 21, 48–49, 66, 74, 75, 78, 80
Perón (Peronist), 167
Peronist MPM (*Movimiento Peronista Montonero*), 65

INDEX

picardía, 148
Pironio, Bishop Eduardo, 78
Pius XI, Pope, 137, 173, 180
Plenary Commission for Latin America, 103
Poirier, José María, 136
Politi, Sebastián, 73
politics, 133, 137, 140, 152; and culture, see Bergoglio, Jorge Mario, on politics
Ponzi finance, 183
poor (people), 93–94, 169, 171–173, 183–184, 198, 204
Pope Francis: four principles unique to, 94–95. *See also Evangelium Gaudium*; *Laudato Si'*; Bergoglio, Jorge Mario
popular religion, 56, 71, 76, 80, 101, 103–104, 106, 128
popular sovereignty (Suárez's theory of), 26–30, 39, 134
Populorum progressio (Paul VI, 1967), 8, 51, 57, 66, 83, 151, 170–171, 184, 186, 198
poverty, 83–84, 94, 171–172, 183
power, 121, 134, 143, 155–156, 157, 200, 204, 205–206
preferential option for the poor, 83, 173
promesa (promise), 21
Puebla (Third General Conference of Latin American Bishops, 1979), 3, 9, 47, 66, 71, 78–81, 83–84, 86, 103–104
el pueblo fiel ("faithful people"), 35, 77–78, 146, 153, 184

Quadragesimo anno (1931 Pius XI), 11, 137, 174, 180
Quechua or *Quichua*, 17
Quiles, Ismael, 120

Ratzinger, Cardinal Joseph. *See* Benedict XVI, Pope
Reductions. *See* Jesuit missions
reflection church, 1, 86
relativism, 10, 95, 114, 119, 160, 161–162, 205, 206; ethical, 161
Rerum Novarum (1891 Leo XIII), 51, 169
restorationism, 75, 78, 108, 198
Revelation (Divine), 156, 200
Río de la Plata, 72
Romero, Archbishop, 61

Rosa de Lima, Saint, 79

Salta, Province of, 106
Santiago del Estero, Province of, 17
San Cayetano (Feast of, August 7), 6, 105, 133, 198
San Martín, General José de, 85, 158
San Miguel (Declaration), 19, 72
Sarmiento, Domingo, 150
Scannone, Father Juan Carlos, S.J., 71, 75, 78
Second General Conference of Latin American Bishops. *See* Medellín
secularism, 10, 89, 95, 160, 162
El Señor del Milagro (The Lord of the Miracle), 106
Simon, Yves R., 29, 181
slavery, 133
Sobrino, Jon, 59
solidarity, 113, 114–115, 116, 118, 143–145, 157, 172, 199, 203
Sollicitudo Rei Socialis (John Paul II), 51
source church, 1, 86, 195
Spain, 1, 30, 36, 39
Suárez, S.J. Father Francisco, 26–30, 134
subsidiarity, 138, 169–170, 170, 179, 189, 199

technology. *See* Bergoglio, Jorge Mario, on technology
technocratic mentality. *See* Bergoglio, Jorge Mario, on technology
Tello, Father Rafael, 71, 74–75, 78
teología del pueblo (theology of the people), 2–3, 5, 9, 72–76, 84, 103, 198
theology of Incarnation, 16
Third General Conference of Latin American Bishops, Puebla, (1979). *See* Puebla
Third World Debt, 183
Toribio, Saint (of Mogrovejo), 109
transcendence, 20, 21, 82, 87, 110, 111, 113, 125–126, 142–143, 198, 199
Treaty of Permuta, 30
Trent, Council of, 16–17
Trinity, 109–110
Tucumán (Argentina), 134

uniform thinking, 32, 87, 119, 128, 204

United Nations, 146, 175
United States, 62, 189; housing market, 183
unity-in-diversity, 23–24, 90, 138
universal destination of goods, 114, 171–172, 173, 189, 200
Urs von Balthasar, Father Hans, 155

Vatican II, 47, 48, 49–50, 59, 66, 74, 80, 197. *See also Lumen gentium*; *Gaudium et spes*
Von Balthasar, Hans Urs, 156

vulture funds, 200

We Drink from Our Own Wells: The Spiritual Journey of a People (Gutiérrez), 81–82
wisdom, 8, 10, 39, 76, 103–104, 107, 124, 126, 128, 148, 160, 203
Word (of God), 23, 57, 82, 83, 89, 206
World Bank, 83, 175
work, 77, 119, 137, 186, 188

Zacchaeus, 144, 199

ABOUT THE AUTHOR

Thomas R. Rourke is professor of political science at Clarion University of Pennsylvania. He is author of several books, including *A Conscience as Large as the World*, *A Theory of Personalism*, and *The Social and Political Thought of Benedict XVI*.

www.ingramcontent.com/pod-product-compliance
Lightning Source LLC
Chambersburg PA
CBHW021849300426
44115CB00005B/73